The Politics of Sacred Rhetoric

Studies in Rhetoric and Religion 12

Editorial Board

Martin J. Medhurst
Editorial Board Chair
Baylor University

Vanessa B. Beasley
Vanderbilt University

Randall L. Bytwerk
Calvin College

James M. Farrell
University of New Hampshire

James A. Herrick
Hope College

Michael J. Hyde
Wake Forest University

Thomas M. Lessl
University of Georgia

John S. McClure
Vanderbilt University

Gary S. Selby
Pepperdine University

THE POLITICS OF SACRED RHETORIC

Absolutist Appeals and Political Persuasion

MORGAN MARIETTA

BAYLOR UNIVERSITY PRESS

© 2012 by Baylor University Press
Waco, Texas 76798

All Rights Reserved. No part of this publication may be reproduced, stored in a retrieval system, or transmitted, in any form or by any means, electronic, mechanical, photocopying, recording or otherwise, without the prior permission in writing of Baylor University Press.

Cover Design by the BookDesigners

Paperback edition first published in 2022 under ISBN 978-1-60258-387-0

The Library of Congress has cataloged the hardcover as follows:

Marietta, Morgan.
 The politics of sacred rhetoric : absolutist appeals and political persuasion / Morgan Marietta.
 275 p. cm. -- (Studies in rhetoric and religion ; 12)
 Includes bibliographical references (p. 249) and index.
 ISBN 978-1-60258-386-3 (hardback : alk. paper)
 1. Religion and politics--United States. 2. Ethical absolutism--Political aspects--United States. 3. Rhetoric--Political aspects--United States. 4. Rhetoric--Religious aspects. I. Title.
 BL2525.M358 2012
 322'.10973--dc23
                    2011032170

For Mark Perlman, teacher

Contents

List of Tables and Figures ix
Acknowledgments xi
Introduction 1

PART I
The Psychology of Sacred Rhetoric

1 Sacred Rhetoric in American Politics 7
2 Values and Value Conflict, Sacred Values and Sacred Rhetoric 25
3 The Reasoning Effect: Sacred Rhetoric and Deliberation 41
4 The Activation Effect: Sacred Rhetoric and Participation 61

PART II
Political Consequences of Sacred Rhetoric

5 "From My Cold, Dead Hands": Sacred Rhetoric and Social Movements 75
6 The Absolutist Advantage: Sacred Rhetoric in the Bush Era 103
7 Sacred Rhetoric from Carter to Clinton: The 1976–1996 Presidential Debates 139
8 Sacred Rhetoric, the 2008 Campaigns, and the Democratic Party 161

Conclusion: "A Cure for Thought and the Diseases It Breeds" 209

Methodological Appendix: Subjects, an Experimental Approach 215
Notes 223
References 249
Index 259

List of Tables and Figures

Tables

3.1	Forms of Political Persuasion	44
3.2	Sacred Values in American Politics	49
3.3	Reasoning Effect Experimental Results	54
4.1	Activation Effect Experimental Results: Intensity	65
4.2	Activation Effect Experimental Results: Engagement	67
4.3	Consequences of Sacred Rhetoric	72
6.1	Sacred Rhetoric in the 2000 Presidential Debates	107
6.2	Sacred Rhetoric in the 2004 Presidential Debates	128
6.3	Valorization Effect Experimental Results	136
8.1	Sacred Rhetoric in the 2008 Democratic Primary Debates	164
8.2	Sacred Rhetoric in the 2008 Republican Primary Debates	166
8.3	Facets of Sacred Rhetoric Employed by Democrats in 2008	179
8.4	Authorities Cited in the 2008 Presidential Primary Debates	180
8.5	Sacred Rhetoric in the 2008 Presidential Debates	191

Figures

7.1	Sacred Rhetoric in Presidential Debate, 1976–2004	140
8.1	Sacred Rhetoric from 1976–2008	195

Acknowledgments

My father taught me to read. My professor and friend Mark Perlman taught me what it was good for. His family has continued to look after me since his passing. I owe many debts, to these souls and others, that I am unlikely to repay but can at least acknowledge.

The origins of this book can be traced to the Honors College of the University of Pittsburgh in the early 1990s, then led by its founding dean, Alec Stewart. He recruited teachers like Professor Perlman to give unique classes like his year-long discussion of the history of economic thought. In that course I found two things: the study of belief systems—grounded in what he called authorities—and a way of life that encompassed the older, better, traditions of scholarship and teaching. After many years of academic meanderings and Perlman's patience I returned to Pittsburgh and discovered the field of political psychology as a means of studying the consequences of belief. There and at other universities I had the opportunity to study with several scholars who added to my thinking and to this volume, including Martin Greenberg and Dick Moreland in psychology, John Markoff in sociology, Gordon Mitchell in rhetoric, and Michael Goodhart in political theory, as well as Jon Krosnick and Tom Nelson in political psychology.

I found the perfect dissertation advisor in David Barker, who believed in my work from the beginning and graciously tolerated my trespasses throughout. Without him I would have neither Ph.D. nor book, and for that and many other acts of kindness I owe him a great debt.

Two other scholars served as both intellectual influences and personal examples. Bert Rockman, of Purdue University, is a gentleman as well as a scholar, who taught me to connect empirical observations to meaningful normative arguments. As his student, editorial assistant, and tennis victim, I have been thankful for his guidance and friendship. Phil Tetlock, of the University of Pennsylvania, is the source of much of my thinking about sacred values, and I have unashamedly stolen and extended his ideas into the realm of political rhetoric. Phil has been more generous with his time and insights than I had any reason to expect when I first sat his courses and realized the significance of absolute values. These two scholars represent what academia has been and should always be.

The Earhart Foundation supported my dissertation research with two years of fellowships, without which this work could not have begun. Ingrid Gregg and Monty Brown deserve special thanks for their support. I was also the recipient of an Umberger Graduate Fellowship at the University of Pittsburgh, for which I am grateful.

Several friends have played invaluable roles in this endeavor, including Jeff Condran, Sam DeCanio, Robert Holzbach, Glenn Kent, and Robert Peluso. For watching this unfold they deserve many sober thanks.

I owe another great debt to the Williams clan, including Alix, Dan, Justin, David, Ken, and especially Abby.

I would like to thank Bob Kraynak, Barry Shain, and Joe Wagner at Colgate University, where I completed my dissertation, as well as the good people of Hamilton, New York, foremost among them Meredith Leland, who knows a great deal about where commas should be. Also Frank Anechiarico and Rob Martin at Hamilton College, and John Maltese, Paul Gurian, and the faculty at the University of Georgia for providing a more than pleasant environment for the editing of the final manuscript.

I am grateful to Martin Medhurst for taking an interest in the project, as well as Carey Newman and the editorial staff at Baylor University Press for their help in preparing the manuscript.

Finally, I would like to thank the several students who read and discussed parts of the project and aided me with commentary and editing, including Will Burgess, Wells Ellenberg, Addie Hampton, Karli Hedstrom, Harrison Newman, Wes Robinson, and Kate Tummarello. Without such excellent students this entire endeavor would be pointless.

Introduction

This book is about the significance of the political sacred, moving beyond the pretense that citizens respond most readily to reasoned arguments geared to their self-interest. Sacredness can be understood as the sense in which a value is absolute, resisting the normal compromises and trade-offs with other values. A sacred political position is akin to Martin Luther's dictum "Here I stand, I can do no other." It is a value for which (in theory) we would rather die than yield. The real choice between yielding and dying rarely comes to pass in democratic politics, but our political rhetoric takes absolutist positions more frequently. The much-noted shift in American politics from the redistribution of wealth to the recognition of cultural differences (from the politics of mine to the politics of me) encourages the expression of unyielding claims that go far beyond the bounds of the religiously or traditionally sacred. Contemporary sacredness has come to comprise both the religious and the secular sacred, grounded in pluralistic sources of authority that establish for different individuals and groups the limits of the tolerable and negotiable, or the boundaries of the sacred. This book examines the nature of sacred rhetoric and its role in contemporary American politics. That role is something of a paradox as sacred appeals are simultaneously beneficial and detrimental to the health of American democracy.

The influence of sacred rhetoric illuminates the tension between the democratic ideals of deliberation and participation. Although scholars often assume that these two political virtues coexist easily, the influence of sacred rhetoric demonstrates that this is not always the case. Sacred rhetoric increases political participation at the same time that it shifts the nature of engagement toward more absolutist and less deliberative forms. But the study of sacred rhetoric also provides significant insight into partisan politics as well as the concerns of democratic theory. The invocation of the sacred yields not only a contradictory influence on democratic health but also an absolutist advantage for the leaders who employ it.

One way to understand the electoral advantage enjoyed by Republicans in recent decades is their more strategic use of language. Perhaps the most prominent proponent of the argument that the Republican advantage resides in language—not in their positions or personalities, but in their more strategic communication—has been George Lakoff. As Lakoff phrases it, language is so significant because it "is far more than a means of expression and communication . . . It organizes and provides access to the system of concepts used in thinking."[1] This book supports Lakoff's essential position that Republicans hold a distinct advantage grounded in language, but disagrees about the nature of its source.

Lakoff offers something unusual among social science scholars—a thematic research agenda with each book building on the foundations of the previous works, leading to a comprehensive view of the role of metaphor in politics. In Lakoff's terms, this makes him more like Republicans than like Democrats. One of his central observations is that Democrats tend to offer a laundry list of policies, while Republicans see the larger connections among their positions and offer a comprehensive worldview that makes them more persuasive and influential. Lakoff's argument is that citizens understand language and argument through metaphor, and the central metaphor in American politics is the nation as family. The Republican worldview is framed around the strict-father metaphor, which sees the world as dangerous, competition as natural, and therefore a disciplined (and disciplinary) father figure as a necessary fixture. This metaphor undergirds and connects many different policies, from the Iraq War to free markets to guns. Liberals are disadvantaged because they fail to attach their policies to their own central family metaphor of the nurturant parent, who sees empathy rather than authority as the highest value.

Lakoff reaches several conclusions that my research supports, especially that "conservative strategists consistently outdo progressive strategists when it comes to long-term, overall strategic initiatives," and that "when conservatives answer liberals' facts and figures with no facts or figures, but with their own morals-based frames presented with emotion and symbolism, their framing will win."[2] This means, as Lakoff phrases it, that "understanding language is not just nice, it is necessary."[3] I agree that differences in language alone provide Republicans with a distinct advantage, but I offer a different perspective on its source. The Republican advantage is grounded in the greater use of sacred rhetoric, invoking absolute values, their explicit boundaries, and moral outrage at their violation. Long-term Democratic success may require more than offering an opposing metaphor; it may require identifying and invoking the authentic sacred values of the left to match the more articulated ones of the right.

The role of sacred rhetoric in electoral and movement politics is one focus of this work. Another is the influence of sacred rhetoric on the nature of American democracy. A third is the psychological mechanisms that underlie each of these dimensions. The first two chapters address the overall argument and the nature of sacred rhetoric. Chapters 3 and 4 examine the influence of sacred rhetoric on political behavior and its meaning for competing theories of democracy. The second part of the book examines political campaigns and strategies of rhetoric. Chapter 5 emphasizes the role of sacred rhetoric in social movements (and by extension the role of social movements in broader politics). Chapter 6 expresses the central argument of the contemporary Republican advantage, while chapter 7 extends this argument to the scope of presidential campaigns since 1976. The final chapter on sacred rhetoric and the Democratic Party will be of particular interest to students and practitioners of political campaigns. Together these chapters address the nature and influence of sacred rhetoric across the concerns of political communication, psychology, democratic theory, and campaign politics.

PART I

THE PSYCHOLOGY OF SACRED RHETORIC

Chapter One

SACRED RHETORIC IN AMERICAN POLITICS

Mircea Eliade, the great historian of religion, wrote that human experience occurs in "a world capable of becoming sacred."[1] Eliade meant that this is true of all human societies, not merely among the explicitly religious. The sacred is not only for the pious. Perhaps more important is his recognition that things—objects, people, ideas—can *become* sacred, which is to say that we can be made to see their sacred aspect. This transition from mundane to sacred has important democratic consequences and imparts to its practitioners a significant partisan advantage.

SACRED LANGUAGE

Some of our best-known political language has centered around what could be characterized as sacred rhetoric. John F. Kennedy's vow that we would "pay any price, bear any burden" is an example that is frequently invoked.[2] Another is Winston Churchill's famous declaration that "we shall defend our island, whatever the cost may be . . . we shall never surrender."[3] The language of the American Founding may best exemplify sacred rhetoric: "I regret that I have but one life to give for my country"; "Give me liberty or give me death"; and "To this we pledge our lives, our fortunes, and our sacred honor." From Martin Luther King Jr.'s "I Have a Dream" at the Lincoln Memorial to Ronald Reagan's "Tear Down This Wall" at Berlin's Brandenburg Gate, many of our most noteworthy speeches have invoked sacred appeals. One of the clearest invocations of sacredness in contemporary American politics is the National Rifle Association (NRA) slogan

"From my cold, dead hands."[4] The literal meaning of this phrase is that gun owners will die before yielding their rights. In symbolic terms, it is a clear statement of a sacred boundary.

The rhetoric of nonnegotiable boundaries—the language of limits—is an important facet of American politics. The shift in contemporary political discourse from a politics of redistribution to a politics of identity has included the prominence of intense, unyielding, and nonnegotiable claims. A great deal of political psychology literature emphasizes that mainstream citizens are often ambivalent, especially when their core values come into conflict.[5] But much of the political rhetoric that citizens encounter is the opposite. It is unconflicted, extreme, and strident, taking positions that ignore compromise or negotiation, upholding a favored set of values while dismissing others.

Clearly the more closely a value is tied to a religion, the more easily it is accorded sacred status. Secular norms often do not seem to hold the same authority as those backed by a divine connection. As Philip Tetlock phrases it, "*Don't do x because I say so* has less impact than *don't do x because God says so*."[6] But it is important to note that while many sacred values are clearly religious, many are not. Sacred in the sense discussed here does not mean holy; it means absolute, which is often but not exclusively religious.[7] Several values within American politics that would be categorized as secular by most observers nonetheless have sacred or absolute dimensions, what could be described as the secular sacred.

Absolutist language has been a facet of American politics from the Founding to abolition to civil rights, but it may have gained particular salience in recent decades. The contemporary importance of sacred rhetoric is connected to three shifts in American politics—the culture wars, the rise of new social movements, and the significance of new media. Although some scholars question the extent of cultural division among ordinary Americans, among political elites the evidence indicates a large and growing split between advocates of progressive versus traditional sources of cultural authority.[8] This division reflects the increasing concentration of American politics on issues of morality and identity—the move from redistribution to recognition, from class to culture. Conservatives and liberals are increasingly characterized by a split between the religious and the secular, rural dwellers and urbanites, clashing on abortion, gay marriage, guns, and public religiosity.[9] Sociologists have characterized this same shift as the rise of new social movements, which work outside of the normal channels of party politics and have cultural rather than economic goals (compared to the "old" social movement—i.e., the labor movement). Prime examples include the women's, peace, and environmental movements.[10] Many of the political issues and actors associated with new social movements also espouse sacred values. As Claus Offe observes, these movements often take uncompromising public positions: "Movements are also unwilling to negotiate because they often consider their central concern of such high and universal priority that no part of it can be meaningfully sacrificed."[11]

Political communication scholars add to this description of contemporary politics the rise of new media and the relative decline in the importance of mainstream sources of news. Beyond the expansion of television news channels such as CNN and Fox News, nontraditional sources of political information and opinion have taken root, especially talk radio and the Internet. The blogosphere is a particularly important source of citizen information and interaction outside of mainstream media, allowing citizens to be simultaneous producers and consumers of information.[12] But bloggers do not need to be measured or reasonable, and may face incentives to be neither. New media allow citizens to restrict their consideration of opposing ideas and increase the stridency and extremism of what they do hear. The combination of these phenomena—the culture wars, new social movements, and new media—has ensured the prominence of sacred rhetoric in American politics.

But what does it mean for democracy if, as W. B. Yeats lamented, "The best lack all conviction, while the worst are full of passionate intensity?"[13] Or could it be that only passionate intensity and its expression can overcome the lethargy of contemporary citizen engagement? To examine the political consequences of sacred rhetoric, I begin by addressing a series of questions: *What is meant by the sacred? How do we conceptualize sacred values and rhetoric in American politics?* And *what are the possible political advantages of moving an argument into the sacred realm?* This will allow later chapters to address two further questions: *How do we explain the mechanics of these influences, or the psychology of sacred rhetoric?* And finally, *what are the ramifications of sacred rhetoric for the nature of American democracy and the prospects of the competing parties?*

The Sacred and the Mundane: The Meaning of Sacredness

By the sacred we mean something set apart for special reverence. The sacred is within the human world but nonetheless imbued with a transcendent quality; it is neither merely human nor fully sublime, but is a bridge between the mundane realm of the material and the unobservable but nonetheless deeply felt realm of higher human values. This understanding of the sacred is drawn from three major social theorists—Emile Durkheim, Mircea Eliade, and Peter Berger—each of whom adds to our understanding of this multifaceted concept.[14] While the primary goal of each of these scholars was to explain the nature of religion (which is *not* our task), they each illuminate the idea of sacredness, a concept that is explicitly derived from religion but not limited to it. When we synthesize the views of these scholars, three aspects of the sacred emerge: (1) *humans tend to divide the world into two distinct spheres of the sacred and the mundane*; (2) *things are made sacred by human labor*, implying the possibility of gradual change in the designation of sacred objects; and (3) *sacredness has not left the contemporary world*.

The Essential Division

All three scholars agree that the sacred is exalted above the human or the material, accessible *to* humans but distinct *from* them. In Durkheim's terms, "sacred things" are "set apart and forbidden"; for Berger, "by the sacred is meant a quality of mysterious and awesome power, other than man and yet related to him . . . The sacred is apprehended as 'sticking out' from the normal routines of everyday life"; in Eliade's language it is "the manifestation of something of a wholly different order, a reality that does not belong to our world."[15] The sacred is the *ganz andere*—the entirely other—that we can be *with* but not *of*.

Durkheim famously argues that all individuals and societies divide their mental world into the two distinct realms of the sacred and nonsacred. These two domains "are always and everywhere conceived by the human intellect as separate genera, as two worlds with nothing in common . . . The two worlds are conceived of not only as separate but also as hostile and jealous rivals," such that "the mind experiences deep repugnance about mingling, even simple contact, between the corresponding things."[16] To read Durkheim is to gain the impression that the sacred and the mundane are not only distinct, but powerfully, permanently, and emotionally so, such that transgressions of the boundaries are immediately and unavoidably troubling. Eliade affirms this essential division, asserting that the "sacred and profane are two modes of being in the world, two existential situations assumed by man."[17]

However, the two existential views are not coequal. The sacred is meaningful, personal, in perhaps a better word, *real*, in a way that most human objects are not. To understand this aspect of the sacred, it is important to take into account the modern reversal of real and unreal. In the pre-Enlightenment view, it is *the sacred that is real, and the mundane that is unreal.*[18] This may appear to be a reversal of our assumptions about the world—to us the observable, mundane world is real, while the unobservable realms of the sacred (along with religion, superstition, or even principles or values) are unreal, even if they are extremely meaningful. However, it is not premodern people but rather ourselves who did the reversing, in the Enlightenment inversion of real and unreal. By pre-Enlightenment assumptions, we cannot know much about a confusing environment. Therefore what we seem to observe is unreal; what lies outside of human apprehension must be what truly exists and is most significant.[19] It is our ignorance of the world that denies it reality; for that we must look elsewhere. Then the Enlightenment claimed the possibility of verifiable human knowledge. Hence now we believe we can know things, and what we can know has become what we think of as real; nondemonstrable beliefs in the supernatural, gods, or God became unreal. But in the sacred worldview, not restricted by the Enlightenment inversion, the original view of real and unreal applies. And if the sacred is the most real, it is also the most meaningful and should be granted the most dignity and respect. The essential division into sacred and mundane is also a division into most and least important.

The Creation of the Sacred: Many Objects, Slow Change

Things are made sacred by human labor. While we may perceive the sacred as a preordained fact that is presented to us, this obscures that a choice of what to consider sacred was made by previous generations. As Berger phrases it, "Whatever else the constellations of the sacred may be 'ultimately,' empirically they are products of human activity and human signification—that is, they are human projections."[20]

Because sacredness is a collective choice made over time, this implies that *a wide range of objects can be made sacred*, such that the objects instilled with sacredness can shift and change. Durkheim observes that sacred things vary remarkably among cultures, such that "a rock, a tree, a spring, a piece of wood, a house, in a word anything, can be sacred."[21] It should be no surprise, especially given their collective nature, that political things—ideas, meeting places, historical events, leaders, national symbols or monuments—can be imbued with sacredness. Moreover, the sacred is not at all limited to the strictly religious. What appear to be fully civil or secular things can be sacred as well. Movements toward secularization may have lessened religion and religiosity in some societies, but not necessarily sacredness and sacred reverence. If religion fades but the impulse to hold something sacred does not, then the secular sacred may rise at the same time that the explicitly religious sacred declines.[22] In this case the sacred is not a given, but must be chosen from among other objects of collective significance. Although sacredness derives from religious thought, it is in no way limited to religion, leaving a wide range for the secular sacred. This might encompass any number of thoroughly secular political positions or ideas.

If sacred objects are in a sense chosen, how does this process work, which is to say, how is the sacred made? Durkheim argues that the range of the sacred is neither small nor stable: "The circle of sacred objects cannot be fixed once and for all; its scope can vary infinitely." The human act of splitting sacred from mundane and enforcing their separation creates and maintains the sacred distinction. Things "are made sacred by groups of people who set them apart and keep them bounded by specific actions; they remain sacred only so long as groups continue to do this. Humans acting collectively make and remake this quality of sacredness but then encounter it after the fact as if it had always been built into objects and was ready-made."[23] This aspect of socially constructed things—that they appear to us to be objective reality—is discussed most clearly by Berger. Building on *The Social Construction of Reality*, his classic written with Thomas Luckmann, he argues that social facts such as sacredness gain their objective quality by being created by one generation and then accepted by the next. This process of socialization "achieves success to the degree that this taken-for-granted quality is internalized." Hence the aspects of society that we perceive as real, fixed, and enduring depend on the discussion that surrounds us; in this way "the subjective reality of the world hangs on the thin thread of conversation."[24]

This view of the sacred implies the possibility or even inevitability of change, but we must be careful of how we understand this process. It is important not to mistake it for being achieved easily or reversed quickly. That social realities are constructed does not mean they can be easily deconstructed. Berger and Luckmann do *not* argue that because things exist in our collective minds, we can simply change our minds and reconstruct reality, a view that can be described as naive reconstructionism. Instead they explicitly argue that because social facts have become real to us, they are extremely resistant to change.[25] This quality of "acquired objectivity" means that "once produced, this world cannot simply be wished away. Although all culture originates and is rooted in the subjective consciousness of human beings, once formed it cannot be reabsorbed into consciousness at will. It stands outside the subjectivity of the individual as, indeed, a world. In other words, the humanly produced world attains the character of objective reality."[26] The creation of a social reality such as a sacredness may be difficult to achieve but even more difficult to dismantle.

It may seem contradictory to argue that aspects of culture such as sacredness are created and therefore changeable, but nonetheless resistant to change. There seems to be no disputing Durkheim's claim that "culture must be continuously produced and reproduced by man. Its structures are, therefore, inherently precarious and predestined to change."[27] But this does not mean that they change quickly or through the efforts of one group. The forces moving a culture may be too large and varied for one group's efforts to make much of an impact. To be rhetorically effective, however, a specific group need not change what is sacred as much as associate their views with what is *already* held as sacred. Sacred rhetoric may be effective primarily by connecting new things with old sacrednesses—not creating the sacred as much as extending it to new realms. Sacred rhetoric may not need to, and likely cannot, create the sacred anew, but it can connect a political position to an existing or latent sacredness. In this sense perhaps the sacred *shifts* more than *changes*. Later we will delve into the exact mechanisms by which invocations of the sacred are effective, but for now it is enough to note that the collective creation of the sacred, with its implications of wide choice and slow change, seems amenable to the influence of sacred rhetoric.

The Persistence of the Sacred

The final facet of sacredness illuminated by these classic works is that *the sacred has not left the contemporary world*. On the contrary, the human impulse to recognize and revere a sacred difference seems alive and well, even when not recognized explicitly. As Eliade notes, our inheritance of a sacred resonance ensures that "something of the religious conception of the world still persists in the behavior of the profane man, although he is not always conscious of this immemorial heritage." The pull toward sacredness suggests that "the man who has made his choice in favor of a profane life never succeeds in completely doing away with religious behavior; even the most desacralized existence still preserves traces of a religious valorization of the world."[28] The objects of reverence may have shifted far from the clearly religious, but the act of reverence remains. If this is the case, then the realm of the secular sacred may be large and influential.

Contrary to many scholars' expectations, the secularization of the Western world is not complete, nor perhaps even still occurring. In *The Desecularization of the World*, Berger argues that "the assumption that we live in a secularized world is false . . . To be sure, modernization has had some secularizing effects, more in some places than in others. But it has also provoked powerful movements of counter-secularization."[29] Outside of western Europe, organized religion remains not only well organized but by many metrics growing rather than declining. The proportion of Americans who state a belief in God is staggering (more than 90% by most respectable surveys), while the proportion who believe that ghosts, spirits, or other aspects of the supernatural exist is almost as high. And it is not religion per se but its remnant in the concept of sacredness that is our concern, whether in religious or secular forms. One way of conceptualizing the sacred in a more secular world is that while we can attempt to ignore sacredness, we can nonetheless be reminded of it. This reminder may occur when violations of the sacred—profanities—are presented to us.[30] In this sense sacred rhetoric could be effective not only by presenting a positive association with the sacred but also by pointing out a negative association with the profane.

Sacredness reveals itself as a seemingly simple concept with several nuanced aspects. Beginning with the question of what is meant by the sacred, we arrive at three important conclusions: that *the sacred and the mundane are two distinct human realms*, though the border between the two is porous; that *things are made sacred by human effort*, changing the objects imbued with sacredness; and that regardless of any secularizing trend, *sacredness has not left the contemporary world*. Taken together, these observations imply that citizens may be influenced to alter their understanding or categorization of certain political issues, ideas, people, or events from one realm to another.

Sacred Values and Sacred Rhetoric

So how do we understand the nature of sacredness in American politics? In this book I take as a starting point the work of Philip Tetlock, building on his research agenda on sacred values and the psychology of the unthinkable—the human intersection of moral absolutes and secular tradeoffs. Specifically, my aim is to expand on the *political ramifications of sacred thinking*. I begin with an understanding of American belief systems that can be termed the Tetlock synthesis: most Americans are conflicted over basic value choices, while a smaller number of citizens hold specific values as absolute, or sacred.[31] This description combines two interrelated aspects of Tetlock's writings: value pluralism and sacred values. In terms of this synthesis, for any given value dimension (such as individualism versus communitarianism), citizens vary along a spectrum of internal value conflict, on which most Americans are characterized by value pluralism (adherence to conflicting values), some citizens have increasing degrees of strong value preferences (less internal value conflict), and usually a minority hold any specific value as sacred (little or no internal value conflict). In this sense internal value conflict is the opposite of sacredness; high internal value conflict allows for negotiability, while the lack of internal value conflict—moral clarity—leads to absolute belief. Sacredness is the sense in which some things are not as negotiable, some rules not as bendable as others. They are inviolable, such that it is offensive to weigh them against other considerations or perhaps even to question their validity. They are special in a nuanced but meaningful sense, in a word, sacred.

A sacred value is a principle that is held to be absolute, resisting trade-offs with other values. Sacredness is the invocation of absoluteness, or the adherence to specific values about which there is little or no question. This definition focuses on the defining trait of sacredness—the absence of internal value conflict. Sacredness may have several other facets with important influences, but it can be defined by this core element.

Sacredness can be conceptualized at several different levels of analysis. In one sense, sacredness is an aggregate or social-level variable that applies to values themselves. A given value may fall anywhere along a range from almost no one holding it as sacred, to a few people or groups, to an important segment of citizens (either in numbers or influence), to near-universal acceptance. This raises the question of what proportion of a population must hold a value as sacred for that value to be accorded sacred status by the culture as a whole. If a critical mass of a population thinks of a value as sacred, the outliers become more likely to refrain from public statements or actions that would antagonize the majority. The spiral of silence and preference falsification perspectives both suggest that total agreement within a society is not necessary for the *appearance* of total agreement.[32] Sidney Tarrow describes this effect as the "costumes of consensus."[33]

In a second sense, sacredness is an individual-level variable. The question in this case is not whether specific values are sacred to society as a whole, but instead whether they are sacred to different individuals. The unit of analysis is the citizen rather than the value itself. In a third level of analysis, and the one on which we concentrate here, sacredness applies to language, or the way in which a domain of thought is expressed in sacred or mundane terms. While it is necessary to begin with the concept of sacred belief, it is the expression of this belief, or sacred rhetoric, that is our specific target. This book examines political rhetoric that invokes sacred values, compared to modes of expression that recognize a greater degree of internal value conflict or negotiability.

What this discussion points to is the flexibility within the value system of a culture, an individual, or a specific discourse, from conflicted to absolute. Whether sacredness is a distinct category or a continuous variable across the spectrum of internal value conflict is a question that needs further empirical clarification. Tetlock suggests that sacredness is more categorical, especially in terms of Alan Fiske's relational theory, which posits that different realms of thinking are discrete and incommensurable.[34] However, there is evidence that the sacred/nonsacred boundary is soft, in that individuals can be framed into reducing sacred claims.[35] This highlights the distinction between sacred and *pseudosacred* values, or those for which citizens will employ sacred claims but will nonetheless compromise. The distinction between sacred and pseudosacred values leads to the observation that sacred beliefs and sacred rhetoric may have distinct dynamics within democratic politics. While holding sacred values may influence how citizens engage in politics, the expression of sacred values in political rhetoric may also alter their behavior. We may not be able to distinguish between the sincere and the strategic sacred rhetoric, but it may have the same influence regardless. And its effects may not depend on changing the distribution of sacred belief among listeners, but instead on activating existing beliefs or reframing arguments in citizens' minds. For this reason, politicians and other opinion leaders may have an incentive to invoke sacred values, and to sacralize those that may not have been sacred before.

Sacralization can be understood as the process by which expressions of the sacredness of a specific value or object increase over time. This could be motivated by an underlying shift in belief (the proportion of people who hold the value to be negotiable decreases while the proportion holding it to be sacred increases). Or it could be the result of greater public expression without a change in the true patterns of belief, either because people became more willing to speak out, or because opinion leaders are altering public rhetoric. Sacralization (or desacralization) could be simply evolutionary, as social values change over time. Or it could occur in response to the intentional efforts of social movement activists or political leaders, what Eric Hoffer refers to as "religiofication—the art of turning practical purposes into holy causes."[36] The sacralization of rhetoric by politicians may be a widespread phenomenon in electoral competition. In this sense rhetoric and belief have related but independent effects and must be examined separately.

One way to describe the intersection of sacred rhetoric and American politics is to illuminate the boundaries of the sacred within different groups of political actors. Sacred boundaries are no doubt distinct for different individuals and groups (forming some of the definitions of group identity). These boundaries are continually in flux, and the social conflicts over their limits form a great swath of contemporary political conflicts. One could certainly make the case that current American political divisions revolve around value conflicts that have sacred dimensions, including abortion, gay marriage, gun rights, military deployments, the death penalty, and environmentalism. This is the case with *both* sides of the abortion debate: pro-life advocates clearly hold the life of a fetus to be sacred, while some pro-choice advocates make seemingly sacred claims about the reproductive rights of women. The second sentence of Justice Harry Blackmun's opinion in *Roe v. Wade* recognizes "the deep and seemingly absolute convictions that the subject inspires."[37] Gun rights advocates argue that the Second Amendment establishes a nonnegotiable boundary. Many citizens hold that patriotism precludes much criticism of military policies during wartime, and especially criticism of military personnel (leading to the almost mandatory preface that one supports the troops even if one criticizes their deployment). The death penalty is for many people an example of a nonconsequentialist value statement—it is not justified by a deterrent effect, but instead is upheld as a moral statement of the requirements of justice (often combined with the biblical injunction of blood for blood).[38] Environmentalism is a clear case where a sacred assertion (protecting a specific species from extinction as an absolute requirement) can be challenged quickly by budgetary realities (how much money will we *really* spend before we reluctantly see the last animal of its kind?). Nonetheless, sacred rhetoric is often heard in regard to the preservation of natural wonders and endangered species. (And we witness remarkable financial commitments. India, for example, though a poor nation per capita, invests a large amount to ensure the survival of its tigers.)

The many possible examples of sacredness in American politics can be concluded with the subject of same-sex marriage. For many citizens this question brings forth immediate feelings about defining acceptable limits, of public homosexuality on one side and of exclusionary practices on the other. For example, the Episcopal Church is experiencing a painful schism over whether homosexuality will be accepted openly within the church hierarchy. Church members are being forced to examine and decide on their sacred boundaries: will they or won't they remain in a church with openly gay leaders, or conversely, one that will not allow them? The degree to which the debate over homosexuality and its public status has become a major political topic and clear dividing line within American politics illustrates the political significance of sacred boundaries.

These examples highlight two concepts that may influence the political efficacy of sacred rhetoric: the underlying degree of conflict or consensus regarding a specific value, and whether only one or both sides of a conflict employ sacred appeals. There may be an important empirical distinction between sacred values that are held in *consensus* within a given society at a given time, and those that are *conflictual* (i.e., some hold the value as sacred while others do not, or even more significantly, some hold a value as sacred while others hold its *opposite* to be sacred). At the most basic level, some consensus sacred values, such as the prohibitions against murder and incest, may be near universals among human societies. But a consensus this broad seems limited to a small number of prohibitions. The larger number of values is likely to achieve a consensus only within a specific subculture.

In contemporary America, a likely candidate for a consensus sacred value is constitutionalism, or the unquestionable authority of the Constitution as the final word in American politics.[39] One way to illustrate that this is a consensus sacred value is to imagine a prominent politician openly suggesting that the Constitution should be disregarded (not a specific interpretation of the document but the document itself), and consider how long he or she would continue being a prominent politician. Even leaders who would attempt to circumvent the Constitution would never admit to it, but instead offer a different view of what the document means. A clear example of this consensus value at work occurred during the 2000 election controversy between George W. Bush and Al Gore. Regardless of the early uproar, any further question of succession ended immediately when the Supreme Court made its ruling; as disliked and criticized as the ruling was, its authority was unquestioned. Although some Democratic supporters continued throughout the Bush presidency to employ the rhetoric of illegitimacy, the issue of succession was effectively over. A sacred value such as constitutionalism can often go unnoticed when a community is in such broad agreement that it forgets about the possibility of dissent. But in few countries would a ruling by nine unelected, largely unknown people in robes immediately and definitively end a major controversy. That Americans find this to be normal is a testament to the degree to which constitutionalism is a sacred consensus value.

An interesting exception to the general rule of public reverence for the Constitution is the rhetoric of nineteenth-century abolitionists. William Lloyd Garrison vilified the Constitution as "a covenant with Death and an agreement with Hell" because of its acquiescence to slavery.[40] (For another example of Garrison's sacred rhetoric, see *Salutatory of the Liberator*: "I am in earnest. I will not equivocate; I will not excuse; I will not retreat a single inch; and I will be heard!")[41] Rather than a case of a sacred value clashing with a negotiable one, this seems to be the more unusual case of one sacred value (abolitionism) clashing with another (constitutionalism). The length and bloodiness of the struggles of the Civil War era can be understood as the product of such juxtapositions.

What may be more politically significant than consensus sacred values are conflictual ones. Given a political world of value pluralism—"the conception that there are many different ends that men may seek and still be fully rational, fully men"—conflict among values may be unavoidable.[42] And the more one group expresses its sacred commitment to a specific value while another group either refuses to recognize its sacredness, or worse, holds its opposite to be sacred, the greater the political consequences that such clashes are likely to have.

Just as some political domains clearly have a greater sacred component than others, the two opposing sides of a given issue may have different degrees of sacredness as well. Sacred values can be thought of as being *single-sided* or *double-sided*. Abortion is likely an area where both camps have sacralized the underlying values. For those on the antiabortion side, the life of the fetus is clearly a sacred value, not to be abrogated by less important things like the rights or desires of the woman. There is also a clear God-ordained backing for this view (a specific boundary sanctioned by a specific authority). But for those on the pro-choice side, the reproductive rights of a woman may take on a similarly sacred status. For both sides, at least for some, their beliefs are nonconsequentialist (other considerations do not matter compared to the rights of the fetus; other considerations do not matter compared to the reproductive rights of the woman).[43] Political domains that are characterized by double-sided sacredness are likely to be highly contested, vitriolic, nondeliberative, and intractable, leading to continual political conflict. Abortion seems to fit this description. Neither side seems to have a rhetorical advantage, however, as both employ sacred rhetoric.

The opposite may be the case when only one side of the argument has been sacralized, reflecting what could be called single-sided sacredness. If sacred rhetoric motivates political engagement, then the sacralized side should have a distinct advantage. This asymmetry in the way the arguments are expressed may not only advantage the sacred side but also affect the nature of political struggle. A situation with two sides on offense creates a different environment than one on rhetorical offense and the other taking a defensive posture. Both sides asserting their protected value is a different situation from one emphasizing values in strident tones and the other discussing consequences, statistics, and policy proposals in measured tones.

The Political Consequences of Sacred Rhetoric

Our discussion of the sacred can be summarized in four observations: that even among modern thinkers it is a common practice to divide the world into the sacred and the mundane; that the sacred is created, meaning that any number of objects may gain sacred status; that the secularization of Western society has far from eradicated the sacred, even fostering a significant realm of the secular sacred; and that the defining feature of sacred values and rhetoric is absoluteness. If these observations are reasonably accurate, then *what advantage is gained by convincing an audience to move a political position from one realm to the other?*

About sacred things we think differently and care more. Both of these aspects have important political consequences, rooted in the sacred's defining feature of perceived inviolability. The sacred is not touched with impunity; its violation has consequences, whether divine, psychic, or social. The psychic consequences include (1) *reasoning and arguing about sacred political domains in a different way*, and (2) *becoming more motivated to engage in politics*. These two effects have important social consequences for the nature of civil society.

The source of the influence of the sacred is its inviolability, which makes a sacred political position unquestionable and its opposition unconscionable. About such absolutes we reason differently. An acknowledged sacredness creates a fixed star by which to navigate a confusing world; once seen, this star is hard to extinguish. Public sacredness also puts good people in a corner, because people who are thought of as good do not question such things (which is a profanity), at least not without raising the public possibility that they are really not that good after all. This social effect is demonstrated in the parable of the emperor's new clothes—if we believe we will be judged negatively for certain expressions, we will cease making them (even going to potentially extreme lengths, as in the denial of the emperor's nakedness).

But this is not to say that the most important effect of sacred rhetoric is the indirect one of altering citizens' *expressed* preferences. The most clear effect is the direct one of altering citizens' way of reasoning and justification, or the process through which they arrive at their *real* preferences. The quality of inviolability is less influential on the *content* of an argument than it is on the *process* of reasoning. Sacredness does not depend on the political position taken or its ideological direction, as one can take a sacred stand against abortion just as one can take a nonsacred stand. The same applies to the antiabortion side, or to stands both for and against the death penalty. Because sacred rhetoric is characterized more by the form of argument than by its ideological direction, it follows that its greatest influence is on citizens' process of reasoning. Sacredness is a cognitive process as well as an outcome. And it is on the method of reasoning that sacred rhetoric has its most discernable effects.

Sacred rhetoric *influences the form of reasoning employed by its hearers*, shifting citizens away from consequentialist reasoning and toward absolutist reasoning. Employing more absolutist reasoning may or may not change the outcome of a citizen's judgment, but the importance of a reasoning shift does not rely on an accompanying shift in outcome. Moving toward a reasoning process that is more absolutist changes the character of political thought and public discourse. If the justifications people give in public are more absolute and less acknowledging of trade-offs, then the character of public debate changes. The citation of authorities and the insistence on boundaries rather than an offering of evidence or a discussion of consequences lead toward a clash of cultural authorities rather than reasoned agreement. Greater invocations of moral outrage engender a more strident form of politics. In this sense the process of reasoning alone is an important aspect of political discourse.

The second consequence of sacred rhetoric is *greater political motivation*. The sacred intrudes on our consciousness in a way that the mundane does not; we feel deeper emotions in its presence and are more concerned about perceived violations. Profanity is more noted and remembered than simple error, falsehood, or failure to maximize. These feelings result in political and personal valorization. Because violation of the sacred is intolerable, rectifying such conditions becomes a noble, valorous act. And political engagement in this service ennobles us not only in our own minds, but perhaps in the minds of those around us. Hence sacredness carries a social as well as internal pressure; violations create not only private disappointment but public shame. It is worth noting that political action may be driven by how we want to be seen by others as well as motivated by sincere belief. Public sacredness creates an expectation of agreement because of the offensive (profane) nature of dissent, generating the incentive not only to care, but to appear to care.

Sacred and valorized ideas are therefore treated differently. They are given more reverence, respect, or dignity. They are, as Durkheim would phrase it, set apart. In addition to the divine command to observe sacred distinctions (as in Exodus 3:5, "Do not come near; put off your shoes from your feet, for the place on which you are standing is holy ground"), there is also the social command to respect others' boundaries and our collective rites. By valorizing such positions and their defense, sacredness allows citizens to construct personal meaning. And this meaning creates political motivation and engagement. About the sacred we simply care more and are therefore more politically motivated.

Both of these effects—that we think differently and care more—deal with political persuasion. But they are not the usual form of persuasion that we consider, or what is thought of as attitude change. These effects are not changing minds, but changing forms of reasoning and levels of political engagement. Increasing engagement is most often referred to as an *activation effect*, or encouraging political action by connecting citizens' previously held beliefs to their political meaning. The other form of persuasion is less frequently considered. It could be called a *reasoning* or *process effect* rather than an outcome effect.

Political engagement is the key not only to the nature of civil society and the vibrancy of democracy but also to the simple mathematics of electoral success. If one party motivates its citizens to participate more than the other party does, this creates a significant partisan advantage. One aspect of the sacred advantage is simply higher voter turnout, but the broader influence is an increase in political discussion. This means not only a greater volume of political conversation but also a discussion of a different tenor—argument in a more strident, absolutist manner that reinforces sacred boundaries and the public pressure to observe them. The partisan advantage is not only a change in the *level* of political participation in terms of voting, donation, or activism, but also a change in the *nature* of political engagement, becoming less deliberative and compromising, more strident and unyielding. If one political party or social movement employs sacred rhetoric to a greater degree than others, it gains these benefits—an absolutist advantage.

The proposed influences of sacred rhetoric can be summarized in these three arguments:

1. *Sacred rhetoric influences citizens' process of justification*, increasing the degree of absolutist reasoning (a process or reasoning effect).
2. *Sacred rhetoric encourages political intensity and engagement* (an activation effect).
3. *The psychological effects of sacred rhetoric advantage the political leaders who employ them*, including social movements on both the left and right, but especially contemporary Republicans, who enjoy a decided lead in sacred appeals.

These empirical propositions represent the psychological dynamics and political consequences of sacred rhetoric, or a shift in public discourse and an increase in political intensity and civic engagement, which create an advantage for the social movements and political parties that express the greater degree of sacredness. These effects influence the health of American democracy as well as the electoral prospects of the contemporary parties. But before examining the evidence for these arguments, we need to address a series of questions about the conceptualization and measurement of sacred rhetoric, to which I now turn.

Chapter Two

VALUES AND VALUE CONFLICT, SACRED VALUES AND SACRED RHETORIC

Conceptualizing sacred rhetoric relies on an understanding of value conflict, the inevitable result of the condition that our political judgments rely on core values that cannot be justified. Sacred values are the most clear form of beliefs for which we make no pretense that their superiority can be demonstrated with evidence or logic. Instead they rely on a sense of self-evident truth. The expression of these values takes a particular form, but to build a clear conceptualization of sacred rhetoric, the underlying concepts of values and value conflict deserve explicit attention.

VALUES

We can begin with the observation that *values cannot be justified, yet we can justify nothing without them*. All of our judgments of right or wrong, better or worse, rely in the end on values, what Isaiah Berlin described as "not means to ends but ultimate ends, ends in themselves."[1] These ends can be thought of as *moral backstops*. If we ask someone to explain a political position, and then press them to justify that justification, and continue in this fashion, the point at which they can go no further is a core value.[2] Hence values—the most reduced form of justification—can only be believed, not justified. These core elements that distinguish one belief system from another cannot be defended rationally; for example, we cannot demonstrate either empirically or logically to someone who does not already agree with us that individualism is superior to communitarianism, or that secularism is superior to religiosity. Even the values of the Enlightenment (the dignity of the individual, the superiority of reason to received wisdom) cannot be demonstrated by Enlightenment methods (empiricism and logic). Our fundamental values, the ultimate source of our political judgments and ideals, are irreducibly Romantic. I suspect that few conditions have as much fundamental political importance as the observation that *we must rely on core values but cannot justify them convincingly to others*. And of course people rely on different ones, which are sometimes incompatible. Hence the basis of our political judgments can be neither justified nor reconciled, leading in many cases to inevitable political conflict.

Their fundamental importance seems to make values more rather than less difficult to define. They also have an intuitive meaning in American discourse (e.g., "family values"), which can lead us to substitute a general cultural understanding for a clear social science definition. The contemporary emphasis on surveys as the standard source of empirical data has also made the study of values more difficult, as they are not articulated easily by most citizens. Nonetheless, definitions have emerged, first from social psychology and then from political science. Foundational definitions in psychology stress the role of values as motivators: "a conception of the desirable"; "the dominating force in life"; or "an enduring belief that a specific mode of conduct or end-state of existence is personally or socially preferable."[3] More recent definitions stress the abstract character of values as "desirable, trans-situational goals" and "abstract trans-situational guides."[4] This highlights an important distinction between *values* as broad organizing principles and *attitudes* as evaluations of specific objects, such as policy proposals. Political science researchers have followed in emphasizing the abstract nature of values as "general principles"; "personal statements regarding the individual's priorities"; or "each individual's abstract, general conceptions about the desirable and undesirable end-states of human life."[5] The consensus view seems to be that values are *standing judgments of preferable social ends*, whether clearly articulated or within an unexamined belief system.

Value Conflict

> "*Conflicts between ends equally ultimate and sacred, but irreconcilable within the breast of even a single human being, or between different men or groups, can lead to tragic and unavoidable collisions.*"[6]

Value conflict can be seen as the inevitable product of the condition that some values are incompatible with others. This condition and its role as a source of conflict are explained clearly by Isaiah Berlin, who provides the philosophical basis for value pluralism—"the conception that there are many different ends that men may seek and still be fully rational, fully men."[7] But values are not only multiple; some are inherently in conflict with others: "What is clear is that values clash," as "some among the Great Goods cannot live together." Hence "in the end, men choose between ultimate values."[8] For any given political value there is most often a directly opposed value—militarism versus pacifism, individualism versus communitarianism, or isolationism versus interventionism. To the degree that we favor one, we automatically and inevitably oppose the other.

When considering value conflict, however, it is important to identify the level of analysis we have in mind. The most obvious form may be *interpersonal* value conflict, which occurs when two clear-minded individuals see clearly in opposing directions. In contrast, two individuals who are both internally conflicted have no real stake in opposing each other, and may even be open to reasoning through their quandary together. It is the lack of this internal value conflict that leads directly to conflict with others. And a short step away from conflict between individuals is conflict between groups within society, as like-minded citizens are drawn together and jointly oppose each other. Sacred value clashes may be deeply connected to Gaetano Mosca's observation that people have an instinct for "herding together and fighting with other herds," creating divisions within society that "occasion moral and, sometimes, physical conflicts."[9]

While interpersonal value conflict may be more observable, the principle form of value conflict may be *intra*personal, which in an important sense explains larger conflicts among individuals and groups. Berlin wrote that "values may easily clash within the breast of a single individual . . . so we must engage in what are called trade-offs—rules, values, principles must yield to each other in varying degrees in specific situations."[10] For most people most of the time these trade-offs may seem reasonable, even if they are difficult or paralyzing.[11] This defines a negotiable value. In his classic book *Political Ideology*, Robert Lane argues that "the healthy person has multiple values, and he finds them often in conflict; his health is revealed in his toleration of the conflict and the means he chooses to reconcile the conflict, not in the way he makes all policy recommendations serve a single value, no matter how economical that might be for him."[12] I find this a pointed description of a negotiable value, though I am less sure of Lane's suggestion that sacred values are unhealthy. On the contrary, sacred values may have beneficial consequences and play a central role in the creation of democratic rights.

Sacred Values

When a belief is unquestionable and its holder unconflicted, it enters the range of a sacred value. Some principles resist trade-offs and demand our absolute adherence. A sacred value as we have defined it is one for which there is no significant intrapersonal value conflict; we enjoy moral certainty rather than quandary, clarity rather than internal conflict. To a sacred thinker, the breach of that boundary is profane rather than merely a difference of opinion or a topic of compromise.

In addition to the core element of absoluteness, sacredness comprises several other important facets. One of these is *noninstrumentality*, or the primacy of reflexive values over calculated self-interest. By instrumentality we mean the difference between being motivated by values and being motivated by interests—the distinction between *what is good* and *what is good for me*. Instrumental thinking is born of deliberate self-interest, while noninstrumental thinking is directed by principle. An important element of instrumentality is calculation, or the degree to which we put mental energy into weighing the alternatives and consequences. In opposition to this is the degree to which we follow gut reactions, predetermined traditions, or what we know to be morally right, without the need for mental computation. Max Weber may have described this best in his distinction between "value rationality" and "instrumental rationality." The first is characterized by "a conscious belief in a value for its own sake," which is pursued "independently of its prospects for success," while the second is a clear-minded connection of means to ends, measured in terms of tangible self-interest.[13] Instrumental thought is calculated and self-interested; noninstrumental thought is reflexive and value driven. In this sense the degree of instrumentality is the opposite of the degree of sacredness.

Another facet of sacredness is the *degree of negotiability*. This can be conceptualized as the perceived degrees of freedom before something becomes simply unacceptable. Negotiability in this sense refers to an *internal* process, or bargaining within one's own mind, rather than external or literal negotiations with other parties. It is the willingness to give credence to opposing positions and to reconsider one's own view. A simple thought experiment should help illustrate this facet of sacredness: Consider your place along a value dimension such as individualism versus communitarianism. You may be anywhere on the spectrum from believing that individuals should be self-sustaining with little help from government, to believing that society as a whole is fully responsible for each individual's welfare. Consider an economic redistribution policy such as greater taxation to fund universal health care, and your immediate policy preference. Given resistance from those who prefer the opposite policy, to what degree would you be willing to accept a compromise? Would you recognize the validity of the opposing value and think it perfectly normal to do so? To the degree that you are comfortable making such trade-offs, individualism/communitarianism is a negotiable and not a sacred value.

Now consider the abortion question. Do you consider abortion on demand to be acceptable (or even necessary to preserve reproductive rights)? If it is acceptable, would you draw a line at late-term abortions? If you were offered a political compromise that would establish your favored position on the tax issue but the opposite of your position on abortion, would you find that compromise acceptable? What about the reverse proposition—the law would reflect your position on abortion, but the reverse on taxation? Would you find this agreement more palatable? The degree to which the first proposition (your view on taxes but not on abortion) is more difficult to accept than the reverse arrangement may reflect a greater degree of sacredness on the moral question of abortion compared to the economic redistribution question of taxes. Now consider something for which there is a near-universal social prohibition, such as incest. If a small sect living in a secluded area of your state were to promote the practice, and the majority party of the state legislature were considering erasing all legal prohibitions (perhaps in return for that group's support on a different issue on which they agree with you), would you feel this was something on which you could compromise? Or would you feel that no public or even symbolic endorsement could be tolerated? Or perhaps that to even consider the gains you could make from such an endorsement would be shameful? Whether a value is fully negotiable, resists negotiation, or is clearly nonnegotiable is an aspect of sacredness. To engage in compromise regarding a sacred value, or even to consider doing so, is seen as illegitimate. Holding a value as sacred entails denying the validity of the normal value trade-offs involved in policy compromises.

In addition to nonnegotiability, another facet of sacredness is *nonconsequentialism*. If a value or principle is sacred, then it stands on its own. It does not require the justification of positive consequences that derive from it, nor is it in any way invalid because of any negative consequences it might have. For example, if free speech is held to be sacred, the negative influences of certain types of speech are irrelevant. If political expression is truly sacred, then the offense that my words create is not only outweighed by my right to say them, but the offense has no weight at all. In this view a citizen who objects to my speech is more wrong to take offense than I am to give it, as he or she is not recognizing the sacredness of free speech. The American Civil Liberties Union has often taken a nonconsequentialist position on the First Amendment, an argument known as free speech absolutism.[14] In this view free speech means precisely that—all speech is protected absolutely and it is not legitimate to weigh speech against its consequences. A similar argument is made from the right of the political spectrum in regard to gun rights— the consequences of gun ownership (violent deaths) are not relevant given that gun ownership is a sacred right. This approach has especially important ramifications for constitutional judgments, because many Supreme Court decisions are grounded in balancing tests rather than absolute principles. If balancing is illegitimate from the start in regard to certain values, this suggests an entirely different decision process. This facet of sacredness is related to Weber's concept of "value rationality" or "value-rational social action," which is characterized by pursuing a value "independently of its prospects for success."[15] Consequences are not relevant if a principle is valid on its own terms. In this sense truly sacred values are noninstrumental, nonnegotiable, and nonconsequentialist; they are not to be calculated, compromised, or opposed with the logic of consequences.

Another facet of sacredness is the setting of *boundaries*. The sacred establishes a limit to thought or behavior. Hence sacred rhetoric entails the language of limits—this cannot be allowed; this kind of relationship is improper; this should never even be mentioned. Cultural relativism and pluralism to the contrary, sacred thinking holds that some things are just not acceptable, delineating the boundaries of the sacred. Although many Americans uphold the importance of tolerance and a nonjudgmental posture, the essence of the culture wars interpretation of contemporary politics is that both traditionalists and progressives have become further apart and less tolerant of each other. In James Davison Hunter's *Culture Wars*, he defines the sacred as "that which communities love and revere as nothing else. The 'sacred' expresses that which is non-negotiable and defines the limits of what they will tolerate."[16]

A boundary is likely not idiosyncratic or random; it is often a boundary sanctioned by an *authority*. In this sense an authority is a recognized source of legitimacy for a sacred claim.[17] It provides the belief system necessary to reinforce a value's sacred status. The authority serves as an answer to the question of why we should accept something as sacred—because X says so. Lacking such an authority, a sacred claim is less likely to be persuasive or to maintain its hold. Consider, for example, a sacred claim that cannot answer the question of why it should be taken seriously. How long will it continue to hold force? In the face of contemporary value pluralism, sacred claims without authoritative backing are not likely to be maintained. By their very nature, value claims cannot rely on empirical evidence or logic for their backing, because "ethical values are not subject to verification" and "are beyond the range of mere logic."[18] Because we cannot demonstrate empirically or logically that one value is superior to another or that one value is truly sacred rather than negotiable, such claims must rely strenuously on appeals to authority. In this sense the sacred is not just a boundary but a *socially reinforced* boundary. One aspect of the sacred is *a specific boundary established by a specific authority*.

However, the degree to which adherence to an authority is truly absolute rather than yielding to important exceptions is a critical question, especially when we consider that there may be many things to which one pays lip service but will compromise nonetheless. The more legitimate and influential the authority, the more persuasive the sacred claim. For example, the Bible is a major religious authority and the Constitution a major secular one. The Book of Mormon, in contrast, is authoritative to some but less so to others, and George Washington's warning against entangling alliances is often cited as a secular political authority but is less authoritative than the Constitution. The degree to which an individual feels bound to the limit established by the authority is a gauge of its sacredness.

In addition to establishing the boundaries of what one will tolerate, sacredness can also influence the boundaries of what one will contemplate. Sacredness can entail taboos against even considering or discussing certain topics. Some options are simply not options to a sacred thinker. In the World War I tract *Instincts of the Herd in Peace and War*, William Trotter describes this effect in regard to the mass movements of that era: "To question it is for the believer to carry skepticism to an insane degree, and will be met by contempt, disapproval, or condemnation . . . There is a quality of feeling which tells us that to inquire into it would be absurd, obviously unnecessary, unprofitable, undesirable, bad form, or wicked."[19] Taking this concept further, Mohammed Arkoun describes the distinction between thoughts that are thinkable and those that are unthinkable.[20] Sacred boundaries limit certain thoughts from consideration, or at least impose high costs to one's morality or decency if one does consider them. Tetlock has demonstrated the social and internal sanctions imposed in response to transgressions against sacred values, including sanctions for just *considering* such transgressions.[21]

A contemporary example of socially enforced boundaries is the conflicting rhetoric surrounding the legitimacy of abortion, which can be observed in the typical discourse within a religious family faced with the unexpected pregnancy of a teenager. Some family members will likely suggest that they should consider how having the child would influence the teenager's education and future. But others may not be willing even to hear that line of discussion—no talk of consequences can be tolerated about something that should be considered only in terms of right and wrong. This strikes me as a particularly cogent example of sacred nonconsequentialism, or a boundary to employing the logic of consequences. A similar phenomenon goes beyond the legitimacy of discussing certain subjects, to the legitimacy of recognizing certain observations. Sacredness may be related to the *denial of sacrilege*, or the refusal to admit the existence of things that should not be the case—what could be termed *sacred blindness*. This could be described as cultivated ignorance for the sake of not having to think unpleasant thoughts, or for the sake of not having to face unpleasant social reactions. In either case, conflating normative and positive (it *should* be this, therefore it *is* this, and I will not pay attention to contrary evidence) may be an important implication of sacredness. In this sense the boundaries of the sacred may have an interesting breadth, extending from action to contemplation to observation.

A final facet of sacred values is *moral outrage*. This may be a powerful element of sacred belief, as the existence of the sacred implies the existence of the profane. Holding a person, place, object, or belief as sacred means that the literal or figurative desecration of that sacred thing is a profanity.[22] To the holder of a negotiable value, the expression of its opposite is merely a difference of opinion, perhaps an annoying but not a fundamentally offensive act. The violation of a sacred value, however, inspires moral outrage.[23] The public denigration of a cherished value results in a negative emotional reaction, which may require defensive public expressions or acts to cleanse. Hence holders of sacred values are likely to be publicly value protective, defending the collective standing or reputation of a sacred value. Tetlock and colleagues describe this as the Sacred Value Protection Model, which predicts that the abrogation of sacred values leads to moral outrage and moral cleansing.[24]

Acts of moral cleansing may involve only public statements, but I hypothesize that they also extend to political participation. Political engagement is a powerful way of distancing oneself from the profane, as an expression both to oneself and to others. This raises the proposition that political engagement is at times fundamentally symbolic, in terms of both its personal meaning and its public intent. Citizens do not need to intend to change public policy in order for their engagement to be meaningful. Symbolic politics and the skirmishes of the culture wars are often described as "the politics of distraction," but while they clearly divert attention from policy proposals in other realms of the political agenda, this is missing the point that *those* issues are a distraction for people who place a high personal value on public symbolism. To sacred thinkers, collective symbolism is not a distraction from what is important, but is instead the more important political statement, both to others and to themselves. The influence of sacred rhetoric may be aided by exactly this connection between moral outrage and political engagement.

Sacred Rhetoric

So how is sacredness expressed, or in other words, what distinguishes a sacred appeal from a nonsacred one? Sacredness does not depend on either the political domain in question or the ideological direction of the position taken. For example, one can take a sacred stand against abortion just as one can take a nonsacred stand. The same applies to the antiabortion side, or to arguments both for and against the death penalty. We can understand sacred rhetoric as a form of reasoning, or a way of thinking through the relation between values and public policy opinions. This form of appeal makes an argument in a manner that sets a political issue apart, reasoning about it in a different way. *Sacred rhetoric employs absolutist reasoning, while nonsacred or negotiable appeals employ a more consequentialist form of reasoning.* Absolutist reasoning is characterized by applying established principles or boundaries to a given situation and then privileging these principles over the consequences of the decision. It may also entail citing specific authorities for the principle, and perhaps engaging in expressions of anger or moral outrage at perceived violations. Consequentialist reasoning, on the other hand, begins from the expected effects or outcomes of the decision and applies a give-and-take form of negotiation, with authorities seen as more pluralistic or nonbinding, and expressions of moral outrage being more limited.

The core difference is illustrated by two competing arguments for why one shouldn't steal—is it because it is wrong, or because crime does not pay? Both argue for the same result, but in a distinct fashion, one absolutist and the other consequentialist. One of my favorite examples of the power of absolutism to conquer consequentialism takes place in Joel and Ethan Coen's remake of *The Ladykillers* (2004), in which Professor G. H. Dorr sees his consequentialist reasoning defeated by the absolutist reasoning of his aged landlady. Professor Dorr tries to convince her to remain quiet about her discovery of the large sum of money that he has stolen. In his consequentialist view, the previous owner of the money was an evil institution (a gambling house), and he will be donating half of the money to her favorite charity (Bob Jones University). More important, there is no victim, as the money will be replaced by the insurance company without even a real cost to the policy holders, each of whom will contribute only one cent. "Think of it," Professor Dorr argues, "one penny from those thousands upon thousands of people, so that Bob Jones University can continue on its mission." Her absolutist response is, "It's wrong. And don't you be leading me into temptation. It's just plain wrong."

At this point we should note that there is a sense in which the distinction between absolutist and consequentialist reasoning is blurred. In the end, even a fully consequentialist position relies on a value judgment regarding the specific consequences at hand. But this reductionist approach ignores some key distinctions between the two modes of thinking and justification. Absolutist reasoning is a critique of actions or beliefs as valid or invalid in and of themselves. Consequentialist reasoning, on the other hand, concentrates on states of affairs that result from these actions or beliefs. Hence one important distinction is whether we begin or end with values. In an absolutist approach, one chooses a value to exalt above others and begins there. A consequentialist approach appeals to values only at the very end, once the chain of consequences is complete. The value that one applies at this point depends on the nature of the consequences at hand. Both modes of reasoning deal with values, but the first *begins* with values that are of one's choosing, whereas the second *ends* with values that one does not necessarily foresee.

Perhaps a more important distinction between the two modes of argument is that in the one it is legitimate or even mandatory to weigh competing consequences, while in the other, such weighing is illegitimate from the outset, identifying the person employing such reasoning as unethical or at least morally suspect. In this sense additional information or facts are helpful or even crucial to consequentialist reasoning, but are at best a distraction to absolutist reasoning. So although there is an important connection between absolutist and consequentialist reasoning, there are also crucial distinctions. It is an important normative point that all arguments reduce in the end to value justifications, but it is also an important empirical point that some arguments arrive there more quickly and immovably than others.

We can define absolutist reasoning more clearly as being characterized by a combination of the following attributes:

1. *Protected status*: placing a value beyond question or set apart from trade-offs with other values
2. *Nonconsequentialism*: privileging values over costs or consequences
3. *Noninstrumentalism*: rejecting calculated self-interest
4. *Nonnegotiability*: denying the legitimacy of compromise
5. *Citation of boundaries*: invoking a boundary of what is acceptable or tolerable
6. *Citation of authority*: invoking an authority for the value or boundary
7. *Moral outrage*: expressing anger at the violation of a value or boundary

As opposed to sacred rhetoric, nonsacred or negotiable political rhetoric emphasizes consequences and outcomes; it cites figures and data rather than principles or authorities. It is phrased in the language of policy experts, concentrating on practical means rather than moral ends. It may well mention or invoke values, but it does so in a nonstrident way. Most important, it employs consequentialist reasoning characterized by the following attributes:

1. *Relativism*: implying value trade-offs or comparability with other competing values
2. *Consequentialism*: invoking costs or consequences
3. *Instrumentalism*: referencing calculated self-interest
4. *Negotiability*: invoking compromise
5. *Denial of boundaries*: denying the validity of a boundary
6. *Denial of authority*: denying the validity of a known authority for the boundary
7. *Denial of moral outrage*: denying the validity of moral anger

This scheme provides a direct means of evaluating any given political appeal or justification. By taking note of each of the elements of absolutist or consequentialist reasoning in a given argument, we can assign it a value from 7 for an extremely absolutist argument (containing all seven absolutist elements) to -7 for a strongly consequentialist argument. Take, for example, the following statement in favor of the death penalty:

The death penalty makes a clear moral statement about what we will and will not allow in our society. Heinous crimes cannot be tolerated. We must be clear about what sort of justice they require. Both the victims and especially their families are due the form of justice that both our religious and secular traditions call for. The Bible is clear about the demands of an eye for an eye, and the Constitution itself specifically mentions capital punishment as part of our legal system. The issue is not deterrence; it is the strongest possible statement of what outrages the community—of what is allowable and what is not.

Protected status	Relativism
Nonconsequentialism	Consequentialism
Noninstrumentalism	Instrumentalism
Nonnegotiability	Negotiability
Boundary	Denial of boundaries
Authority	Denial of authority
Moral outrage	Denial of moral outrage

This appeal invokes at least five elements of absolutist reasoning (protected status, nonconsequentialism, citation of a boundary, citation of authority, and moral outrage [marked in italics], representing a 5 on the reasoning scale). Compare this to the following statement, also in favor of the death penalty:

The death penalty is our last line of defense against the most violent and dangerous criminals in our society. Some argue that capital punishment is not a deterrent to crime, but common sense tells you that at least some potential murderers will be stopped by the knowledge that they may be put to death. We must also protect society by removing the most vicious criminals from our midst, which cannot be done with certainty by imposing long prison sentences that later parole boards can lessen. Opponents argue that if one innocent man is executed then the system must be stopped. But how different is this from one innocent man who is held in prison for the rest of his life? We cannot stop from determining justice only because a mistake might rarely be made. Even if an innocent man is executed in the rare case of a mistake, this is more than balanced by the number of lives saved by making sure that the most vicious criminals cannot kill again.

Protected status	*Relativism*
Nonconsequentialism	*Consequentialism*
Noninstrumentalism	*Instrumentalism*

Nonnegotiability	Negotiability
Boundary	Denial of boundaries
Authority	Denial of authority
Moral outrage	Denial of moral outrage

While this appeal argues for the same policy as the first one, it does so in a consequentialist fashion, employing at least three elements of consequentialist reasoning and none of absolutist (-3 on the reasoning scale). This procedure for assessing the nature of reasoning can be applied to any given appeal or justification (and will be employed in our experimental studies).

Consider the case of differing arguments in favor of gun possession. Although one can take a consequentialist position in favor of guns, the more common arguments made by the National Rifle Association employ absolutist appeals, as in the following statement:

> The ability to keep and bear arms is a protected right of free citizens. The Constitution gave us that right because our forefathers knew that it must be preserved against future encroachments. It is this principle that counts. The Second Amendment is no better or no worse than the other parts of the Bill of Rights. We must preserve it just as we must preserve First Amendment rights to free speech, and Fifth Amendment rights against self-incrimination. We should be angry at the efforts by false leaders to take away our long-standing freedoms, and refuse to allow ourselves to go down the slippery slope of one concession after another. We cannot negotiate away our sacred rights.

Protected status	Relativism
Nonconsequentialism	Consequentialism
Noninstrumentalism	Instrumentalism
Nonnegotiability	Negotiability
Boundary	Denial of boundaries
Authority	Denial of authority
Moral outrage	Denial of moral outrage

This argument scores a 6 on the reasoning scale. Compare it to a more consequentialist way of making an argument in the same direction, which scores a -4 on the scale:

> Citizens must be allowed to keep firearms in order to protect themselves. Allowing citizens to own guns is simply a matter of weighing the consequences of law-abiding citizens having them versus what would happen if solid citizens did not have guns. Having firearms may lead to some

accidental deaths by those who do not store their guns properly or teach their children how to respect them. But the consequence of not upholding gun rights is the inability of citizens to protect themselves against criminals, as well as the increased boldness of criminals because they know that home owners are not armed. This would result in a much larger number of deaths and a more violent society. It is simply not true that we can rely on the police to protect us. They do not, and we must be able to protect ourselves.

Protected status	*Relativism*
Nonconsequentialism	*Consequentialism*
Noninstrumentalism	*Instrumentalism*
Nonnegotiability	*Negotiability*
Boundary	Denial of boundaries
Authority	Denial of authority
Moral outrage	Denial of moral outrage

These two arguments make very different appeals for maintaining private gun ownership, and their influence may be quite different as well.

Sacred Rhetoric in Movements and Parties

The examples just given come from the language of social movements, an important source of sacred rhetoric. Social movements may be one of the most common mechanisms through which sacred rhetoric influences American politics and enters partisan discourse. Moreover, this form of appeal may be inextricably connected to the nature of social movements themselves. I argue later that in some ways it is difficult to fully understand one without the other. More important, their success may be mutually reinforcing; the success of a social movement increases the dissemination of sacred rhetoric, while the employment of sacred appeals may be one of the key factors in a movement's success.

Aside from the province of social movements, where do we find sacred rhetoric? Is it sprinkled throughout American political speech, or is it concentrated within specific domains or in the rhetoric of certain actors? In addition to these questions about contemporary American politics, it may be instructive to wonder whether our political rhetoric is more sacred now than in the recent past. Although the historical question of how we compare with other eras is outside the scope of this study, it is nonetheless significant to note why sacred rhetoric may be an important characterization of our time. If we are living in a period of relatively prevalent sacred rhetoric, this may be because of the divided nature of our current politics, or as Mark Brewer and Jeffrey Stonecash phrase it in their 2006 book, our "split." The culture wars thesis argues that beginning in the 1980s, we have become a more culturally divided nation along progressive versus traditionalist lines. To the degree that the culture wars thesis describes contemporary politics, we have shifted emphasis toward moral rather than economic questions (framing even economic issues as moral causes). And sacred rhetoric is likely to be more prevalent in the realms of morality and identity. Redistribution questions are by their very nature monetized and therefore amenable to negotiated division. Moral questions, however, are more likely to be attached to deeply held principles, and offer no easy way to split the difference.[25] Claims of identity recognition are also hard to reconcile by dividing the spoils. These conflicts lead more frequently to clashing authorities than to negotiated compromises.

Whether the newer cultural divisions have replaced or only added to the older economic division is unclear. But what remains of the economic divide may have increased as a result of the recent wealth expansion among the upper strata of society. It is important to note that the American economic division is *not* about having or not having wealth, but rather about *the attitude toward wealth*. Many Americans in the higher economic strata are now politically liberal, and there is a strong base of economic individualists among poorer citizens, which is not coincidentally the base of Evangelicalism.[26] Rather than a conflict between the "haves and have nots," the American division is over the attitude toward having. To these divides we can add the more recent post-9/11 split over the response to Islamist terrorism. Hence we have three major separations that map onto the current party structure (divided by the response to traditional culture, individual wealth creation, and warfighting). For these reasons, along with the rise of new social movements and new media discussed earlier in chapter 1, we may well be living in a relatively sacralized era.

Perhaps one of the most important questions is whether sacred rhetoric is employed equally by the two major parties. Is it the case that sacred language is more prominent on the right? Or do the sacrednesses of the left create a substantial degree of sacred rhetoric from Democrats as well? More than just a matter of understanding partisan beliefs and tactics, this question has important implications for the electoral success of the competing parties. If one party employs a substantially greater degree of sacred rhetoric, then it will accrue the activation advantages of sacredness. In the close political environment of the current day, this may provide a critical margin for one party over the other, what could be called the absolutist advantage. However, the role of sacred rhetoric is greater than just the advantages that it provides to social movements and political parties. Its influences raise broader questions about the quality of American democracy, points to which I now turn.

Chapter Three

THE REASONING EFFECT

Sacred Rhetoric and Deliberation

The form as well as the content of an appeal can affect how we perceive its message. An example of the influence of rhetorical form is the negative reaction of many American citizens to flag burning during the protests of the 1960s and 1970s. The same message without the same emotional response could have been achieved through other symbolism. For example, if protestors had engaged in *flag washing*, symbolically cleansing the flag (and hence the nation) of its improper acts, they could have made a similar point without giving the same offense.[1] Flag burning was offensive because it is a profanity to many citizens, which prevented them from seeing any effective political message beyond the desecration of a sacred symbol. In his dissent in *Texas v. Johnson* (1989), the decision that narrowly upheld flag burning as constitutionally protected speech, even Justice John Paul Stevens, who was considered one of the most liberal justices on the Court at the time of his retirement in 2010, wrote that "the question is unique . . . Even if flag burning could be considered just another species of symbolic speech under the logical application of the rules that the Court has developed in its interpretation of the First Amendment in other contexts, this case has an intangible dimension that makes those rules inapplicable."[2]

The flag-burning example illustrates that the sacred element changes the impact of the message. Certain forms of rhetoric can either limit or increase the acceptability of an argument or act. An example of facilitating rhetoric is the use of the term "harvest" in organ donation. "It's time to cut out the deceased's heart" puts a brake on the whole procedure, while "It's time to harvest the deceased's heart" invokes an entirely different reaction that allows it to proceed.[3] Each of these examples makes the same point—that language and symbolism count. The same argument made in a different way may no longer be the same argument, which is to say that it has an entirely different effect.

The Psychology of the Sacred Appeal

Not merely the content of political opinion but also the form of its expression is meaningful for the health of American democracy. The positions citizens take affect our collective decisions, but the justifications they offer affect the nature of public discourse. Reasoning that is absolute or inflexible allows little room for compromise or mutual agreement. This is particularly significant for the prospects of a more deliberative democracy. Hence the reasons for citizens' opinions can be as important as the opinions themselves in terms of their influence on the nature of political conflict and the functioning of civil society.

Sacred rhetoric may be particularly important in this regard because it is intimately connected to a specific form of reasoning, or a way of thinking through the relation between values and public policy opinions. This form of appeal makes an argument in a manner that sets a political issue apart, reasoning about it in a different way. *Sacred rhetoric employs absolutist reasoning, whereas nonsacred or negotiable appeals employ more consequentialist reasoning.* Absolutist reasoning is characterized by identifying established principles or boundaries and then privileging these concerns over the consequences of a decision. It may also rely on specific authorities for the principle, and perhaps engage in expressions of anger or moral outrage at perceived violations. Consequentialist reasoning, in contrast, concentrates on the expected effects or outcomes of the decision, focusing on cause-and-effect relationships or cost-benefit calculations. Authorities are more likely to be seen as pluralistic and expressions of moral outrage are limited.

In this sense sacredness is a cognitive *process* as well as an outcome. Because sacred rhetoric is characterized more by the form of an argument than by its ideological direction, it may follow that its greatest influence is on citizens' process of reasoning rather than on the outcome of opinion. Specifically, I argue that sacred rhetoric *influences the form of reasoning employed by its hearers*, shifting citizens away from consequentialist reasoning and toward absolutist reasoning. This is one facet of what we mean by persuasion, a multifaceted concept comprising several distinct aspects, some of which are more significant than others for the psychology of the sacred appeal.

Contagion

In *The End of the Affair* we hear the complaint, "I've caught belief like a disease. I've fallen into belief like I fell into love."[4] Graham Greene is not alone in arguing that beliefs can be caught. Emile Durkheim describes sacredness as a contagion that imposes itself onto objects, ideas, and minds whenever the sacred comes into contact with the mundane: "The sacred world is as though inclined by its very nature to spread into the same profane world that it otherwise excludes. While repelling the profane world, the sacred world tends at the same time to flow into the profane world whenever the latter world comes near it."[5] This process may require neither explicit effort nor an object of any specific character. If sacredness has settled in one locale, "it naturally spreads from the object to all the others it finds nearby—that is, to all that some cause has brought close to the first in the mind."[6] That cause may be sacred rhetoric. The spread of the sacred may not require much effort or explicit argumentation because of "the extraordinary contagiousness that sacredness has. Far from remaining attached to the things that are marked with it, sacredness possesses a certain transience. Even the most superficial or indirect contact is enough for it to spread from one object to another."[7] Mere juxtaposition will do.

In this view sacred beliefs "are like an oil slick; they spread to all the other mental states that occupy the mind."[8] As discussed in chapter 1, sacredness may grow in almost any field.[9] By juxtaposing sacred elements with a political cause or position, sacred rhetoric may lead its hearers to think of this object in sacred ways. And what they think *of* it changes how they think *about* it. Recategorizing political domains through sacred contagion represents a distinct way of conceptualizing political persuasion.

Outcome and Process: The Several Facets of Persuasion

We can define persuasion broadly as simply *any inducement of one individual's choices by another.*[10] The most obvious form of persuasion is *attitude change*, or altering a citizen's opinion of a policy, candidate, or other object. If we identify the different forms of persuasion in the political psychology literature, it is clear that most concentrate on outcome effects, or the final opinion that citizens hold or express. But as table 3.1 illustrates, several other aspects of political persuasion have more subtle influences, including *framing, priming, preference falsification,* and *activation*.[11]

TABLE 3.1
Forms of Political Persuasion

Effect	Definition	Source	Type
Attitude Change	altering a policy choice or political opinion	Eagly and Chaiken; Petty and Cacioppo	Outcome
Activation	increasing political engagement in accord with pre-existing beliefs	Finkel	Outcome*
Preference Falsification	inducing changes in public expression without changing underlying beliefs	Kuran	Outcome
Valorization	enhancing perceptions of a speaker's virtue	Current Work (chap. 6)	Outcome
Framing	shifting the weight given to different considerations	Nelson	Outcome & Process
Priming	introducing a new factor into consideration	Krosnick and Kinder	Outcome & Process
Reasoning Shift	shifting the form of reasoning or justification employed	Current Work (chap. 3)	**Process**

* *In this case the outcome is political action rather than belief; there is no outcome effect on opinion or attitude, but there is one on engagement.*

A less recognized persuasive effect could be called a *reasoning shift*. Most of the time we are concerned about the effect of language on citizens' opinions, or the outcome of their political judgments. But we can make a distinction between effects on *outcome*, or a citizen's final position, and effects on *process*, or a citizen's form of reasoning. What do we make of a change in a listener's way of thinking that is distinct from a change in attitude—that is, a difference in process but not necessarily in outcome? I propose that this can be termed a *reasoning effect* or a change in *cognitive method*, shifting the modes or forms of reasoning that citizens employ. But how stable is a citizen's form of reasoning? Are reasoning styles malleable, in the sense that exposure to different rhetorical forms can shift them? Or are cognitive methods more like habits, in the sense that citizens are likely to have a default mode of reasoning that they apply to most political domains regardless of external influences?

The degree to which a trait is malleable can be understood in two different empirical senses. The first is whether exposure to a specific treatment, such as a particular form of rhetoric, can shift a citizen's thinking.

The second is whether that shift is maintained over time or whether the citizen reverts back to his or her original position, and how quickly. If we think through the ramifications of these two stages, there are important problems for the argument that messages are persuasive. The most glaring research problem is that most often we are testing only the first form of malleability—whether the treatment influences citizens in the immediate term. It is much more difficult to determine whether the effects are lasting. But there is also a logical problem for this sort of argument. If citizens are not malleable in the immediate term, then the appeals seem to be ineffective. If citizens *are* malleable, however, then the shift created is unlikely to be maintained for long because the citizen will be shifted again by the next message to come along. The catch-22 is that we can demonstrate that citizens are either immovable or that they are inconstant, bending with each new wind. What we really mean to suggest is that citizens are somewhere in the middle—they have some of the characteristics of a habit in the sense that they carry past influences with them, but these habits are not so ingrained that they cannot be moved by small increments. If sacred rhetoric or other forms of appeal have political importance, it is not because they affect citizens' decisions only immediately after they are heard. Their importance relies on a longer-term effect resulting from repeated exposures. For sacred appeals to have long-term importance, reasoning processes must be malleable enough to be influenced, but still have some of the character of a habit so that repeated incidences of this influence will accumulate into a long-run shift. Repeated exposure to sacred rhetoric may shift a citizen's default process toward more absolutist reasoning. The more often a citizen is exposed to a particular form of reasoning, the more normal, accepted, and expected it becomes, and the more likely he or she is to employ it.

A form of persuasion that entails both a process and an outcome effect is *framing*. Framing can be understood most clearly as the way in which differences in language change the relative weight given to competing considerations.[12] Several prominent studies have concluded that the wording of political or media messages can produce substantial framing effects.[13] The frequently cited studies conducted by Tom Nelson employ the example of the relative importance of free speech or public-safety considerations when deciding whether to support an application by the Ku Klux Klan to hold a rally. Although framing often affects the outcome of an individual's judgment, its direct effect is on how an individual weighs competing arguments. Studies of framing have shown that its effects are not based on simple accessibility, or the degree to which different arguments are readily available in a citizen's mind, but are instead dependent on the conscious weighing of alternatives.[14] Hence framing is more or less effective depending on the degree to which an argument matches the audience's predispositions; listeners respond to cues that produce positive reactions, but reject cues that produce negative ones.[15] In addition to individual differences such as value predispositions, framing is conditioned by contextual factors such as engaging in discussion with others or exposure to the competing frame.[16] Because the effects of framing may be limited by these factors, we could summarize by saying that the power of framing is maximized when the recipient is exposed to the framed message *repeatedly* and *without the opposing frame*.

Although citizens will be exposed to both frames in regard to many political questions, the ideological specialization of media into clearly conservative and liberal outlets may mean that many citizens are increasingly hearing only one side of framed messages. As selective exposure to only limited media sources becomes more prevalent, several persuasive mechanisms should become more effective. But even among citizens who absorb multiple sources of news, the nature of sacred rhetoric leads to an important exception to the pattern of exposure to both competing influences. Political domains involving sacred values can be characterized as *single-sided* or *double-sided*, depending on whether only one or both sides of the issue have sacralized the underlying values in question. In political domains that are single-sided, citizens hear only one sacred appeal. Citizens may hear opposing arguments phrased in negotiable rhetoric, but the particular effects of sacredness apply to only one side of the debate. Hence sacred appeals may be particularly effective in some political domains.

The Reasoning Effect of Sacred Rhetoric

Attitude change is clearly an outcome effect, and framing entails a process effect that often leads directly to a different outcome; but a reasoning shift represents a pure process effect. A powerful influence of sacred rhetoric is on citizens' cognitive method rather than on their final opinion, *increasing their reliance on absolutist reasoning* rather than persuading them to agree with the content of the message (Argument 1, on p. 23). Sacred rhetoric may be no more persuasive than mundane rhetoric on outcome (opinion), while having a substantial effect on process (the form of reasoning employed and the justifications given). Psychologists argue that humans have a strong natural propensity to be "cognitive misers," expending only the minimum amount of mental energy sufficient to the task at hand. In this view citizens rely extensively on shortcuts or rules of thumb known as heuristics, especially in regard to decisions made with chronically low levels of information. Political decision making by most citizens definitely falls into this category given their scant political knowledge.[17] In this sense absolutist reasoning may be more efficient. Citizens do not have to weigh alternatives or consider competing consequences that are hard to verify. It is much less cognitively taxing to default to principles, rules, and norms that provide established judgments. The cognitive misery of citizens suggests that political reasoning would be prone to absolutism, and therefore that citizens should be vulnerable to sacred appeals.

This may be the case regardless of whether citizens agree with the message. One of the most important tests of the reasoning effect is whether the change in process applies to *all* listeners, even those who continue to disagree with the message. If only those who agree with the appeal are affected, then the role of sacred rhetoric is more limited. But if even listeners who oppose the appeal are still led to employ more absolutist reasoning, then the influence of sacred rhetoric is stronger and more pervasive. A process effect regardless of citizens' expressed opposition we can consider *Argument 1a: Sacred rhetoric increases absolutist reasoning even among listeners who disagree with the message.*

We should consider, however, how this could be moderated by the single- or double-sidedness of the issue. If the issue is double-sided sacred, then listeners have a ready default of absolutist arguments on either side. If they take up the absolutism of a message, they can apply it easily in the direction of their original inclination. However, if the issue is only single-sided sacred, then listeners who disagree with a sacred appeal do not have a ready example of absolutist arguments on the opposing side. Because of this distinction, we can expect greater absolutist reasoning by those who disagree with a sacred appeal, but only in regard to double-sided political domains.

If "the contagious quality of sacredness" operates through sacred rhetoric, then we can expect significant persuasion effects, though not the ones we are most accustomed to examining.[18] A powerful influence should be on reasoning, emphasizing process as well as outcome effects. The effect on cognitive method is a purely process effect, which has received less attention in the political psychology literature. This may be because its significance is less obvious. It is an effect on the nature of discourse rather than the direction of opinion, but the manner of expression and the tone of political speech have much to do with the functioning of civil society and the health of American democracy. To fully understand these effects and their political meaning, we need to turn to the empirical evidence, which in this case suggests an experimental approach.

The Experimental Design

Our empirical test of the influence of sacred rhetoric relies on a straightforward experimental manipulation that allows us to compare the effects of sacred versus nonsacred rhetoric. The methodological appendix provides further details of the experimental approach employed, but here it is important to note the basic design of the study. The experiments asked a group of participants to read and consider a set of political appeals and then respond to a series of questions about their opinions and justifications. For each political domain, participants were randomly exposed to either sacred or negotiable rhetoric arguing for the same political position. The sacred rhetoric statements contained at least five of the seven elements of absolutist reasoning described in chapter 2, while the nonsacred statements contained none (see the appendix for the wording of the sacred and nonsacred appeals). The statements were designed to mimic actual language employed by public advocates of those political positions, and are similar to common political rhetoric that citizens encounter.

To test the effects of sacred rhetoric, we need to concentrate on a few specific political domains. (Rather than *issue*, *attitude*, or even *value*, I prefer the term *domain* to connote simply an area of thought or political concern, within which a citizen may or may not apply those other constructs.) Table 3.2 lists several prominent political domains in which advocates regularly employ sacred rhetoric. Three different criteria seem important in winnowing down an appropriate sample on which to concentrate—the sidedness, obviousness, and source of authority for the potentially sacred values. Chapter 1 discussed the single- or double-sidedness of political domains, which refers to whether only one or both sides of a political struggle have sacralized the underlying values. Domains that I suspect are double-sided include abortion, gay marriage, and the death penalty. However, several other domains are likely only single-sided, from either the left or the right. These include free speech, environmentalism, animal rights, and pacifism on the left, and gun rights, flag burning, and public religiosity (such as school prayer and displaying the Ten Commandments) on the right. The domains of the study include each of these categories: two double-sided, one single-sided from the left, and one single-sided from the right.

THE REASONING EFFECT 49

TABLE 3.2
Sacred Values in American Politics

Domain	Apparent Sidedness				Obviousness*		Source of Authority	
	Double-Sided	Single Left	Single Right	Consensus	More Obvious	Less Obvious	Religious	Secular
Abortion^	x				x		x	
Gay Marriage	•				•		•	
Death Penalty	•					•	•	•
The Environment		•				•		•
Free Speech		x				x		x
Post-9/11 Civil Liberties		x				x		x
Animal Rights		x				x		x
Pacifism		x				x		x
Gun Rights			•			•		•
Flag Burning			x		x			x
Public Religiosity^Σ			x		x		x	
Constitutionalism				x		x		x

The political domains examined in the study are in bold and represented in the table by dots rather than xs.

* The degree to which political domains are obviously sacralized influences whether our empirical tests are more meaningful. The less obvious cases provide a more conservative test.

^ Abortion is the central topic of a broader domain characterized by the religious, ethical, and humanistic ramifications of interventions into human fertility, centering in one sense on the status of humans before they are born, and in another on public attitudes toward sexual mores. Stem cell research is a related issue that is focused more on the first root question. Sex education in schools and the distribution of contraception is another issue that centers more on the second concern.

Σ Public religiosity includes such issues as prayer in school, the "under God" controversy in the Pledge of Allegiance, evolution versus creationism in public schools, and the display of the Ten Commandments in courts. These could be thought of as separate domains, but they seem to share the same question of whether Christian values and symbols are excluded from/or given a noted place in public institutions.

Another criterion is obviousness, or how clearly sacralized the domain is in contemporary politics. Some areas of political conflict have more obvious sacred connections than others. In choosing areas on which to focus, we would not want to avoid the obvious domains entirely, as they are politically important. But the argument should not rely only on obvious cases. Abortion may be the most prominent example of a domain characterized by sacred values, but it may be too much so, providing only a narrow test of the role of sacredness. Moreover, abortion has also received a great deal of scholarly attention. Less obvious examples provide a more conservative test, and if successful, argue for a broader range of the influence of sacred rhetoric.

The third criterion is the source of authority, whether religious or secular. Because one of the important questions regarding the nature of sacredness is the division between the religious and secular sacred, as well as the role of an established and legitimate authority in backing up sacred claims, it would be unwise to concentrate solely on domains characterized by either religious or secular sources.

Balancing these different criteria leads us toward four specific domains: *gay marriage, the death penalty, environmentalism,* and *gun rights.* Gay marriage is potentially double-sided, more obvious, and clearly religious. It is also an important contemporary political issue, taking up a respectable portion of public issue-space. The sacred element of the anti-gay marriage position is seen both in terms of an established authority opposing the public legitimacy of homosexuality, and in terms of drawing boundaries of the acceptable. Opposition to gay marriage is framed by its very nature as defining limits and roles: What are the boundaries of what we call marriage? What are the appropriate roles for men and for women? What is acceptable in public and what in private? For the opposing side the sacred element is less clear, but still quite possibly influential. It is a different framing of limits, in this case the limits to bigotry or exclusion. The potentially sacred value is inclusiveness, equal treatment, and nondiscrimination.

The three remaining domains are less obviously sacralized and therefore provide more conservative tests of the influence of sacred rhetoric. Another potentially double-sided domain is the death penalty, which has both religious and secular sources of authority on both sides of the question. Some opponents of the death penalty base their opposition on the Christian sanctity of human life. Employing this reasoning, some antiabortion advocates also oppose the death penalty on the same grounds, while other abortion foes do not. However, this is not necessarily a contradiction; foes of abortion who advocate the death penalty are opposed to the taking of *innocent* lives, which does not extend to those who have earned a death sentence. Advocates of the death penalty also cite a sacred religious authority, based on explicit biblical sanction.[19] Some anti-death penalty activists take a more secular sacred position that killings by the state should be forbidden because they brutalize the state itself. This position is distinct from the concern over errors, which is a consequentialist argument that applies only when errors are made; brutalization is an absolutist argument that applies universally. But supporters of the death penalty also take a secular sacred view that the death penalty makes an unequivocal statement of right and wrong, of what is considered most heinous by our society, regardless of any deterrent or nondeterrent effect. In this sense the death penalty provides a domain with several different sources of religious and secular authority on both sides of the question.

The third domain is environmentalism, which is potentially single-sided from the left (the absolute requirement to save natural resources, wonders, or species). It is generally secular, though there are some religious foundations as well.[20] The antienvironmental side seems to be more consequentialist than sacred.[21] This may be because the motivation is not really an opposition to the environment but is instead pro-economic development or pro-business, a distinctly consequentialist position. Opponents of environmentalism are not in favor of destroying natural resources but are simply not willing to pay the costs of their preservation, in terms of either government spending or forgone business revenues. Although I know many people with a sense of affection or protectiveness toward specific endangered species, I know no one with a personal animosity toward spotted owls or any other animal; they simply do not want to pay for their upkeep given other priorities.

The final domain is gun rights, which is potentially single-sided from the right and secular. The language of gun rights is clearly sacred, invoking boundaries, authority, and absolutes. From their cold, dead hands to the invocation of a very slippery slope, gun advocates take some of the strongest secular sacred positions in American politics. Together these four political domains provide us with a broad enough range to note differences, but a small enough group to examine fully.

After considering the sacred or negotiable appeals in each of these domains, two of the most important questions for the participants were about their opinion on the issue and their justification for that position. One question was simply, "What is your opinion on [gay marriage/the death penalty/the environment/guns]?" Responses were along a seven-point scale anchored by the following statements: "Laws should be changed to allow gay marriages; Gay marriages should not be allowed," "The death penalty should be ended; The death penalty should be continued," "We need greater controls on damage to the environment; We do *not* need greater controls on damage to the environment," "Gun rights should be more limited; Gun rights should be more protected." The gauge of participants' form of reasoning for this opinion is based on their response to the subsequent open-ended question, "Can you explain why you hold the view that you hold?" As described in chapter 2, the seven facets of sacred rhetoric provide us with a scheme to gauge the presence of absolutist reasoning in these responses. By taking note of each of the facets of absolutist or consequentialist reasoning present in a given response, we can assign it a value from 7 for an extremely absolutist argument (containing all seven absolutist elements) to –7 for a strongly consequentialist argument.

Rhetoric and Reasoning

We can test the causal connection between rhetoric and reasoning by examining this experimental evidence of the comparative effects of sacred and negotiable appeals. An initial question is whether the sacred rhetoric manipulation was successful, in the sense that readers saw the ostensibly sacred appeal in that light and reconsidered their view of the topic. Citizens may use different terms for the distinction between sacred and nonsacred concerns, but the essence is that the domain is special in an important way that demands it be dealt with differently; it is determined by transcendental authority and is not up to majority vote. Directly after their random exposure to a sacred or negotiable appeal, participants were asked, "How would you describe [gay marriage/the death penalty/the environment/gun ownership]? A) It is the same as most political issues. It should be decided through the normal democratic politics of discussion and negotiation, or B) It is not like most political issues. It is too important or sacred to be decided by the normal democratic politics of discussion and negotiation." Participants in the sacred rhetoric condition were significantly more likely in three out of four domains to choose option B, the indication of sacred status. In regard to the environment there is no discernable effect, but we see significant differences with gay marriage, the death penalty, and guns.[22] This provides initial evidence that the rhetorical manipulation was successful, leading citizens to alter their view of the domain in question and recategorize it as sacred or set apart from normal issues.

The larger question is the influence of sacred rhetoric on reasoning. It is important to note that the meaningful comparison is between the group exposed to sacred rhetoric and the group exposed to negotiable rhetoric, rather than a true control group exposed to no argument at all. Comparing the sacred rhetoric group to a group that receives no message does not address the real question at hand—whether sacred rhetoric has different influences than a nonsacred appeal that provides the same message but in a more measured and negotiable form. In other words, does the sacred rhetoric associated with the culture wars, new social movements, and new media have different effects than the usual political rhetoric of mainstream parties and politicians?

Table 3.3 displays the empirical results of the first experiment. At the outset it should be noted that sacred rhetoric is not more persuasive than nonsacred rhetoric in the sense of altering policy opinions to a greater degree; both were persuasive, but neither one more so than the other. Opinions on gay marriage, the death penalty, the environment, and gun rights were not altered more on average by sacred appeals than by negotiable ones. Instead, the distinctive influence of sacred rhetoric is on the process of reasoning. The most important finding of the experiment is that compared to negotiable political rhetoric, sacred appeals shift the listeners' reasoning styles toward absolutism. After reading the political appeals, participants were asked, "Please tell us more about your thinking on this question. Can you explain why you hold the view that you hold?" Their responses (which averaged forty-two written words) were coded for their form of reasoning in the fashion described previously, resulting in a scale from 7 (employing each of the facets of sacred reasoning) to -7 (employing each of the facets of negotiable reasoning).[23]

A few examples should serve to illustrate the sorts of results obtained (quotations are in the citizens' own language, including grammatical and spelling errors):

Gay Marriage:

> "Well I recently got saved and am into church. The Bible says woman and man, not woman and woman. I think it is gross and unacceptable. Homosexuality is a choice, and a very wrong one at that." (Scale = 3 [boundary, authority, moral outrage])

> "I hold my view because I don't feel that marriage is so sacred that it should only be one man–one woman. People get married and divorced

so quickly now that marriage is not such a traditional and holy thing. Besides, if a gay couple got married, how could that affect me one way or another?" (Scale = -2 [denial of boundary, instrumentalism])

"I believe that as individuals we should have the right to marry who we want to. According to the constitution this is supposed to be the land of the free. We as a people do not have to answer for another persons sins. Let them marry." (Scale = 3 [protected status, citation of authority, noninstrumentalism])

TABLE 3.3
Reasoning Effect Experimental Results

Dependent Variable	Issue Area			
	Double-Sided Sacred		Single-Sided Sacred	
	Gay Marriage	Death Penalty	Environment	Guns
	Sacred v. Negotiable Rhetoric	Sacred v. Negotiable Rhetoric	Sacred v. Negotiable Rhetoric	Sacred v. Negotiable Rhetoric
Argument 1: Sacred Rhetoric Increases Absolutist Reasoning				
Opinion	F = 1.32 (p = .25)	F = 0.62 (p = .43)	F = 0.80 (p = .37)	F = 0.99 (p = .32)
Absolutist Reasoning	**F = 9.37 (p = .01)**	**F = 15.93 (p = .01)**	**F = 16.56 (p = .01)**	**F = 8.37 (p = .01)**
Argument 1a: Even among Listeners Who Disagree				
Reasoning by Those Who Disagree	**F = 5.35 (p = .02)**	**F = 6.61 (p = .01)**	F = 0.39 (p = .53)	F = 0.52 (p = .47)

Results in each of the tables are F statistics derived from a one-way analysis of variance (ANOVA), comparing the sacred rhetoric treatment to the negotiable rhetoric treatment. Statistically significant results are in bold ($p < .05$).

"Opinion" is reported along a seven-point scale, where lower scores are more ideologically liberal. Absolutist Reasoning is gauged along a scale of consequentialism to absolutism, based on the participant's answer to the open-ended question, "Please tell us more about your thinking on this question. Can you explain why you hold the view that you hold?" Answers ranged from -2 (consequentialist reasoning) to 3 (absolutist reasoning).

"Reasoning by Those Who Disagree" is restricted to participants who disagreed with the direction of the appeal (i.e., responded from 1 to 3 on the seven-point scale of opinion). N = 107, 72, 48, and 137 respectively. Positive results indicate that even listeners who disagreed with the content of the message were influenced by its form, shifting them toward absolutist reasoning.

Death Penalty:

"I believe in the principle 'An eye for an eye'" (Scale = 1 [citation of authority])

"I think the death penalty should be used—and used often. If we just let murderers sit in jail for a life sentence how is that going to stop others from murdering." (Scale = -1 [consequentialism])

"I do not believe in the death penalty. Yes the Bible says an eye for an eye but it also says though shalt not kill. What as individuals gives us the right to decide if he should die, leaving there blood on our hands. What if yrs down the road they find that the person didn't do it—you can't bring him back. But if sentenced to life with no parole he could be released." (Scale = -3 [denial of authority, relativism, consequentialism])

When we compare the form of reasoning employed by the two groups, we find consistent and strong evidence that exposure to sacred rhetoric increases the degree of absolutist reasoning. In all four domains there is a statistically significant and substantively influential effect.[24] We can state with confidence that there is a strong effect of sacred rhetoric on reasoning process.

Disagreement and Absolutist Reasoning

But how pervasive is the reasoning effect? One of the important questions about sacred rhetoric is whether the reasoning shift applies to *all* listeners or only to those who agree with the message. If listeners who oppose the appeal are still influenced toward employing more absolutist reasoning, then the influence of sacred rhetoric is more politically significant (*Hypothesis 1a*). To test this hypothesis, I limited the sample to those who disagreed with the statement and again tested for differences between the sacred and nonsacred groups. For example, in regard to the anti-gay marriage statements, I selected only participants who gave opinions in favor of gay marriage (a 1, 2, or 3 on the seven-point scale). The same procedure was applied to the death penalty, environment, and guns. In two out of four domains, citizens who were exposed to sacred rhetoric but disagreed with its message still employed absolutist reasoning at higher rates than those exposed to nonsacred rhetoric.[25] Their form of argumentation was significantly affected even though they continued to dispute the appeal itself. This is particularly strong evidence that sacred rhetoric influences the reasoning process of its listeners, even while not changing opinions—or despite blatant disagreement.

Had we not been considering the single- or double-sidedness of the issues, it might appear that sacred rhetoric is ineffective half of the time among those who disagree. Because the effect is in evidence only in regard to gay marriage and the death penalty but not the other two domains, this could suggest a weak or partial effect. But on reflection, the effect should be moderated by the nature of the domain. We can expect greater absolutist reasoning by those who disagree with a sacred appeal, but only in regard to clearly double-sided political domains. The likely single-sided nature of the pro-gun rights and pro-environment positions provides a persuasive reason that we should not expect absolutist reasoning among those who disagree with the sacred appeals in regard to these domains. Both opposing arguments are grounded in consequentialist positions—the one because of the deaths resulting from gun ownership and the other because of the loss of economic output caused by environmental regulation. Hence the lack of result in the gun and environmental domains but a strong effect in the cases of gay marriage and the death penalty provides strong support for the argument. The finding that sacred rhetoric affects reasoning processes within double-sided domains even among listeners who disagree with its message is strong evidence of its influence.

The Importance of Political Reasoning and Public Justification

The psychological importance of the findings is that a specific form of political appeal—sacred rhetoric—has a significant effect on citizens' reasoning process even in the absence of any unusual influence on aggregate opinion. The distinctive effect of sacred rhetoric is on the reasons offered rather than the opinions held, an influence on public discourse rather than public opinion. Sacred rhetoric increases the prevalence of absolutist reasoning based on principles and authorities, boundaries and moral anger, while decreasing citizens' reliance on arguments grounded in consequences for public welfare. The influence of sacred rhetoric is pervasive, operating even among listeners who disagree with the direction of the message. Because effects on reasoning process are more subtle than direct persuasion effects, they may be overlooked by political researchers concentrating on political opinions. But process rather than outcome effects represent a significant and underappreciated facet of political persuasion.

Differences in reasoning process may be important because they could lead to differences in opinion, but they are also meaningful in and of themselves because they change the ways that citizens justify their positions. One of the most important consequences of sacred rhetoric may be for democratic deliberation and the nature of public discourse within civil society. One focus of contemporary political science is the ongoing debate about the state of American democracy, or the degree to which our democracy matches the different principles of representation in which we traditionally believed or have more recently come to hold. Several normative and empirical research agendas converge on the central question of the degree to which our political system lives up to the norms of representation and citizen engagement to which it aspires, or the degree to which it is healthy or malfunctioning. Different aspects of this conversation take divergent perspectives on the health of American democracy, the causes of its maladies, and the prescriptions for its improvement, but they are all part of what Theda Skocpol and Morris Fiorina describe as the general agreement "that social dynamics are closely intertwined with the health of democracy."[26] Two of the most prominent arguments are from the perspectives of a more participatory or a more deliberative democracy.

The *deliberative democracy* approach argues that all forms of political engagement within the organizations of civil society are *not* created equal; the form of civic engagement matters. In this view the most appropriate form of civic engagement is unrestrained discussion leading toward reasoned agreement. The central requirement of democratic legitimacy is deliberation in public by members of all sectors of society. Grounded in the work of Jurgen Habermas, deliberative democracy emphasizes the importance of communication within the public sphere.[27] Because deliberation exists within this realm, it relies directly on the organizations of civil society and the motivation of individuals to engage within them. Deliberative theorists emphasize the importance of reciprocity, or the norm of employing political reasoning that is mutually justifiable. Reciprocity requires that citizens are motivated to come to an accord that is acceptable to all parties. A necessary element for this sort of atmosphere is a mutually agreed standard on which to base arguments, such as their consequences for public welfare. Political theorists such as Amy Gutmann, Dennis Thompson, and Seyla Benhabib argue that the prevalence of essential value conflict is a major challenge for productive deliberation.[28] In this sense sacred rhetoric may have significant ramifications for the prospect of a more deliberative democracy.

As distinct from the deliberative approach, advocates of *participatory democracy* emphasize the value of direct political action among all sectors of society.[29] Participation includes all facets of political engagement, as well as the extension of democracy into collective institutions such as the workplace. The essence of democracy in this view is full participation, which develops more competent and civic-minded citizens. Although both deliberative and participatory democrats emphasize increased citizen involvement, the form of engagement is different. An important distinction between the participatory and deliberative traditions is that participatory democrats expect citizens to have recognized interests and fully formed opinions, while deliberative democrats emphasize the willingness to engage in discussion, rethink views, and find a consensus rather than a victor.

The participatory and deliberative approaches to democracy are often seen as espousing compatible virtues, as both advocate greater civic engagement. However, recent empirical work demonstrates that the two are in important senses antithetical. Deliberation discourages participation because it increases ambivalence and forces citizens to reveal political positions that can exact social costs. On the other side of the coin, greater participation also discourages deliberation because engaged citizens become more politically extreme and committed, limiting their own and others' consideration of alternatives. An excellent discussion of these tensions can be found in Diana Mutz' *Hearing the Other Side*.[30] As Mutz argues, people often value social harmony more than political expression, and consequently increased exposure to deliberation can decrease participation. Among those who do participate actively, their social networks discourage deliberation with others who might disagree, concentrating political discussion among citizens with homogeneous beliefs. John Hibbing and Elizabeth Theiss-Morse argue that it is specifically the exposure to conflict and discord that turns many Americans toward apathy and alienates them from our political institutions.[31] Hence the two democratic virtues of participation and deliberation are at times empirically contradictory.

Communication within the public sphere requires a commitment to only limited forms of conviction, allowing room for compromise and most importantly for respect toward opposing positions. Intransigent positions and absolute convictions are inimical to open discussion and the formation of consensus. In this sense consequentialist and absolutist reasoning have very different influences, especially for the deliberative norm of reciprocity, or employing political reasoning that is mutually justifiable. Hence consequentialist reasoning is a much stronger basis for a deliberative public culture. Absolutist reasoning, in contrast, begins from foundations that are far from mutually agreeable. The expressions of intransigent values can only increase the difficulties of deliberation and consensus. To be clear, it is not just the extremity or content of sacred rhetoric that is significant but also its form of expression. Not only opinions but also their justifications affect the nature of public discourse. Reasoning that is absolute, inflexible, or strident allows little room for negotiation, compromise, or mutual agreement.

In some senses the reasons a citizen gives for an opinion are as important as the opinions themselves. The mode rather than content of an argument determines whether public debate is civil or strident, negotiable or intractable. Starting from cultural authorities as a foundation for an argument means that a citizen can accept either one side's authorities or another's; no compromise is possible. Absolutist positions that insist on the primacy of certain principles leave little room for conciliation. To win adherents, their advocates can only become more strident, more shrill, more insistent. The difference in the prevalence of the two forms of reasoning is a difference in the nature of our public culture.

Chapter Four

THE ACTIVATION EFFECT

Sacred Rhetoric and Participation

The shift from mundane opinion to sacred value signals not only a change in how citizens reason but also a change in how they engage in politics. The sacred shift engendered by absolutist rhetoric may have important consequences for American democracy, increasing citizen engagement at the same time that it lowers the capacity for deliberation. In this chapter we examine the empirical evidence for the activation effect of sacred rhetoric, grounded in the psychology of the sacred.

SACRED MOTIVATION

Why some citizens engage in politics more than others is a central question for our understanding of democratic representation, but the motivation to participate has never been especially clear. In the view of more rationalist approaches, differences in participation are tied to disparities in the calculated benefits to be received. In Anthony Downs' famous formulation, the profit to be found in political knowledge or engagement for most people is quite low, which explains the persistence of both political ignorance and apathy.[1] Rational ignorance and the collective action problem can be overcome by offering citizens exclusive benefits for participation, as famously suggested by Mancur Olson.[2] However, those who read to the end of *The Logic of Collective Action* note that Olson makes a clear distinction in the final chapter between economic interests and those that are guided by other motives. In regard to value-driven politics,

> the theory is not at all sufficient where philanthropic lobbies, that is, lobbies that voice concern about some group other than the group that supports the lobby, or religious lobbies are concerned. In philanthropic and religious lobbies the relationships between purposes and interests of the individual, and the purposes and interests of the organization, may be so rich and obscure that a theory of the sort developed here cannot provide much insight . . . Where non-rational or irrational behavior is the basis for a lobby, it would perhaps be better to turn to psychology or social psychology than to economics for a relevant theory.[3]

The role of sacred motivation may provide more traction in explaining the politics of belief. Political engagement relies on the connection between belief and a call to individual action, which the potentially successful politician or social movement leader must make clear. If we concentrate not merely on the question of what motivates citizen engagement, but on motivations that can be influenced by political activists, we arrive at the role of rhetoric. Rational incentives to participate are mostly outside of the control of political leaders or social movement entrepreneurs. Other potential explanations for the differences in levels of participation also center on mechanisms that are largely out of the control of political actors, including resource availability (citizens who are more affluent in money and time are more likely to participate) and social norms of participation (citizens who see voting or other forms of participation as a social duty are the ones who are most active). Rhetoric, in contrast, is within the province of political movements. The choice of language, symbol, and frame is under their control and may be their best avenue of influence.

One powerful rhetorical influence open to political actors may be the shifting of the sacred in the minds of citizens. Interestingly, Olson himself identifies an alternative explanation for political engagement that dovetails with the role of sacred rhetoric: citizens are motivated by "an individual, non-collective satisfaction in the form of *a feeling of personal moral worth*, or because of *a desire for respectability or praise.*"[4] The psychology of the sacred suggests that these are the two key mechanisms that lead to engagement—valorization and cleansing. Participation in the service of the sacred is valorized, increasing our sense of dignity, righteousness, or honor. And participation allows us to morally cleanse any disquieting or disreputable affiliation with the profane. As Olson suggests, political participation is not merely a personal but also a public act. It allows us to establish or reestablish our moral standing, both private and public. For these two reasons, sacred status offers the combination of carrot and stick to encourage civic engagement—the benefit of personal valorization and the detriment of contamination if one does not morally cleanse.

Antisacred acts or opinions are not merely wrong: they are a violation. If sacred rhetoric can create this shift in citizens' minds, from seeing political opposition as ordinary wrongheadedness to perceiving it as an indecent act, then participation grounded in valorization and moral cleansing should follow. Rectifying a violation allows us to improve our self-image, creating personal meaning and identity through a political act. In the formulation of the Sacred Value Protection Model (SVPM), Tetlock argues that exposure to violations of sacred values will lead citizens to "engage in symbolic acts of moral cleansing designed to reaffirm their solidarity with their moral community."[5] Previous experiments reveal that this effect is not limited to literal acts or opinions that violate sacred boundaries, but is triggered by *mere contemplation*. Citizens who even considered whether boundaries such as legalizing prostitution or selling human body parts should be violated were more likely to both express moral outrage and to seize opportunities to engage in moral cleansing such as volunteering for an organ donation campaign. The mere contemplation effect is a powerful suggestion that sacred rhetoric alone may be an agent of influence, given the peculiar psychology of the sacred.

The Activation Effect of Sacred Rhetoric

Along with the process effect of greater absolutist reasoning, we can expect *an activation effect of sacred rhetoric, leading to greater intensity and engagement* (*Argument 2*). Activation would be considered an outcome effect, although the outcome is not a different opinion, but greater political involvement. Beliefs may not change, but citizens connect existing beliefs to their political significance.[6] About sacred objects we not only think differently but care more. Their violation is less tolerable, and political effort to rectify such a situation is valorized. A successful sacred appeal can therefore be expected to increase the perceived political importance of the issue at hand. Even though the citizen's opinion may remain the same, the issue itself is of greater note.

Activation can be conceptualized in several different ways. Along with the increased importance ascribed to a political issue, activation is reflected in greater political engagement, such as the intention to vote, to take part in political discussions, and to participate in campaigns. Activation can also be observed in greater intensity of feeling toward one's own political position and a decline in the perceived legitimacy of opposing arguments. If sacred rhetoric influences both citizens who agree with its message and those who disagree, then we should see greater extremism in each direction. Even while not creating greater attitude change in the intended direction of the message, sacred rhetoric may push opinions away from the center. Although I argue that the central effect of sacred rhetoric is on process rather than outcome, a related outcome effect that may occur is polarization rather than persuasion.

To test the activation effect, it is important to see whether sacred rhetoric exerts influence across a wide spectrum of possible variables. These can be divided into effects on *citizen engagement* (the intent to vote, to take part in political discussions, to attempt to convince others of your position, or to contribute to political campaigns) and effects on *political intensity* (the extremity of opinions, perceived importance of the issue, or perceived legitimacy of opposing arguments). Even though sacred rhetoric does not shift opinion any more effectively than negotiable rhetoric, it may polarize opinion by increasing intensity in both directions simultaneously. Just as sacred rhetoric increases absolutist reasoning by both those who agree with its message and those who disagree, it may lead to extremism on either side as well. Sacred rhetoric should push opinions away from the center at the same time that it increases reliance on authorities, boundaries, and absolutes. This emphasis should also increase citizens' perceptions of an issue's importance or its centrality to their political conclusions and actions.

Opposing views, by contrast, should be granted less legitimacy. The greater the degree that one's values are absolute and unquestionable, not to be weighed against competing concerns, the less one has to view opposing positions with any respect. Sacred rhetoric is likely to lessen the perceived legitimacy of challenges to a sacred position because of its appeals to absolutism and nonconsequentialism. These appeals represent an extreme form of framing effect, as they do not just lessen the weight assigned to the opposing values or consequences, but argue that they have no weight at all.[7] A successful absolutist argument changes the reasoning process from one of weighing competing considerations into one of identifying the appropriate principle and isolating it from consequentialist challenges. A successful nonconsequentialist appeal gives listeners a basis for eliminating all concern for the results of their position; the principle is all and the consequences emphasized by the opposing side are nothing. In sum, sacred rhetoric should be accompanied by greater political intensity, revealed by more extreme opinions, opposition to which is seen as increasingly illegitimate, about issues that are increasingly important.

If we compare the extremity of citizens' opinions when exposed to sacred and nonsacred rhetoric, in three out of four domains the sacred group has more extreme opinions toward *both* sides (only opinions on the environment do not show polarization) (table 4.1). Fewer citizens remain in the middle, while there are both more people strongly in favor and more people strongly opposed to the sentiment of the appeal. The effect of sacred rhetoric is to polarize its listeners, creating a more divided and strident environment.

TABLE 4.1
Activation Effect Experimental Results: Intensity

Dependent Variable	Issue Area			
	Double-Sided Sacred		Single-Sided Sacred	
	Gay Marriage	Death Penalty	Environment	Guns
	Sacred v. Negotiable Rhetoric	Sacred v. Negotiable Rhetoric	Sacred v. Negotiable Rhetoric	Sacred v. Negotiable Rhetoric
Extremity of Opinion	**F = 13.46 (p = .01)**	**F = 7.82 (p = .01)**	F = 0.29 (p = .59)	**F = 11.08 (p = .01)**
Importance of the Issue	**F = 4.46 (p = .03)**	F = 1.58 (p = .21)	F = 0.11 (p = .74)	**F = 6.93 (p = .01)**
Illegitimacy of Opposing Arguments	F = 0.61 (p = .44)	**F = 5.97 (p = .02)**	F = 3.33 (p = .06)	F = 0.24 (p = .62)

Results are F statistics derived from a one-way analysis of variance (ANOVA), comparing the sacred rhetoric treatment to the negotiable rhetoric treatment. All statistically significant results are in bold ($p < .05$). N = 237.

"Extremity of Opinion" is tested by folding the opinion scale, such that moderate opinions are the low end of the scale and extreme opinions the high end (4 = 0; 3 or 5 = 1; 2 or 6 = 2; and 1 or 7 = 3). "Importance of the Issue" is reported along a four-point scale: 1 = Not at all important; 2 = Somewhat important; 3 = Important; 4 = Very important. "Illegitimacy of Opposing Arguments" is recorded along a seven-point scale derived from "Opponents of same-sex marriage argue that it would degrade traditional marriages. How legitimate is that argument?" 1 = Legitimate; 7 = Not Legitimate. The wording for other domains was: "Opponents of the death penalty argue that it does not deter crime; Opponents of environmental controls argue that it lessens economic growth; Opponents of gun rights argue that gun ownership leads to more violent deaths."

Table 4.1 also demonstrates the influence of sacred rhetoric on the perceived importance of the issues discussed and the perceived legitimacy of opposing positions. Participants were asked, "How important to you is [gay marriage/the death penalty/the environment/guns] as a political issue?" In two out of four domains (gay marriage and guns), sacred rhetoric increased perceptions of the importance of the issue. After reading the political statements, participants were also asked about the legitimacy of opposing arguments. For gay marriage the question was, "Opponents of same-sex marriage argue that it would degrade traditional marriages. How legitimate is that argument?" Responses were along a seven-point scale anchored by Legitimate (1) and Not Legitimate (7). The wording for other domains was, "Opponents of the death penalty argue that it does not deter crime," "Opponents of environmental controls argue that it lessens economic growth," and "Opponents of gun rights argue that gun ownership leads to more violent deaths." Citizens exposed to sacred rhetoric were significantly more likely to consider the opposing positions to be illegitimate in two out of four domains (death penalty and environment). Although each test was not upheld in each domain, there is a clear pattern of increasing intensity. Of the several different tests, there are statistically significant effects in seven out of twelve cases. Each of the facets of intensity—the extremity of opinion, the perceived importance of the issue, and the perceived illegitimacy of opposing arguments—is increased by exposure to sacred rather than negotiable rhetoric.

To test aspects of political engagement as opposed to intensity, a second experiment was designed to focus on these effects. In this experiment, participants were randomly selected to receive either sacred or negotiable messages for all four domains, rather than randomizing each exposure. If the exposure to sacred or negotiable rhetoric were mixed as in the first experiment, we could not determine an overall effect on participation, but in the second experiment the causal influence is clear. After reading the arguments, participants were asked about various aspects of political engagement, including how likely they were to vote, to engage in political discussions, to try to convince someone they know to support their political views, and to contribute money to a candidate who supports their views during the next campaign season.

As illustrated in table 4.2, we find significant effects of sacred rhetoric in two of the four aspects of civic engagement. Citizens' intent to discuss politics moved on average from 5.3 to 6.0 on the seven-point scale, and their intent to convince others to see things their way jumped from 4.0

TABLE 4.2
Activation Effect Experimental Results: Engagement

Dependent Variable	Total	Agree	Disagree
Intent to Vote	F = 0.68 (p = .41)	F = 0.15 (p = .90)	F = 0.94 (p = .34)
Intent to Discuss	**F = 6.19 (p = .01)**	**F = 6.87 (p = .01)**	F = 0.29 (p = .59)
Intent to Convince	**F = 8.94 (p = .01)**	**F = 4.02 (p = .05)**	F = 0.03 (p = .88)
Intent to Contribute	F = 1.94 (p = .17)	**F = 6.50 (p = .02)**	F = 2.13 (p = .15)

Results are F statistics derived from a one-way analysis of variance (ANOVA), comparing the sacred rhetoric treatment to the negotiable rhetoric treatment. All statistically significant results are in bold ($p < .05$).

In the first round of experiments, each political domain was randomly sacred or nonsacred, so the final questions regarding intent to participate would not be related to the overall exposure to sacred rhetoric. The second round was designed to test these effects by exposing participants to only sacred or nonsacred rhetoric for all four domains. N = 136.

The Agree group is restricted to participants whose opinion agreed with the direction of the argument in at least three out of the four domains (N = 38). The Disagree test is identical in the opposite direction (N = 44).

Intent to Vote, Discuss, Convince, and Contribute are gauged with seven-point scales derived from "How likely are you to vote in the next national election?," ". . . engage in political discussions in the next campaign season?," ". . . try to convince someone you know to support your political views during the next national campaign?," ". . . contribute money to a candidate who supports your views during next campaign season?" (1 = Very Unlikely, 7 = Certainly)

to 5.0 on the scale. The differences for voting and contributing were also higher in the sacred rhetoric condition (by 0.2 and 0.4, respectively), but these increases were not statistically significant. However, there is a strong indication of why voting in particular did not demonstrate a significant effect: respondents are already clustered at the top of the scale, with more than half of the participants in each condition recording a 7 on the scale, indicating that they were "certainly" going to vote. Survey and experimental participants generally overstate their likelihood to vote, not allowing enough variation for the rhetorical influence to show an effect. However, for both discussing politics and attempting to convince others, exposure to sacred rhetoric has a strong influence.

The Backlash Question

But is there a backlash effect? Does sacred rhetoric activate only citizens who support its cause, or does it also activate those in opposition? If a sacred appeal is equally motivating to those who are impressed and those who are annoyed, there may be no net benefit for its advocates. The overall level of political engagement would rise, but the partisan advantage of political activation would be lost. To test this possibility, we can split the sample into those who are in agreement with the appeals and those who are in dissent. For the four domains, I identified the participants who agreed with at least three of the four appeals. In the group that agreed with the messages, the influence of sacred rhetoric is equally positive in regard to their intent to discuss politics and to convince others. Although the influence of sacred rhetoric on the intent to contribute to campaigns was not statistically significant in the whole sample (moving up only 0.4 on the seven-point scale), in the group more in agreement with the messages it jumped more than two points on the scale, from an average of 2.2 to 4.4, an extremely statistically significant difference. On the whole, sacred rhetoric has remarkable effects when we concentrate on citizens who resonate with its message. However, in the group that largely disagreed with the appeals, there were no effects at all within all four forms of political engagement. The numbers employed in these tests were necessarily small, meaning that we cannot have the same degree of confidence in these findings.[8] But the disparity between the agreeing and disagreeing groups is so striking that it is highly suggestive that the activation effects are contingent on agreement. The initial evidence at least indicates that a backlash effect is unlikely.

Sacred Rhetoric and Participatory Democracy

The activation effect of sacred rhetoric provides an insight into the role of principled belief in political thought and motivation. While citizen engagement is often seen as a matter of socioeconomic status and resources—those with greater education, wealth, and time participate more in politics—this ignores the potentially important connections between political engagement and sacredness. Regardless of the consistent performance of socioeconomic variables in statistical analyses of participation, the increasing levels of average education and wealth within the American public in the second half of the twentieth century did not lead to higher levels of citizen engagement during that period. Resource-based approaches certainly provide some insight into our political process, but they shed more light on why some citizens *can* have more influence, rather than the process of how some *choose* to do so but most (even in the higher socioeconomic ranges) do not. Regarding the crucial question of who has influence in democratic politics, for each given issue it may be the people who care the most rather than those who have the most resources.

Sacred rhetoric is not only an advantage to the partisans who employ it. It has a broader effect of engendering a more participatory democracy. One of the more striking features of American politics is the sheer lack of interest among our citizens. In the battle for the public's attention, citizens' own immediate lives are more compelling than the concerns of remote politicians; the pursuit of happiness in a market economy is more absorbing than public policy. In Robert Weissberg's phrase, "The Home Shopping Network inevitably trumps C-SPAN."[9] Anything that cuts through the public's inattention, increases its political intensity, and leads to civic engagement is likely to be seen as beneficial by many democratic theorists.

However, sacred rhetoric has a more complex effect. It *increases participation* at the same time that it *decreases deliberation*. One way to discuss the meaning of this contradiction is to focus on the competing goals of deliberative and participatory democrats. Deliberative democrats emphasize the importance of collective discussion on the basis of the discourse principle—that decisions should be made only if all affected by the decision would agree.[10] The ideal requires that no concerned citizens be excluded and no power relations distort the discussion. The norm of reciprocity assumes that all citizens are equally motivated to come to an accord that is acceptable to all parties. A central requirement for this sort of atmosphere is a recognized standard on which to base arguments, such as their consequences for public welfare. Under these circumstances the governing factor is, in Jurgen Habermas' phrase, "the forceless force of the better argument." In this sense deliberative democracy offers a particular standard for a healthy democracy—what is legitimate is only *what is deliberated to consensus by the people collectively*.

The main object of deliberation in public, and of deliberative democracy itself, is legitimacy. The theme that haunts discussions of deliberative democracy is the nagging doubt about government legitimacy following World War II. In her volume *Democracy and Difference*, Seyla Benhabib identifies three public goods that "complex modern democratic societies since the Second World War face the task of securing."[11] The second and third of these are economic welfare and collective identity, but the first among them is legitimacy. The method of gaining this political good is deliberation: "I will argue that legitimacy in complex democratic societies must be thought to result from the free and unconstrained public deliberations of all matters of common concern."[12] Habermas himself defines deliberative democracy as the "democratic procedure that lends legitimating force to lawmaking under conditions of social and ideological pluralism."[13] Deliberative democrats argue that only through deliberation is democracy freed from the weight of past custom and the tyranny of current elites. As John Dryzek phrases it, "Communicative rationalization frees the lifeworld from the dead hand of custom, myth, and illusion on the one hand and the domination of specialists and manipulators on the other."[14] Even Alexis de Tocqueville, whose focus was on equality, notes that legitimacy is a major democratic concern, but for deliberative democrats it is their central concern.[15]

Legitimacy, however, is far from the only democratic virtue. The central point of participatory approaches, which distinguishes them from deliberative perspectives, is that democracy inherently means full democracy, of all able citizens in all aspects of representative governance. Less-than-full participation is less-than-full democracy. Participation is not less valued if citizens come to the process with inflexible opinions. It is not the development of consensus but the expression of opinion that is paramount. Political engagement is valued not merely as a means to representation, but instead is seen as an end in itself. Participation is to be valued as a means of expression, which is part of what it means to be human (a political animal); hence a sense of political community is a good in its own right.

The important point this illustrates is that each of these democratic approaches wishes to maximize a different virtue. Participatory approaches see political engagement (as both a means toward representation and as end in itself) as the thing to be valued most highly, while deliberative democrats believe it is legitimacy, which they argue is best achieved through discourse. When trade-offs are to be made, each approach argues for a different virtue to be privileged.

The legitimacy claims of deliberative democrats are not without criticism. Why is deliberation the only or primary source of legitimacy? Consensus sacredness and traditional authority also provide legitimacy. It may be an odd pretense that deliberation is its only source. Habermas argues that this is the case because we "no longer legitimate maxims, practices, and rules of action simply by calling attention to the contexts in which they were handed down."[16] But this observation is more and less true in different political cultures. To understand the origins of deliberative theory, it is important to note that the concern about the legitimacy of basic institutions is a syndrome more European than American. Legitimacy is often grounded in historical weight—the older, more hallowed, and more traditional it is, the more legitimate an institution becomes. In the European context, entire governments were delegitimized in the eyes of their people in the aftermath of World War II (as were the Communist governments of the Soviet bloc in the succeeding generations). History and past practice (one of the usual sources of legitimacy) hence had little force for many citizens, and the nagging doubt over what was legitimate and how it could be identified has been a central focus of European thought since the war. Americans, in contrast, do not have this problem. American politics is grounded in a reverence for the Founding and our political past. Contrary to Habermas' assertion that institutions are no longer legitimized by calling attention to the context of their origins, this is precisely what Americans tend to do, and what American law does.[17] Political legitimacy is grounded in constitutionalism as one of the strongest American consensus sacred values. Legitimacy in the sense of public certainty about the form and justification of institutions is not an American problem; that Habermas is a member of the postwar German generation that has that problem is not a coincidence.

Participatory democracy likewise has its own failures in what it values most. The Achilles' heel of a participatory system is the refusal to admit that not all political engagement is positive. One of the usual assumptions of the civil society literature is that all participation is good participation; greater citizen engagement is by definition superior to less. But this should not be an unexamined assumption. In a liberal democracy, too much engagement by the extremely committed, unyielding, or illiberal may be a detriment, just as too much apathy is. Instead of seeing it as an unmitigated good, some commentators such as Jacques Barzun define participation differently: "Participatory democracy is in fact direct minority rule, a kind of reverse democracy for coercing authority by protests, demonstrations, sit-ins, and job actions in order to obtain the rapid satisfaction of new demands."[18] Rather than the vices of apathy, we may wish to be concerned about those of extremism. What degrades democracy more: apathy and lack of involvement or the strong, even violent, passions that curtail meaningful deliberation, make reasoned agreement difficult, and discourage participation by moderates?

Sacred rhetoric is connected to the nature of democracy in two fundamental ways: (1) sacred rhetoric encourages absolutist reasoning, influencing the *nature* of civic engagement and degrading the prospects for deliberation, and (2) sacred rhetoric encourages political intensity, influencing the *degree* of civic engagement and increasing the prospects for participation. Through its influence on the degree and nature of civic engagement, sacred rhetoric may have simultaneously positive and negative effects, a complex legacy. The implications for the quality of democracy depend on whether sacredness is encouraging citizens to rise from a state of apathy or descend into a state of unreason; it is a complex, even paradoxical observation that intensity is simultaneously necessary and detrimental for democratic health. Table 4.3 illustrates the central ways that the political consequences of sacred rhetoric can be conceptualized, emphasizing the influences on both democratic health and partisan politics. The contradiction engendered by sacred rhetoric is further complicated by the disparities in the use of sacred appeals by different political groups. As we shall see in the following chapters, sacred rhetoric creates a partisan advantage as well as a democratic quandary.

TABLE 4.3
Consequences of Sacred Rhetoric

Democratic Effects

Effect	*Mechanism*
Positive for Participation	Sacred rhetoric activates citizens, encouraging political intensity and engagement
Negative for Deliberation	Sacred rhetoric increases absolutist reasoning, changing public discourse

Partisan Effects

Advantages the Republican Party	Republicans tend to employ more sacred rhetoric, increasing the absolutism and engagement of listeners
Advantages Social Movements Employing Sacred Rhetoric	Increases the absolutism and engagement of movement supporters

PART II

POLITICAL CONSEQUENCES OF SACRED RHETORIC

Chapter Five

"From My Cold, Dead Hands"

Sacred Rhetoric and Social Movements

Social movements throughout American history have not shied away from sacred commitments. Prominent examples include abolition, free silver, temperance, women's suffrage, and civil rights, to name only a few. Contemporary movements grounded in sacred rhetoric include both the pro-life and pro-choice movements; both gay rights and the political rise of the religious right that opposes challenges to traditional family arrangements, especially gay marriage; the peace and anti-death penalty movements; and the environmental and gun rights movements. In this chapter I examine the role of sacred rhetoric in how social movements succeed in their aim of changing prevailing social norms. The focus is on social movements as proponents of ideas. In this sense the discussion of social movement politics lays the groundwork for our later examination of partisan politics. Although social movements tend to focus on cultural change, and political parties on electoral victory, they overlap in the realm of language and persuasion. The effective use of sacred rhetoric by social movements mirrors and explains the employment of the same approach by some but not most political actors.

While the discussion in this chapter takes into account several social movements, the focus is on the rhetoric of gun rights: its invocation of sacredness, its connection to the master frame of rights, and the important but often overlooked connections between the gun rights and civil rights movements. To develop this argument, I first examine the nature of social movements as contests over public ideas, and then describe the mechanisms through which sacred rhetoric advantages movements in this endeavor.

Social Movements as Ideas

Social movements can be understood most clearly as explicit attempts to advance specific ideas or values. In this sense social movements can be defined as collective attempts to alter the balance of beliefs in society. Academic approaches that focus on the organization, resources, or political opportunities of movements, rather than the ideas they promote, limit our understanding of what social movements do and the role of rhetoric in their success. A useful definition of a social movement may be *cultural vanguardism*, attempting to lead a change in prevailing social norms by altering the dominant discourse. This interpretation gives us a clear view of the central tools and purposes of social movements (to employ language to change ideas), as well as a definition of their success or failure (whether cultural change takes place).

Culture is an elusive and contested concept, though such a powerful one that it is hard to ignore. It may be enough to define a culture as the pattern of beliefs and norms of a group with a shared identity, in its broadest sense the "symbolic expressive aspect of human behavior."[1] A culture comprises not only positive influences but also negative constraints—the perceived limits to belief and action that group association creates. In a pluralistic society, when we speak of a dominant or mainstream culture, this presupposes subcultures that dissent from the common pattern. But the broader cultural constraints remain meaningful for all members of society, whether they embrace or attack them. Subcultures define themselves against the broader culture, remaining highly aware of its power. The goal of a social movement is to influence others to alter the beliefs, behaviors, and language of the mainstream culture, either to move closer to the movement's preferences or at least to increase the respect and recognition given to its views.

There are many subgroups within American society that adopt distinct beliefs and ways of living but do not constitute a social movement, specifically because they are attempting to depart from the larger culture rather than change it. An example is the Montana Freemen, who do not form a social movement because they are not making a sustained campaign to alter our prevailing social norms; they simply want nothing to do with them. We hear little about the Freemen, because they do not care what other Americans think and are not trying to change them. In contrast, Evangelical movements care a great deal about prevailing norms and popular beliefs, and make sustained efforts to influence society rather than avoid it. Much of this has to do with language, or a contest over the words that are used in public expression. The essence of cultural vanguardism is contesting the prevailing discourse, altering culture by influencing the day-to-day language of other members of society.

This conceptualization provides a clear distinction between social movements and interest groups, which are often confused. The target of social movements is the belief systems of society; the target of interest groups is government policy. Of course these may overlap: the pro-life cause involves both a social movement and interest groups, but this is not necessarily the case. The AARP is a clear interest group, with no discernable "pro-older Americans" social movement aimed at changing prevalent attitudes or social norms. An example of the reverse—a social movement without an interest group—would be the free love movement of the 1960s. While it was clearly a movement aimed at changing social mores toward sexuality, I am not aware of an interest group of free love advocates intent on changing government policy. In this sense social movements and interest groups are distinct in conceptual and empirical terms, even though they often overlap.

There is no doubt that social movements have a strong ideational component, but defining them in this way has not always been in the mainstream of social movement scholarship. More orthodox interpretations of social movements focus on resource mobilization, political opportunities, or other materialist foundations that neglect the cognitive nature of social movements.[2] Although the interpretation of social movements as ideas is not widely recognized, several strains of contemporary scholarship support it, beginning with Michael McGee's 1980 article on the ideational rather than material origin of social movements. As he describes it, "the issue was materialism versus idealism: The dispute was over *what* 'moves' in history—the material things which are our physical environment or the human ideas which mediate and interpret the facts of our experience."[3]

In the following decades, the more Hegelian view of social movements developed further, understanding them as the vanguard of ideational change.[4] As Bert Klandermans phrases it, "Organizers are 'social reconstructionists'; they construct an alternative view of social reality."[5] This is especially true of what have come to be described as new social movements, which have more cultural than economic goals and work outside of the normal channels of party politics. Several of the issues in American politics characterized by sacred rhetoric are the same issues associated with new social movements, such as abortion, gun rights, peace, the death penalty, and environmentalism. An ideational approach is especially meaningful when we take into account that many scholars argue that the influence of social movements on government policy runs from marginal to counterproductive.[6] Their larger influence is on social thought rather than policy change.

An ideational approach can incorporate many important elements of previous studies of social movements, even as it reconceptualizes movements as organized efforts to change prevailing social norms. Two powerful concepts are Charles Tilly and Sidney Tarrow's idea of a *contentious repertoire*, and David Snow and Robert Benford's notion of a *master frame*. A social movement employs tactics from a known bag of tricks, sometimes referred to as its contentious repertoire, or the "arrays of contentious performances that are currently known and available within some set of political actors."[7] Social movements employ many tools, such as petitions, letter campaigns, marches, demonstrations, sit-ins, pamphleteering, media interviews, various tactics of fund-raising, demonstrating numbers by wearing identifying marks of dress, or gaining celebrity endorsements. A more recent innovation is creating movies that promote a movement, such as Al Gore's *An Inconvenient Truth* (2006). The concept of a repertoire highlights a movement's cultural limits as well as possibilities: once a new element of contention is innovated by one movement, it can enter the set of cultural possibilities of all movements, but only if they see it as within their bounds of appropriate behaviors. For example, the more aggressive or violent tactics of the radical environmental group Earth First! are not seen as acceptable possibilities for other groups. The displays of humor or ridicule employed by some groups are not thought to be sufficiently high-minded for other movements, who would see such displays as decreasing the seriousness of their cause. One of the elements of a contentious repertoire that is most available, and most in control of movement leadership, is the style of rhetoric a movement employs. Sacred rhetoric is an effective contentious technique, but only for those who see its possibilities and accept its validity.

Another aspect of social movement theory that dovetails into an ideational approach is the concept of a master frame. In this view one key to success is choosing the most influential way of connecting a movement's specific claims to a larger concept of claim making that is already understood by the audience.[8] Sacred rhetoric taps into two distinct master frames: sacred status and rights. Sacredness is implicitly understood within a broad range of American culture. Sacred rhetoric simply attempts to shift the movement's claim into that realm, changing its nature. The concept of rights also gives an argument a special role and power. The goal of many movements is to shift their claim from a debatable preference to a recognized right. As we will see, there is a clear connection between sacredness and rights creation.

To the degree that scholars underappreciate the ideational foundations of social movements, they also miss the role of sacred rhetoric in the public sacralization of a movement's values and the resulting encouragement of citizen engagement to advance a movement's goals. Tilly and Tarrow define a social movement as "a sustained campaign of claim making"; I argue that making sacred claims lends a movement particular influence, especially in what Hank Johnston and Bert Klandermans call "a movement's cultural work."[9] Social movements show great variation in organization, methods, constituencies, motivating beliefs, and opportunities within existing institutions.[10] However, several of the most influential movements of post–World War II American politics have a unifying feature: an imbalance in the rhetorical sacredness of the opposing sides. This is the case with the civil rights, environmental, and gun rights movements, each of which makes sacred rhetorical claims against the consequentialist reasoning of opponents. For social movement activists, the most effective rhetorical frame may be a sacred one. Movements that request little may be less successful than movements that request much. In the phrase credited to Daniel Burnham, the innovator of the pathbreaking Chicago World's Fair of 1893, "Make no little plans; they have no magic to stir men's blood."

Mobilizing the Faithful, Cowing the Opposition, and Creating Rights

Sacred rhetoric advantages social movements in their cultural contest primarily by increasing mobilization. The two unique influences of sacred rhetoric have a contradictory effect on democratic health as a whole, but both play a positive role for social movements. The increased reliance on absolutist reasoning decreases the prospects for democratic deliberation, but this same form of unyielding reasoning is exactly what drives social movement activists. And the greater intensity and engagement inspired by sacred rhetoric increases democratic participation, advancing social movements just as it does other aspects of politics. Social movements rely on the numbers and commitment of their members, so the psychology of sacred rhetoric creates significant advantages for activists.

In addition to mobilizing the faithful, two other effects that we have not yet discussed also connect sacredness with the success of social movements. Sacred claims may have additional influences on the public at large as well as on the members of the movement, specifically in cowing opposition and creating perceptions of rights.

Cowing the Opposition

There are two obvious targets of social movement rhetoric: supporters to be rallied and potential supporters to be convinced. A third target is nonsupporters who offer activists no hope of conversion. Those citizens may never agree with the movement, but what they think about the movement's supporters is nonetheless critical: Are they perceived as passive or energized? Are they reasonable and negotiable, or likely to take offense and become morally indignant? There are different forms of disagreement with a movement's goals, from adamant and vocal opposition to a passive difference of opinion. The more a social movement can influence its detractors toward the passive end of that spectrum, the less real opposition they will face. Sacred claims may be highly effective in reducing opposition because of a cowing effect.

One purpose of sacred rhetoric is to increase the broader awareness of the sacredness of a movement's position. The point is not only how this influences those who agree, but how it affects those who do not. Violation of a sacred boundary creates a public stigma, placing opposition in a different moral position. Ideas become harder to oppose if many people think of them as moral issues rather than policy matters. Opposition is no longer respectable disagreement, but illegitimate standing; detractors of gay marriage are bigots, opponents of the civil rights movement are racists, adversaries of the pro-life movement are murderers. But this is only the case if citizens know that a movement's supporters will take public offense and think ill of those who oppose them. Hence it can be in a movement's interest to portray its members as absolutists. If other people will be offended, and your own social standing may be hurt by taking a public position, it becomes easier simply to be quiet. Private opposition may not decrease, but public opposition will.

This may be a subtle effect, but it is supported by other scholarship. Theorists from Alexis de Tocqueville to Antonio Gramsci to Michel Foucault have emphasized the pervasive power of conformity to group norms, fueled by the desire to avoid public disapproval. Contemporary empirical researchers in social psychology have also documented the political aspects of individual reactions to group beliefs, especially in the literatures on *accountability*, the *spiral of silence*, and *preference falsification*.[11] Tetlock's studies of accountability demonstrate that citizens faced with speaking to a dissenting audience will take several steps to lessen confrontation, including modifying their position or avoiding speaking altogether. The spiral of silence is an especially significant perspective, because it includes a dynamic element in its effects. A perceived majority will cause some citizens in opposition to be silent; this creates the appearance of a larger majority, which causes even more people to be silent. This can result in the appearance of a near-uniform society even in the face of considerable underlying disagreement. The same outcome of a distinct difference between public appearance and true opinion is documented by Timur Kuran in his work on preference falsification. He argues that dramatic shifts of opinion that appear to occur in both totalitarian and democratic societies are the result of sudden changes in the public perception of what it is acceptable to express. They are not dramatic changes in mass opinion, but instead the sudden public expression of what was previously said only in private. Cowing the opposition into silence is especially likely to occur when the sacred is involved. Social pressure alone may be powerful enough, but adding a sacred element can only increase the effect.

Creating Rights

Another advantage of sacred rhetoric relates to the perception of rights. A common reaction to conflict in American politics emphasizes only a short-run appraisal. For this reason, conflict is generally seen as a negative influence—it is disruptive and seems to have high costs. But in the longer run it may be only conflict, even of the most disruptive kind, that leads to the expansion of democratic freedoms and rights. Aside from the short-term influences of conflict, we must take into account that *the expression of sacred values may also encourage rights creation and maintenance* through the mechanisms of civil society, a long-term influence on democratic prospects. American history is full of examples of conflicts that were seen at the time as negative, dangerous, and highly costly, though in retrospect we see their outcomes as positive advancements. The Civil War is the looming example. Abolitionism is one of the historical belief systems that can be categorized most clearly as sacred, and it surely fits the description of a contemporary negative influence on democratic stability that is seen as exactly the opposite in historical perspective. The history of women's suffrage, the labor movement, and the civil rights era are other excellent examples of contemporary costs and long-term gains. The American Revolution itself fits the same description. It is easy to emphasize the democratic advantages of day-to-day normality rather than the necessity of conflict, but only historical judgment can determine which conflictual sacred values will be negative influences now *and* later, and which will be redeemed. It is said that Zhou Enlai, the Chinese revolutionary and first foreign minister of the People's Republic (1949–1958), was once asked if the French Revolution had been a success; he responded that it was too early to tell.

Advancements in democratic rights are often brought about through collective action but have also relied on the role of individuals who stood up alone against prevailing social norms. Sacredness may be connected to rights creation through the more individual process of acts of *civil courage*. A quintessential example is Rosa Parks, whose refusal to give up her seat to a white person at the cost of her subsequent arrest led to the Alabama bus boycott, a milestone of the civil rights movement.[12] Even more dramatic examples include the Germans who hid Jews during the Holocaust, or American Southerners who hid runaway slaves along the Underground Railroad. Individual acts of this nature can be described as civil courage, or "to dare to act because of one's conviction, even at the risk of paying a high price for this conviction."[13] The term is not in common usage in American social science, but Richard Swedberg argues that it should enter the lexicon as a parallel to the term *civil society*, connoting specifically individual acts of conscience, which have great social and political importance.

Acts of civil courage can support causes that are either positive or negative depending on our perspective. A prominent current example is the interference with the operation of abortion clinics practiced by those who believe, counter to the prevailing law, that abortion is murder. Standing up for their beliefs against the current norm, and potentially accepting arrest as a result, surely counts as an act of civil courage. Whether it will be judged in a positive or negative light by future generations is something of a historical question; in other words, it depends on which direction society goes on the issue. But the origin of acts of civil courage seems to be tied to the sacralization of a cause. Recognizing the absolute or uncompromising nature of sacred boundaries provides a reason, even a commandment, to stand up when those values are violated. That acts of civil courage are rare indicates that additional factors are involved, but sacred rhetoric and civil courage are likely to be strongly linked, as are civil courage and the evolution of rights.

I do not, however, want to digress too far into the complex literature on theories of rights creation. Two relatively uncontroversial points should demonstrate a connection between sacredness and the expansion of rights.

The first is that nonnegotiable and nonconsequentialist values are akin to our understanding of rights. The American constitutional conception of a right can be summarized as a recognized privilege or immunity.[14] Rights establish boundaries to government action, or individual spheres that cannot be abridged. Both sacred rhetoric and rights employ the language of limits. Because they are operationally similar, they may be easily conflated. What one thinks of as sacred, one can easily think of as a right; what is a right may over time become sacred.

The second point is that the evolution of consensus values is connected to the recognition of rights by our political leaders (both elected and judicial). The origin of our rights is a matter of some controversy, but in general when we speak of a right we rely on social recognition as a benchmark—our rights are those that have been upheld by the Supreme Court and are recognized in society, or at least those that we believe *should* be recognized.[15] On the one hand, rights can be understood as being God given and preceding political organization (as in the natural rights tradition), or on the other hand, rights can be conceptualized as fully socially constructed (we have the rights that we collectively think we do). But in either case, the *recognition* of rights changes over time, as citizens either become aware of them (if they are preexisting) or create them among themselves (if they are socially constructed). Scholarship on the rights revolution of the second half of the twentieth century makes the explicit point that it was driven by the increasing rights consciousness of the public and by the explicit efforts of advocacy organizations within civil society.[16] In either way of thinking about rights, the history of their expansion has been a story of struggle and advocacy. The operations of civil society rely on certain democratic freedoms, especially the rights of free speech and assembly. Moreover, it is not merely the specific or legalistic freedoms that allow civil society to thrive, but also a culture that tolerates if not encourages free discussion and dissent.[17] It is no coincidence that civil society relies on democratic rights, just as it is civil society that expands them.

Our assessment of the role of sacred rhetoric, civil courage, and rights creation depends greatly on the historical judgment of the justice of each cause. Whether rights movements, from abolition to pro-life, are positive or negative depends entirely on our long-run assessment of the movement in question. As the noted constitutional scholar Alexander Bickel argued, "The mob, like revolution, is an ambiguous fact. The mob is bad when it is wrong; it may be heroic when it is right."[18] The same applies to contemporary social movements, from the peace movement to gun rights. In the case of our central example of gun rights, how we assess the goals of the movement is a separate matter, but we can see through its history how sacred rhetoric has played a significant role. Its advancement has been encouraged by each of the mechanisms we have discussed: conceptualizing a cause as sacred, mobilizing political engagement, cowing opposition, and maintaining perceptions of rights.

The Gun Rights Movement

The only person to be president of both the United States and the National Rifle Association (NRA) was Ulysses S. Grant, elected the eighteenth U.S. commander in chief in 1868 and the eighth leader of the NRA in 1883. The NRA was founded by former Union officers following the Civil War and was led by several of the most famous surviving Union generals, including Ambrose Burnside, Winfield Scott Hancock, and Philip Sheridan in addition to Grant. These officers had been disappointed by the inducted soldiers' lack of military knowledge and wanted to foster greater skill with firearms among American citizens before future conflicts. For approximately the first hundred years of its existence, the NRA was a shooting and sportsmen's association, but during the 1970s it shifted focus dramatically toward its current role as a civil liberties organization, committed to protecting the ownership of firearms as well as promoting their efficient use. This transition from rifle marksmanship to rights maintenance is crucial to understanding the NRA and its use of language.

The person most noted for his leadership of the NRA is not U. S. Grant, but Charlton Heston, who served three terms from June 1998 to April 2003. A less remembered president is Sandy Froman (2005–2007), who is female, Jewish, and a Harvard Law graduate, traits more closely associated with mainstream social movements on the left rather than the populist right perception of the NRA. But in some aspects of perspective and rhetoric, the contemporary NRA is more akin to those organizations than to grassroots populism. Similar to other prominent social movement organizations, the NRA leadership is media savvy and highly aware of its use of language. In my judgment, however, the NRA is more skilled than many other groups. It is more effective at employing language to make explicit sacred claims that mobilize its base, cow opposition, and maintain perceptions of rights. In the terminology of Tilly and Tarrow's influential work on social movements and contentious politics, the NRA successfully *appropriated* (converted previously nonpolitical networks into political actors) the *social movement base* (network of participants and their cultural traditions) of the large body of American gun owners into a *social movement campaign* (a sustained challenge to power holders through displays of unity, numbers, and commitment).[19] I argue that its central tactic was ideational as much as organizational, to create a rhetorical campaign aimed at changing prevailing social norms regarding the respect for and justification of gun ownership.

The language of gun rights advocates—who have been remarkably successful in advancing and sustaining their cause—is certainly framed in sacred terms: the common NRA slogan "[You can have my gun when you take it] From my cold, dead hands" is one of the clearest statements in contemporary American politics of an absolute principle that refuses any sort of trade-off. The NRA takes a strong nonconsequentialist position that the accidental or violent deaths that result from gun ownership are not germane to the issue, as the right to bear arms is a principle that transcends these concerns. It is inviolable.

Another way of phrasing this is that the higher-order consequences of gun ownership in terms of maintaining individual freedoms and preventing government tyranny outweigh the lesser-order or temporal consequences such as a limited number of deaths—or as Charlton Heston put it in his 2000 NRA annual meeting remarks, "The doorway to all freedoms is framed by muskets." Many free speech advocates employ the same logic in terms of the higher-order consequences of free speech (individual freedom and the prevention of tyranny) that outweigh the lesser-order or short-term consequences of public disruption, threats to minorities (as in the Skokie case), or damage to national security (as in the Pentagon Papers case). Whether the beliefs match the rhetoric in terms of true sacredness is an interesting empirical question. But sacredness is *not* a central facet of the antigun position, which is about cause and effect rather than transcendent principle. Supporters of antigun positions must be convinced of negative consequences to be avoided rather than principles to be upheld.

This raises an interesting question about the comparative power of the pro- and anti-gun rights positions. True or not, many commentators view the NRA as the most influential single-purpose lobbying organization in Washington. How it gained this status of real or perceived influence is a vital question. It is often assumed that the power of the NRA comes from its large coffers. An alternative hypothesis about the source of its power is the advantage gained by a sacred position opposing a consequentialist one. The gun rights position may enjoy a belief system and rhetorical advantage over its detractors. This comports with two broad observations about the politics of issues characterized by single- versus double-sided sacredness. Gay marriage, like abortion, is a back-and-forth battleground, with no clear advantage on either side. Gun rights, in contrast, have had little electoral or constitutional challenge; the politics of gun rights weigh decidedly in supporters' favor. This could be because of the power of the NRA as a lobby, but it could also in part be due to the form of belief system and rhetoric involved. A second observation is the comparative power of organizations on either side of the controversy. For abortion, both sides have prominent and well-funded organizations (e.g., Operation Rescue on one side and NARAL on the other). For guns, nothing matches the prominence and influence of the NRA; antigun organizations exist, but none is close to the NRA in status. The Brady Campaign to Prevent Gun Violence (formerly Handgun Control, Inc.) describes itself as "the nation's largest national, non-partisan, grassroots organization leading the fight to prevent gun violence," but it is dwarfed in membership and funding by the NRA. This could be due to the particularities of these domains and their issue publics, but it could also in part be due to the prominence of sacred arguments on one side but not the other. It may be more than a simple matter of membership and money, but also worldview and language.

The NRA Argument

Before analyzing the NRA's rhetoric, it is important to understand their argument in order to see the use of language in its defense. On one level their position is obvious: favoring gun ownership and opposing gun control. But the justifications for this are more complex and for many people counterintuitive. It is instructive that an intuitive grasp of the NRA's position is simply lacking for many citizens, especially residents of the cities and coasts, a strong illustration of the disconnect between red and blue America. While for many issues, such as abortion or the death penalty, citizens at one end of the spectrum can articulate the reasoning of their opponents, frequently this is not the case in regard to opponents of the NRA. (It has been a fascinating realization in the course of discussing this book with academic colleagues at many institutions how few can describe the NRA understanding of the Second Amendment.) For readers who oppose gun ownership, a thought experiment may be useful: can you articulate clearly the NRA justification for gun rights? Not simply that the Constitution protects the right to bear arms, but why that is a good thing and the reason our basic political document explicitly does this?

My impression from conversations with NRA members and nonmembers is that the NRA view of the Second Amendment tends to be seen as either obvious or a great mystery, with fewer citizens in the middle of the spectrum. There is a bumper sticker that can be found in red America that reads "God + Guns = Freedom." If this equation does not seem to add up, it is important to note that for many Americans the meaning of the slogan is clear. That a large number of citizens understand it intuitively while many are mystified is a testament to our current cultural divisions. The meaning of the slogan is that God gave us our rights (the Lockean interpretation of God-given natural rights to life and liberty), and guns, in the final analysis, are what protect our rights. Without either one, freedom dissolves. Hence liberty relies on the conjunction of public religion and private firearms, without which we would neither have rights nor be able to keep them. The equation is understandable once the underlying premises are made clear, but like many beliefs, they may be opaque to the uninitiated.

Connecting God, guns, and freedom may be counterintuitive in two different senses. First, it seems to suggest that God has a positive feeling toward guns, which in this worldview is not entirely false. This idea is more alien to a kindly New Testament Redeemer (God is love) than to a hard-nosed Old Testament Creator (God is judgment). Moreover, while it may contradict a sense of Christian goodwill, it is in line with other common interpretations of God's respect for those who strive against opposition, defend his laws, and perhaps most important, help themselves. A second sense in which the equation may seem counterintuitive is that religious commandment is often seen as a force aligned *against* personal freedoms rather than supporting them. But the slogan is referring to our *collective* freedoms as well as our individual ones. In the most basic sense, a free society is a people not beholden to a foreign power or to a tyrannical government. Only in such a case can individual freedoms be exercised. However, those who privilege individual freedoms too much may put our collective freedom at risk by weakening our ability to resist invasion and tyranny. A religious culture also prevents anarchy, a severe threat to maintaining rights. So a godly society both enshrines individual rights and protects collective freedom (previously from godless Communists and now from overzealous Islamists), while gun ownership ensures individual freedoms. Both a free society and a free individual rely on two bulwarks. Without God to help us and guns to help those who help themselves, freedoms vanish. Hence God + Guns = Freedom. Once explained, it is a clear argument, but beforehand it may seem nonsensical. If many readers do not readily understand the bumper sticker's position, but we recognize that a large group of Americans grasp it immediately, this points to an important disjuncture in contemporary American political culture.

If our deeply held political values have become more divided and conflictual, as the culture wars argument suggests, one of the central value divides is between individualists and communitarians.[20] This value clearly separates advocates of gun rights from advocates of restrictions. If you assert that society is organized around individuals, who should do what is in their (and their family's) best interests, then having a gun for self-protection is a clear option. Communitarians, in contrast, assert that even if this is the case for a given individual, what increases safety for all of us is to ban guns from criminals and law-abiding citizens alike. Each side sees empirical flaws in the opposition: gun rights advocates respond that keeping guns from criminals is simply not possible (hence, as the saying goes, if guns are outlawed, only outlaws will have guns), while restriction advocates argue that keeping a gun in the home is more likely to result in harm to family members than to criminals. Individualists assert that the communitarian premise that police will protect individuals adequately is simply false; personal protection is dependent on individual action, not faulty collective institutions. Communitarians respond that the individualist premise that personal weapons lead to positive outcomes is mistaken in more cases than not.

The NRA position, however, is *not* that its value preferences or empirical premises should win the day. If this were the battleground, then a majority of citizens might disagree, and their political representatives in Congress or in state legislatures could restrict gun ownership. Instead it is a question of rights rather than majority will. And the *right* to hold weapons as opposed to a simple preference comes down to the meaning of the Second Amendment. There is a vast literature on the amendment, but what is important here is not who is right, but instead what position the NRA takes and how it communicates that position. Simply put, the argument is that the right to bear arms is the bedrock of all other rights (the "first freedom"), because it ensures that an armed populace can assert and defend all of its rights against the possibility of a tyrannical government. When the Second Amendment states that "the right of the people to keep and bear arms shall not be infringed," this reflects an individual right that adheres to all citizens, just as rights to free speech, against unreasonable search and seizure, and other rights held by "the people" refer to individual rights.

The preceding clause of the amendment is not a limit to this right, but a justification. The translation in contemporary American English of the eighteenth-century statement "A well regulated militia being necessary to the security of a free state, the right to keep and bear arms shall not be infringed" is "*Because* a well-regulated militia *is* necessary to the security of a free state, the right to keep and bear arms shall not be infringed." The opening clause is a constitutional curiosity, because the document does not justify itself in other places. For example, the separation of powers into distinct branches of government is merely stated but not justified, nor is the right of free speech given its own reason, but the right to bear arms is. The justification of the Second Amendment in this view is that when the government holds a monopoly of force, no rights are safe. Individual armed citizens who can organize at need to protect their liberty are the guarantor of a state remaining free.[21] The National Guard cannot be what the amendment protects because the Guard rose many decades after the Founding and comprises only a fraction of the citizenry rather than all able-bodied men of the community, as the militia is defined. Most important, the National Guard is commanded by the government itself, and therefore cannot possibly usurp or replace the grant of the Bill of Rights, which is directed *against* the government. As another popular bumper sticker makes the point, "Politicians Prefer Unarmed Peasants."[22]

In other words, the Bill of Rights says that the first and last defense of rights (the most important and the last resort) is the individual armed citizen, not any collective, and certainly not the government itself. Bearing arms is not a preference, a value, or a negotiable demand, but a guaranteed, inviolable right, on which all other rights ultimately rest. This view may sound strange to many citizens who are not steeped in the rhetoric of gun rights or the constitutional arguments about how to interpret the Bill of Rights, but it is nonetheless intellectually legitimate, well articulated, and most important for our purposes, strongly believed by NRA supporters.[23] As we shall see, it also makes the gun rights position another aspect of civil liberties, and makes its defenders—such as Charlton Heston—civil libertarians, akin to protectors of free speech, freedom of religion, freedom from government searches, and even more significantly, civil rights.

Charlton Heston and the Rhetoric of Gun Rights

Taylor (Charlton Heston): Do you have any weapons? Any guns?
Cornelius (Roddy McDowall): The best. But we won't need them.
Taylor: I'm glad to hear it. I want one anyway.

Planet of the Apes (1968)

That Charlton Heston became the most famous leader and spokesman of the NRA was not serendipitous. Like another famously effective conservative, he was president of the Screen Actors Guild (1966–1971, soon after Ronald Reagan's last term in 1960). Heston was also an early supporter of the civil rights movement, had marched with Martin Luther King Jr., and saw no contradiction between this political activism and the gun rights movement. A central facet of the contemporary NRA is Heston's synthesis of rights, religion, and protest, drawing on the rhetoric of the civil rights movement. His personal history prepared both his rhetoric and his public perception to build an effective persona for NRA leadership. Several elements combined into an unusually effective whole, so it is important to illustrate the disparate elements of the Heston synthesis, especially his film roles and political activism.

Heston is noted for roles in two settings: biblical and apocalyptic. His most famous early characters are Moses in *The Ten Commandments* (1956), the title role in *Ben-Hur* (1959), and John the Baptist in *The Greatest Story Ever Told* (1965). These performances established not only gravitas but also righteousness. It is not a flippant observation that it is hard to dispute the persona of Moses. Following these films, the famous Heston movies of the late 1960s and early 1970s explored landscapes of the primitive future, in which humans cannot count on peace or stability so must be individually armed. The two most striking and best-known examples of this genre are *Planet of the Apes* (1968) and *The Omega Man* (1971).[24] In the second film, the last man on Earth spends his days driving enviable cars through the streets of a deserted Manhattan, well-armed and stylishly dressed (for the 1970s), shooting from his convertible at movement in the shadows. His nights are spent violently defending his bunkered retreat from the repeated onslaught of mutants intent on his destruction.

Planet of the Apes is known for two politically liberal themes: a cautionary tale about nuclear holocaust or other environmental catastrophe, and a racial allegory about blind prejudice and countercultural heroes who stand up against prevailing norms (displaying civil courage). But it is also blatantly pro-gun, which is not a contradiction. The heroes need weapons to be effective against a tyrannical state as well as to protect themselves in a primitive world. When he escapes captivity with the help of one of the more enlightened apes (Roddy McDowall as Cornelius), Heston's first question is, "Do you have any weapons? Any guns?" When Cornelius responds, "The best. But we won't need them," Heston says, "I'm glad to hear it. I want one anyway." This is a perfect representation of the NRA position: the need for guns is not dependent on immediate need. It is a good thing that we are safe, but the call for guns will arise nonetheless, in this generation or the next. (In gun culture parlance, it is better to have a gun and not need it than to need a gun and not have it.) Cornelius, of course, turns out to be wrong; Heston ends up needing a gun sooner rather than later. In both the apocalyptic and biblical movies, Heston's film work reflects his own personal politics to a remarkable degree.

In what is probably his best-known political speech, at the 2000 NRA annual meeting in Charlotte, North Carolina, Heston recounts how he became president of the association. His version is significant because it illustrates the origin of the visual symbol of his rhetoric. It also offers the story of his growing commitment to the cause as an example of political mobilization, to be emulated by supporters of the movement:

> I remember a decade ago at my first annual meeting in St. Louis. After my banquet remarks to a packed house, they presented me with a very special gift. It was a splendid hand-crafted musket.
>
> I admit I was overcome by the power of its simple symbolism. I looked at that musket and I thought of all of the lives given for that freedom. I thought of all of the lives saved with that freedom. It dawned on me that *the doorway to all freedoms is framed by muskets.*[25]
>
> So I lifted that musket over my head for all to see. And as flashbulbs popped around the room, my heart and a few tears swelled up, and I uttered five unscripted words. When I did, that room exploded in sustained applause and hoots and shouts that seemed to last forever.
>
> *In that moment, I bonded with this great Association.* And in thousands of moments since, I've been asked to repeat those five words in airports and hotels and rallies and speeches across this land.[26]

Those five words are, of course, "From my cold, dead hands." In NRA lore, that simple statement is tied not only to the clear setting of a sacred boundary, but also to the image of a moral man defiantly holding above his head the symbol of his own freedom—the combined visual and verbal symbolism of the movement. Heston repeated those two symbols on countless occasions. They are not only a statement of defiance, but a call for others to follow, to join and stand for the movement. The raised gun is a totem, an iconic image, a statement of pride, and a symbol of protest. It evokes what the movement admires (and Heston was): soldier, leader, defender of faith and tradition, man of certainty and commitment. The image is powerful not only because of its emotional and ideational content but also because of its cultural resonances, invoking military, religious, and historical motifs from across the American cultural spectrum.

Heston's Sacred Rhetoric: Gun Rights, Civil Rights, and Sacred Boundaries

When Heston became NRA president in 1998, he began a significant media campaign, aided by his own notoriety. The campaign included interviews, letters to newspapers, and perhaps most interestingly, speeches at major universities. His target was both current and potential supporters of the NRA, but also the public perception of the movement. A letter to the *New York Times* printed on May 12, 1998, presents the core argument of an inalienable right: "The Founders' intent in framing the Second Amendment is perfectly clear and undeniable. Thomas Jefferson wrote, 'No man shall ever be debarred the use of arms.' Some anti-gun elitists declare this notion outdated. However, many constitutional scholars from this country's most prestigious universities agree that the Founders' intent is clear and irreversible: To 'keep and bear arms' is a right for all law-abiding citizens."

Heston spoke directly to university audiences on several occasions, perhaps most notably at Harvard Law School in February 1999 and the Yale University Political Union in April.[27] These appeals to a clearly non-NRA audience emphasized sacred boundaries but also addressed the audience on its own ground of free speech. His talks are about political correctness on campus as much as gun rights. The theme of the speeches is sacredness and disobedience, or the things on which you should not compromise and what you should do if the authorities try to force you to abandon your rights: disobey.

Both speeches begin and end with references to Martin Luther King Jr. and civil disobedience, explicitly making the connection between gun rights and civil rights. It may surprise people outside the NRA and the gun rights movement how often Heston spoke of King. At the beginning of his speech to the Yale Political Union he said, "I marched with Martin Luther King in 1963, long before Hollywood found it fashionable. Supporting civil rights then was about as popular as supporting gun rights is now." The final sentence of both speeches is, "If Dr. King were here, I think he would agree." One might object that King is best known for nonviolence, which makes him a questionable authority for gun rights. But that is the hook of the argument: King stood for the Bill of Rights and the ideals of liberty espoused by the Founders. In this view King is more about liberty than nonviolence. Just as King's movement relied on the First Amendment right of assembly, he would support the Second Amendment right of bearing arms against tyranny.[28] This is an important juxtaposition, as it establishes the gun rights movement's progressive credentials at the same time that it ties the Second Amendment to the broader realm of social justice. Just as King explicitly connected the newer argument of civil rights to the Founding symbolism of liberty, Heston ties gun rights to both.

This is more than clever rhetoric: it is a way of placing the gun rights movement in the stream of rights movements, expansions of civil liberties, and righteous protests from the Founding forward, from abolition to suffrage, free speech, and gay rights. Heston defined himself more than anything else as a civil libertarian, from civil rights to guns. The main thrust of his university speeches is not gun rights directly, but freedom of speech. More than an appeal for gun ownership, his pitch is in favor of free expression on campus and against political correctness stifling the advocates of gun rights. He accuses his audience at the Harvard Law School of being cowards who have allowed implicit campus speech codes to erode their birthright of free speech: "I submit that you, and your counterparts across the land, are the most socially conformed and politically silenced generation since Concord Bridge. And as long as you validate that, and abide it, you are, by your grandfathers' standards, cowards." The answer to this oppression is the same as it has always been in America: "But what can you do? How can anyone prevail against such pervasive social subjugation? The answer's been here all along. I learned it 36 years ago, on the steps of the Lincoln Memorial in Washington, D.C., standing with Dr. Martin Luther King and two hundred thousand people. You simply disobey." When faced with a violation of sacred values, we resist: "When told how to think or what to say or how to behave, we don't. We disobey social protocol that stifles and stigmatizes personal freedom. I learned the awesome power of disobedience from Dr. King, who learned it from Gandhi, and Thoreau, and Jesus, and every other great man who led those in the right against those with the might."

He ends his Yale speech with these lines:

> I ask you, in Lincoln's words, "so that this nation may long endure," please, do what you must to reveal, and then revere, truth. Expect and accept the consequences of your actions and those of your nation, and every day, test what you see with what you know is right. And when it's dishonest, defy it. Follow in the hallowed footsteps of the great disobedience movements

of history that freed exiles, founded religions, defeated tyrants, and in the hands of an aroused rabble in arms and a few great men, by God's grace, built this country. If Dr. King were here, I think he would agree. Thank you.

Each of the elements of sacred rhetoric appears in these relatively short speeches (2,100 and 2,000 words, respectively, with significant overlap in the arguments). He invokes the protected status of nonconsequentialist values, especially freedom: "your own sense of liberty, your own freedom of thought, your own compass for what is right . . . your birthright to think and say what resides in your heart." Rather than instrumental reasoning or promised benefits, he urges noninstrumentality and the virtue of sacrifice: "But be careful, it hurts. Disobedience demands that you put yourself at risk. Dr. King stood on lots of balconies. You must be willing to be humiliated, to endure the modern-day equivalent of the police dogs at Montgomery and the water cannons at Selma." He invokes nonnegotiable boundaries: "Don't let America's universities continue to serve as incubators for this rampant epidemic of new McCarthyism . . . I am asking you to disavow cultural correctness with massive disobedience of rogue authority, social directives and onerous law that weaken personal freedom." Both free speech and gun rights are not just limits, but ones we should guard zealously against intrusion. Moreover, they are tied together, as free speech allows us to defend gun rights, just as in the final analysis, gun rights allow us to defend our freedom of speech: "I don't care what you think about guns. But if you are shocked at that, I am shocked at you. Who will guard the raw material of unfettered ideas, if not you? Who will defend the core value of academia, if you supposed soldiers of free thought and expression lay down your arms and plead, 'Don't shoot me'?"

Heston cites at least seven different authorities for his position, including God, the Old Testament, Lincoln at Gettysburg, Martin Luther King Jr., Thoreau, Gandhi, and Jesus. But it is moral outrage that is perhaps most evident throughout his language. The tone of both speeches is disgust. Heston cites example after example of why he is angry, and at Harvard concludes, "What does all of this mean? It means that telling us what to think has evolved into telling us what to say, so telling us what to do can't be far behind. Before you claim to be a champion of free thought, tell me: Why did political correctness originate on America's campuses? And why do you continue to tolerate it? Why do you, who're supposed to debate ideas, surrender to their suppression?" He turns this disapproval on the Yale audience members themselves: "You there, listening politely while you plan your next date and your first million, are you willing to put that all aside—just as thousands of good men did sixty years ago—and go fight? Or are you thinking, as I suspect, that it's some lesser person's job?" Sacred rhetoric is often neither polite nor undemanding. It often provokes listeners, perhaps shaming them into action rather than reasoning them into agreement.

The Convention Speeches

"A nation cannot gain safety by giving up freedom. This truth is older than our country. Those who would give up essential liberty to purchase a little temporary safety, deserve neither liberty nor safety." Those words could have been said by any civil libertarian opposing the Patriot Act. But they were said by Charlton Heston in his 1999 NRA speech in Denver, following the school shooting at Columbine. His reasoning is identical to any number of thinkers on the progressive side of American politics, until his next sentences: "If you like your freedoms of speech and of religion, freedom from search and seizure, freedom of the press and of privacy, to assemble and to redress grievances, then you'd better give them that eternal bodyguard called the Second Amendment. The individual right to bear arms is freedom's insurance policy, not just for your children but for infinite generations to come."

In his speeches to NRA members, Heston is even more clear about the sacredness of his position. His most known and noteworthy speeches may be the addresses at the 1999 convention in Denver and the 2000 convention during Bush's first presidential campaign. The 1999 NRA meeting stands out because it was planned to begin on May 1, eleven days after the most shocking and publicized school shooting to that time. Columbine focused the national conversation on the direct human costs of the availability of firearms in contemporary society, compared to the more abstract political claims of the gun rights movement. The convention's location attracted a great deal of criticism, framed as an insult to the local community and a celebration of guns in the face of the destruction they bring about. This placed the NRA leadership in a delicate position for the public perception of the movement: should they cancel the meeting or stand their ground? Would canceling be perceived as proper respect, or an admission of guilt? Would continuing as planned be perceived as callous or courageous? This was a critical moment in the history of the movement, and the NRA's rhetoric aimed toward an unusually attentive media is significant.

They decided to stay and conduct business meetings but cancel the normal festivities and exhibitions that are a large aspect of NRA gatherings. In other words, state their rights, but not celebrate in a period of national mourning ("It's fitting and proper that we should do this," Heston said in his opening remarks, "because NRA members are, above all, Americans"). Heston did not avoid the controversy, and addressed it directly in his opening and closing speeches. The opening lines of his second speech were "I have been admonished not to be here, not to speak to you here. It's not the first time. In 1963 I marched on Washington with Dr. Martin Luther King, long before Hollywood found civil rights fashionable. My associates advised me not to go. They said it would be unpopular and maybe dangerous. Thirty-six years later my associates advised me not to come to Denver. They said it would be unpopular and maybe dangerous. But I am here." He argues to the membership that the best thing to do is not be cowed, not buy into other groups' constructions of the movement and the meaning of their meeting in Denver. Both the civil rights protests and this one are demonstrations for freedom, both against the prevailing view of what is correct.

His speech had three main points: the movement will not accept blame for Columbine and be cast into the role of villain; the country should be united rather than divided, bound together by the Bill of Rights as our definition of America; and the Bill of Rights places sacred boundaries on gun rights as the bedrock of the system. First of all, the movement should not be cast on the defensive:

> The countless requests we've received for media appearances are in fact summons to public floggings, where those who hate firearms will predictably don the white hat and hand us the black . . . Their story needs a villain. They want us to play the heavy in their drama of packaged grief, to provide riveting programming to run between commercials for cars and cat food. The dirty secret of this day and age is that political gain and media ratings all too often bloom upon fresh graves. I remember a better day, when no one dared politicize or profiteer on trauma.

Heston wanted his listeners to remember that even though the media may make it appear otherwise, the NRA is with the majority of Americans:

> One camp would be the majority—people who believe our Founders guaranteed our security with the right to defend ourselves, our families and our country. The other camp would be a large minority—people who believe that we will buy security if we will just surrender these freedoms. This debate would be accurately described as those who believe in the

> Second Amendment, versus those who don't. But instead it is spun as those who believe in murder, versus those who don't. A struggle between the reckless and the prudent, between the dimwitted and the enlightened, between the archaic and the progressive, between inferior citizens and elitists who know what's good for society . . . And we're often cast as the villain. That is not our role in American society, and we will not be forced to play it.

Heston argues that the only result of this division is weakness, instead of unity behind an American vision enshrined in the Bill of Rights.

> Such hateful, divisive forces are leading us to one awful end: America's own form of Balkanization. A weakened country of rabid factions, each less free, and united only by hatred of one another . . . Too many on both sides have forgotten that we are, first, Americans . . . because so much more connects us than divides us. And because tragedy has been and will always be with us. Somewhere right now, evil people are scheming evil things. All of us will do every meaningful thing we can do to prevent it. But each horrible act can't become an axe for opportunists to cleave the very Bill of Rights that binds us.

His final point is that maintaining the Bill of Rights requires an unwavering commitment to freedom of arms:

> Our mission is to remain a steady beacon of strength and support for the Second Amendment, even if it has no other friend on the planet. We cannot let tragedy lay waste to the most rare and hard-won human right in history . . . Our essential reason for being is this: *As long as there is a Second Amendment, evil can never conquer us. Tyranny, in any form, can never find footing within a society of law-abiding, armed, ethical people.* The majesty of the Second Amendment, that our Founders so divinely captured and crafted into your birthright, guarantees that no government despot, no renegade faction of armed forces, no roving gangs of criminals, no breakdown of law and order, no massive anarchy, no force of evil or crime or oppression from within or from without, can ever rob you of the liberties that define your Americanism . . . Let me be absolutely clear. *The Founding Fathers guaranteed this freedom because they knew no tyranny can ever arise among a people endowed with the right to keep and bear arms.* (emphasis added)

Even in the face of Columbine, Heston understands the Second Amendment as an absolute on which all other rights rest; this is "its singular, sacred beauty."

The 2000 speech has a similar focus but adds other elements of authority, moral outrage, and sacrifice. It begins by invoking George Washington, Franklin D. Roosevelt, and Reagan as moral leaders who stayed the course in adversity. It extols the sacrifices of the NRA members who have contributed to the movement. And more is asked of them. The many reasons to be morally offended lead to one important conclusion—make sure everything possible is done to ensure that Al Gore is defeated in the coming election:

> Which leads me to that one mission left undone: Winning in November. That's why I'm staying on for a third tour of duty. Today I challenge you to find your third term, and serve it. Find your extra mile, and walk it. Only you know what you can do between now and that decisive November day to turn the tide of these elections in favor of freedom. I ask you to find it and fulfill it. Go the extra distance, find that extra member, write the extra check, knock on one more door, work one more hour, make one more call, convince one more friend, turn the other cheek if you must, but find your third term and serve it.

The speech ends with the iconic pose and the clear symbolism at the heart of the movement: the belief in the sacred status of a right that is absolute and nonconsequentialist, that sets a nonnegotiable boundary, violations of which inspire moral outrage, and for which members are willing to sacrifice. "That's why those five words issue an irresistible call to us all, and we muster. So as we set out this year to defeat the divisive forces that would take freedom away, I want to say those words again for everyone within the sound of my voice to hear and to heed, and especially for you, Mr. Gore: From my cold, dead hands!"

Gun Rights and Totemism

A final note about the rhetoric of gun rights is the role of totemism. In Emile Durkheim's classic definition, religion is not distinguished by ritual, belief in the supernatural, or an explanation of man's origins or destiny, but by the demarcation of the sacred from the profane. The most basic form of religion in this view is totemism, or the organization of groups or clans around a common emblem. The totem is "the species of things that serves to designate the clan collectively . . . It is the very archetype of sacred things."[29] Whether an animal or an inanimate object, it holds sacred significance for the group members and is part of their personal and collective identity. According to Durkheim, "This theory of totemism will provide us the key to a curious trait of the human mind that, although more pronounced long ago than now, has not disappeared."[30]

The significance of the gun for the NRA can be described as a mild but meaningful form of totemism. When Heston speaks of the "sacred stuff in that wooden stock and blued steel," he is placing the gun in a particular role, "when ordinary hands can hold such an extraordinary instrument."[31] To be clear, this totemism is not as developed as the beliefs of the Native American or Australian tribes documented by the classic sociologists. But Durkheim argues that the two central facets of totemism are the sacredness of a specific object and the social organization around it by its identifiers. The gun rights movement comprises mild elements of both, which increases the power of its sacred rhetoric.

It may be instructive to consider the term *gun culture* as it is employed and understood in contemporary America. The term evokes the social networks and worldview of gun owners, whose families often include hunters and soldiers, in rural and suburban areas throughout the nation but concentrated in the South, Midwest, and West. Gun culture does not necessarily mean that everyone within it shoots or hunts, but instead suggests familiarity and ease with guns and people who have them. The distinction might be that if one were visiting an acquaintance's home and noticed a shotgun on the wall, the first question that came to mind would more likely be, "Is that a twelve or a twenty gauge?" rather than, "Why in the world are there guns here?"

This subculture may have more identity and cohesion than one might initially think. There are certainly many subcultures in the United States that have distinctive values, norms, symbols, and everyday behaviors. These can be grounded in ethnic or geographic connections, such as Latino or southern culture. One could speak of distinctive cultures or traits among occupational groups such as doctors, or among class groups such as socialite or blue-collar culture. Sport or associational groups may have their own culture, such as football culture or fraternity culture. But few are as totemic, centered around an object with a sacred dimension. Many of the subcultures mentioned could have centered around an object in similar fashion, but do not. The football itself does not have the same sacred dimension. Neither does the fraternity house, or any specific object within Latino, medical, or blue-collar groups. But the centrality and sacredness of a totemic object is an unusual and powerful element of gun culture.

The NRA connection to the military also adds to the symbolic meaning of the gun as totem. The official NRA emblem of the eagle and rifle is not coincidentally patriotic. It is worth mentioning the mildly totemistic nature of the rifle within Army and especially Marine culture. The U.S. Army enforces a powerful norm of soldiers not being separated from their rifle at any time while in the field, which on one hand is practical training, and on the other hand is a symbolic connection to the weapon. In Marine culture the symbolism is more advanced, connected to the view that every Marine regardless of specialty is first and foremost a rifleman. This is reflected in the basic training mantra, repeated countless times: "This is my rifle. There are many like it, but this one is mine . . . My rifle without me is useless. Without my rifle, I am useless." Of course, military culture has a significant overlap with gun culture, in membership, mutual respect, symbolism, and totemistic leanings.

It is important to note that totemism, or the most basic, essentialist form of religion, sees the totem as a sacred object but not a worshiped one. It is not equivalent to holy objects in Christianity such as the cross. The regard for the totem is "by no means that attitude a believer has toward his god."[32] Instead, the totem is the representation of the group and the individual. A member of the group sees totems as "kindly associates, whose help he believes he can count on. He calls them to his aid, and they come to guide his hand in the hunt and avert dangers that he may encounter."[33] This is a surprisingly apt description of American gun culture attitudes toward firearms.

Even a mild form of totemism, or the treatment of guns as a quasi-sacred object, provides several advantages to a movement. It solidifies an emotional connection among the group. It establishes a negative reaction to violations of the sacred object and generates the will to come to its defense. It increases group attachment and recognition. And it provides a means of effective symbolic communication, all of which add up to a powerful source of political motivation.

Social Movements and the Sacred

The rhetoric scholars Stephen Lucas and Martin Medhurst compiled a list of the top one hundred American speeches of the twentieth century.[34] The rankings are based on the selections of 137 other scholars specializing in rhetoric and public address, grounded in the impact and artistry of the speeches. The three presidents who appear the most are Franklin D. Roosevelt, John F. Kennedy, and Ronald Reagan, who are tied with six appearances each. Some of their most famous words are clear examples of sacred rhetoric: "Don't ask what your country can do for you; ask what you can do for your country." "Mr. Gorbachev, tear down this wall!" Kennedy's inaugural address and Reagan's speech at the Brandenburg Gate come in respectively at numbers 2 and 92 on the list (Reagan also appears as high as number 8). These speeches invoke boundaries, limits, protected values, and the sacrifices we must undertake to defend them. Kennedy minced no words about sacred boundaries: "Let every nation know, whether it wishes us well or ill, that we shall pay any price, bear any burden, meet any hardship, support any friend, oppose any foe, in order to assure the survival and the success of liberty." Reagan was clear about his moral outrage at the tyrannies of communism: "The totalitarian world produces backwardness because it does such violence to the spirit, thwarting the human impulse to create, to enjoy, to worship. The totalitarian world finds even the symbols of love and worship an affront."[35]

The American speech rated as the most influential of the last century, however, is not from a politician, but from the leader of a social movement: Martin Luther King Jr.'s "I Have a Dream" speech of August 28, 1963. King did not stand in front of the hundreds of thousands of people on the National Mall in Washington that day and say, "I have a plan." If he had done so, the speech would have joined the countless number of forgotten political moments. Instead he invoked a far-reaching vision, a call for commitment to nonnegotiable boundaries, fueled by the moral outrage of generations. More than anything else, the speech is grounded in the authority of the Declaration and the Constitution. It is a call to recognize the "sacred obligations" that our Founding tradition requires, spoken in "this hallowed spot." It invokes explicit boundaries of what can and will be tolerated: "We can never be satisfied as long as our children are stripped of their selfhood and robbed of their dignity by a sign stating 'For Whites Only.' We cannot be satisfied as long as a Negro in Mississippi cannot vote . . . No, no, we are not satisfied, and we will not be satisfied until 'justice rolls down like waters, and righteousness like a mighty stream.'" King explicitly states the nonnegotiable nature of his position, emphasizing "the fierce urgency of Now": "It would be fatal for the nation to overlook the urgency of the moment. This sweltering summer of the Negro's legitimate discontent will not pass until there is an invigorating autumn of freedom and equality . . . There will be neither rest nor tranquility in America until the Negro is granted his citizenship rights."

The religious elements of his speech are undeniable, including biblical references, an interweaving of traditional spirituals, and the distinctive cadence of Protestant preaching, but they are in the service of secular goals, invoking religious feeling about secular objects. Heston also employs religious references, from explicit appeals to God and religious tradition, to invocations of the "sacred stuff in that wooden stock and blued steel," a reference to the wooden cross and iron nails of the crucifixion. This is subtle enough to be missed by the irreligious but clear enough to be meaningful for the devout. Religious juxtaposition is influential specifically because it is not an explicit argument, but instead evokes a religious feeling without being overbearing. It does not state that the secular should be thought of as religious, but simply ties the two together in the mind of the audience.

Both the civil rights and gun rights movements gained strong advantages by employing sacred rhetoric, and the gun rights movement accrued additional advantages by connecting itself to civil rights. The contentious repertoire of American social movements provides many options, but the one perhaps most in the control of movement leadership is a choice of rhetoric and symbolism. Without being privileged to the strategy sessions of contemporary movements, I suspect that the choice of sacred rhetoric is often calculated as well as organic. A foundation of sacred appeal benefits a movement in several ways. The choice has powerful effects in fostering mobilization and increasing the absolutism of a movement's participants. It may be effective in cowing opposition, as sacred positions are more likely than nonsacred ones to shame opponents into silence, increasing the political influence of a movement. Opposition becomes even more difficult if a movement can tap into the master frame of rights and the sacredness of the Founding. This ties a movement's goals to the consensus sacred values of the Constitution, rather than the conflictual ones of a divisive social conflict. Even the greatest divisions in our history, such as slavery and abolitionism, take on a different aspect when connected to constitutional rights. The visual similarity between Heston's iconic pose, musket raised above his head, and the famous depiction of John Brown with a raised rifle in his right hand is striking.[36] An important difference is that Brown has a Bible in his other hand. But in a metaphorical sense, so did Heston, and so did King. The tie of a secular cause to sacred rhetoric gives it greater power in American politics.

Although this has been understood by many leaders of social movements, the same cannot be said in our electoral politics. The leaders of our political parties have not always recognized the advantages of sacred rhetoric. The contemporary presidential candidates have varied widely in their use of absolutist appeals, creating an advantage for the more sacred party. In the following chapters we examine the partisan consequences of sacred rhetoric.

Chapter Six

THE ABSOLUTIST ADVANTAGE

Sacred Rhetoric in the Bush Era

The significance of value language may be more clear to rhetoricians than to politicians. A popular rhetoric text from the 1960s concluded with this "moral law" of speaking:

> *Always act to provide conditions most favorable for mutual understanding between yourself and all concerned.*
>
> Speaking, if it is to be ethical, must create conditions favorable to the expansion of symbolism and mutual understanding and influence. We define ethical rhetoric as *the discovery of the means of symbolism which leads to the greatest mutual understanding and mutual influence.*
>
> The highest values have the highest consequences. When we use these values in speaking, we may enable man to transform himself and his society. To this end, speaking must commit itself if it is to serve us best.[1]

A clear example of language that commits itself is sacred rhetoric. This language has certain advantages in the fractured communication process between ideological elites and an inattentive public. But sacred rhetoric may be understood and employed by some politicians more than others. The question I address in this chapter is whether there is a partisan distinction in the use of sacred rhetoric. Is it simply the case that Republicans are the more sacred party, given their propensity for religious foundations and traditional sources of authority? Or do Democrats have their own sacrednesses, also employing the language of limits? If one party employs sacred rhetoric significantly more than the other, it inspires greater intensity and engagement, promotes nonnegotiable and intransigent reasoning by its supporters, and valorizes its candidates. In short, it gains the absolutist advantage.

Sacredness in Presidential Rhetoric: The 2000 Bush–Gore Debates

To evaluate the comparative degree of sacredness across the breadth of party rhetoric would be a daunting task. Even limiting the inquiry to recent years, the total amount of political speech is staggering, including the presidential addresses, party convention speeches, and news conferences and their rebuttals, as well as the campaign speeches, television ads, and public discussions for multiple offices at national, state, and local levels. Even a fair assessment of who represents each party would be difficult to identify. Rather than claim to examine a cross section of party language, it may be more advisable to choose a quintessential form of competing party rhetoric and limit ourselves to one clear example. For this task, the presidential debates may be the most meaningful test of partisan differences. They are a straightforward case of attempted persuasion, pitting the two party leaders in direct competition. They take place on a national stage and perhaps have more direct influence on voters than any other single exchange between the parties. They are generally not limited to a single event but take place in consecutive broadcasts separated by extensive commentary and analysis. This forum is also one of the only cases of an explicit simultaneous comparison of the two parties, when they face each other directly, rather than the more usual form of partisan rhetoric in which citizens hear only a single appeal at a time from one side or the other, such as a political advertisement, presidential news conference, or party convention. The 2000 debates between George W. Bush and Al Gore may be especially significant because of their historical timing. They represent an important watershed in political eras and perhaps in party rhetoric: the end of the Clinton era, the return to Republican-dominated national politics, and the solidified influence of the Evangelical movement within the Republican Party. The Bush–Gore debates represent an important initial test of partisan rhetoric in their attempt to persuade, their visibility and impact, their historical timing, and their direct comparison of the two parties.

As a means of party comparison, the debates also offer an additional advantage. Mainstream party politicians may be less likely to employ sacred rhetoric than more fringe politicians or the elements of the party more attached to social movements or interest groups. Concentrating on the two party leaders provides a conservative test of partisan differences, because expressions of sacredness are likely to be more muted in the presidential debates than other elements of party rhetoric. By contrast, if we were to compare the speeches at the respective party conventions, we would likely find a greater difference in rhetorical styles. By concentrating on the presidential debates we can make a meaningful and conservative test of the differences in the two parties.

"That Wonderful Note of Disagreement": Contrasting Partisan Styles

"On that wonderful note of disagreement, we have to stop here," was the moderator's way of bringing the first debate of the 2000 presidential contest to a close. Jim Lehrer was referring to the candidates' clash over public funding of political campaigns, but their "note of disagreement" perhaps describes rhetorical styles more than simple policy difference. To see the rhetorical difference between the two candidates, we need only compare their closing sentences of the final debate, the last impression each made on the viewers:

> *Gore*: We've made some progress during the last eight years. We have seen the strongest economy in the history of the United States. Lower crime rates for eight years in a row. Highest private home ownership ever, but I'll make you one promise here. You ain't seen nothing yet. And I will keep that promise.
>
> *Bush*: Should I be fortunate enough to become your president, when I put my hand on the Bible, I will swear to not only uphold the laws of the land, but I will also swear to uphold the honor and the dignity of the office to which I have been elected, so help me God. Thank you very much.

Both candidates offered promises, but they are commitments of a very different nature. The first is to reach certain results or consequences, while the second is to uphold certain values and boundaries. Gore's promise dealt with the economy, crime, and home ownership—personal standards of living—whereas Bush's dealt with public dignity, or personal values. In one sense Bush's words are a reference to the previous Democratic president's indiscretions as well as an invocation of traditional religious values. In another sense his entire concluding statement can be understood as a series of simple values and limits: "There is a big difference between big federal government and somebody who is coming from outside Washington who will trust individuals"; "A promise made will be a promise kept should I be fortunate enough to become your president"; "I don't think the surplus is the government's money. I think it's the people's money"; "I will swear to uphold the honor and dignity of the office." The two candidates did not always disagree on policy, but they did contrast in their style of rhetoric.

To examine the degree of sacred rhetoric employed by each candidate, I conducted an analysis employing the same strategy used to discern sacred rhetoric in the experiments discussed earlier. For this test we move away from the causal methods of the experiments toward more direct empirical observation. Because we have an explicit definition of the elements of sacred rhetoric that we can distinguish and observe, this leads toward a content analysis, or an empirical method for counting and comparing the use of distinct words, phrases, or ideas within a given discourse. This approach allows for a quantitative gauge, which introduces a more specific means of comparing the differences between the parties. Because the debates are divided into a series of exchanges on distinct topics, we can examine the degree of sacredness in each exchange. For each candidate for each question, I recorded the use of any of the seven facets of sacred rhetoric:

1. *Protected status*: placing a value beyond question or set apart from trade-offs with other values
2. *Nonconsequentialism*: privileging values over costs or consequences
3. *Noninstrumentalism*: rejecting calculated self-interest
4. *Nonnegotiability*: denying the legitimacy of compromise
5. *Citation of boundaries*: invoking a boundary of what is acceptable or tolerable
6. *Citation of authority*: invoking an authority for the value or boundary
7. *Moral outrage*: expressing anger at the violation of a value or boundary

This creates a scale from 0 (employing no elements of sacred rhetoric) to 7 (employing each element).[2] The results ranged from 0 to 4, with a great deal of variation across issue areas. Table 6.1 illustrates the results of this analysis for each of the three debates.

The most important finding is that Republican appeals entail a greater degree of sacred rhetoric. For each exchange, Bush's language averaged 1.3 more elements of sacred rhetoric than Gore's in the first debate, 1.2 in the second, and 1.8 in the third. The overall average was 1.5 more elements of sacred rhetoric for Bush in each exchange. This is clearly a statistically

TABLE 6.1
Sacred Rhetoric in the 2000 Presidential Debates

Topic	Bush	Gore	Difference	Reversals
DEBATE 1				
Social Security	3	1	2	
Oil Supply and Environment	0	1	-1	x
Abortion	4	2	2	
Yugoslavia	0	0	0	
Use of Force	0	2	-2	x
Domestic Political Philosophy	3	0	3	
Education	2	0	2	
Financial Crises	1	1	0	
Social Security	2	1	1	
Character	3	0	3	
Closing Statements	4	0	4	
AVERAGE	2.0	0.7	1.3	
DEBATE 2				
U.S. Power	1	3	-2	x
Racial Profiling / Hate Crimes	2	2	0	
Gay Marriage	3	0	3	
Guns	4	0	4	
Health Insurance for Kids	1	0	1	
Environment	1	3	-2	x
Closing Statements	4	0	4	
AVERAGE	2.3	1.1	1.2	
DEBATE 3				
HMOs	0	0	0	
Drug Prices	0	0	0	
National Health Care	2	1	1	
Educational Accountability	3	0	3	
Teachers	2	0	2	

cont. on next page

TABLE 6.1 (CONT.)

Topic	Bush	Gore	Difference	Reversals
DEBATE 3 (cont.)				
Middle East	2	1	1	
Military Preparedness	1	0	1	
Guns	3	0	3	
Family Farms	2	0	2	
Inheritance Tax	4	0	4	
Morality & Hollywood	2	0	2	
Youth Apathy	2	0	2	
Inclusiveness	2	0	2	
Taxes	2	0	2	
Capital Punishment	1	0	1	
Closing Statements	3	0	3	
AVERAGE	1.9	.1	1.8	
TOTAL AVERAGE	2.0	.5	1.5	
Average Difference Without Democratic Reversals			1.9	
Average Difference of Morals, Guns, Taxes, and School			3.0	
Average Difference of Closing Statements			3.7	

Topics in bold indicate especially noteworthy differentials in sacred rhetoric.

significant difference, even though the numbers involved are relatively small (a total number of thirty-four meaningful exchanges).[3] When we compare only the candidates' closing statements—the most prepared language of the debates—the difference is even more stark, with Bush employing an average of 3.7 more elements of sacred rhetoric.

While it is clear that Republican rhetoric was more sacred on the whole, this was not the case with every topic, nor was there always a great difference. The areas in which Bush displayed the more decisive difference were predictably the moral issues (abortion, gay marriage, character, and public morality), but also issues of principled disagreement such as guns and taxes. The exchanges involving the inheritance tax and public school accountability entailed some of the greatest distinctions in rhetorical style as a result of Bush's invocation of strong boundaries, limits, and standards compared to Gore's discussion of policy consequences.

To understand these differences it is important to move beyond the raw data to examples of the candidates' competing rhetoric. One of the best ways to compare the candidates is not in their answers to questions chosen by the moderator or audience members, but in their closing statements, which they had ample time to prepare and to phrase in their preferred fashion. The closing statements from the first debate follow. They are given in full because they illustrate major differences in the candidates' rhetorical styles. The text that follows is verbatim, with especially illustrative passages in italics.

> *Bush:* Thank you, Jim. Thank the University of Massachusetts and Mr. Vice President, thank you. It has been a good, lively exchange. There is a huge difference of opinion. Mine is *I want to empower people in their own lives.* I also want to go to Washington to get some positive things done. It is going to require a new spirit. A spirit of cooperation. It will require the ability of a Republican president to reach out across the partisan divide and to say to Democrats, let's come together to do what is right for America. It's been my record as governor of Texas. It will be how I conduct myself if I'm fortunate enough to earn your vote as president of the United States. I want to finally get something done on Medicare. I want to make sure prescription drugs are available for all seniors. And I want seniors to have additional choices when it comes to choosing their health care plans. I want to finally get something done on Social Security. I want to make sure the seniors have *the promise made will be a promise kept,* but I want younger workers to be able to manage some of their own money, some of their own payroll taxes in the private sector under certain guidelines to get a better rate of return on your own money. I want to rebuild our military to keep the peace. I want to have a strong hand when it comes to the United States in world affairs. I don't want to try to put our troops in all places at all times. *I don't want to be the world's policeman,* I want to be the world's peacemaker by having a military of high morale and a military that is well equipped. I want antiballistic missile systems to protect ourselves and our allies from a rogue nation that may try to hold us hostage or blackmail our allies and friends. *I want to make sure the education system fulfills its hope and promise.* I've had a strong record of working with Democrats and Republicans in Texas to make sure no child

is left behind. I understand the limited role of the federal government, but it could be a constructive role when it comes to reform, *by insisting that there be a strong accountability systems.* My intentions are to earn your vote and earn your confidence. I'm asking for your vote. I want you to be on my team. And for those of you working, thanks from the bottom of my heart. For those of you making up your mind, I would be honored to have your support.

Gore: I want to thank everybody who watched and listened tonight because *this is indeed a crucial time in American history. We're at a fork in the road. We have this incredible prosperity, but a lot of people have been left behind. And we have a very important decision to make. Will we use the prosperity to enrich all of our families and not just a few?* One important way of looking at this is to ask who are you going to fight for? Throughout my career in public service, I have fought for the working men and women of this country, middle-class families. Why? Because you are the ones who have the hardest time paying taxes, the hardest time making ends meet. You are the ones who are making car payments and mortgage payments and doing right by your kids. And a lot of times there are powerful forces that are against you. Make no mistake about it, they do have undue influence in Washington, D.C., and it makes a difference if you have a president who will fight for you. I know one thing about the position of president, it's the only position in our Constitution that is filled by an individual who is given the responsibility to fight not just for one state or one district or the well connected or wealthy, but to fight for all of the people, including especially those who most need somebody who will stand up and take on whatever powerful forces might stand in the way. There is a woman named Winifred Skinner here tonight from Iowa. I mentioned her earlier. She's seventy-nine years old. She has Social Security. I'm not going to cut her benefits or support any proposal that would. She gets a small pension, but in order to pay for her prescription drug benefits, she has to go out seven days a week several hours a day picking up cans. She came all the way from Iowa in a Winnebago with her poodle in order [to] attend here tonight. I want to tell her, I'll fight for a prescription drug benefit for all seniors and *fight for the people of this country for a prosperity that benefits all.*

Bush opens with "there is a huge difference of opinion." This may be true, but there is also a substantial difference in style of argument. When given free choice of words and unconstrained by a questioner, Bush begins with a value statement: "I want to empower people in their own lives." In other words, individualism is paramount, such that government is not to be trusted compared to individual decision makers. Gore, in contrast, opens quite differently: "I want to thank everybody who watched and listened tonight because this is indeed a crucial time in American history. We're at a fork in the road." In other words, what happens next is what counts the most; it is the direct consequences of our actions we should consider. Especially now, when the consequences are high.

Later in the debates Gore continues to focus on instrumentalist appeals and the logic of consequences. One of his clearest appeals to instrumental calculation appears in the third debate on the subject of taxes:

> Look, this isn't about Governor Bush, it's not about me. It's about you . . . If you want somebody who believes that we were better off eight years ago than we are now and that we ought to go back to the kind of policies that we had back then, emphasizing tax cuts mainly for the wealthy, here is your man. If you want somebody who will fight for you and who will fight to have middle-class tax cuts, then I am your man. I want to be. Now, I doubt that anybody here makes more than $330,000 a year. I won't ask you, but if you do, you're in the top 1%.

On the topic of presidential character, Gore also attempts to shift the conversation to consequentialism: "You may want to focus on scandal. I want to focus on results." In this exchange, Bush cites moral outrage and appropriate boundaries of conduct:

> I think the thing that discouraged me about the vice president was uttering those famous words, "No controlling legal authority." I felt like there needed to be a better sense of responsibility of what was going on in the White House. I believe that, I believe they've moved that sign, "The buck stops here" from the Oval Office desk to "The buck stops here" on the Lincoln Bedroom. It's not good for the country and it's not right.
>
> I think people need to be held responsible for the actions they take in life. I think that, well, I think that's part of the need for a cultural change. We need to say we each need to be responsible for what we do.

In response, Gore moves immediately away from broader concepts of character or values to a specific policy proposal:

> I think the American people should take into account who we are as individuals, what our experience is, what our positions are on the issues and proposals are. I'm asking you to see me for who I really am. I'm offering you my own vision, my own experience, my own proposals. And

incidentally, one of them is this. This current campaign financing system has not reflected credit on anybody in either party. And that's one of the reasons I've said before, and I'll pledge here tonight, if I'm president, the very first bill that Joe Lieberman and I will send to the United States Congress is the McCain-Feingold campaign finance reform bill.

Bush's focus on boundary setting is clear in his first closing statement quoted earlier. In it he cites at least three boundaries: "The promise made will be a promise kept"; "I don't want to be the world's policeman"; "I want to make sure the education system fulfills its hope and promise . . . by insisting that there be a strong accountability systems." This trend continues throughout the debates. For example, in regard to health reform: "I'm absolutely opposed to a national health care plan." In regard to taxes: "Everybody that pays taxes is going to get tax relief." On the inheritance tax: "I just don't think it's fair to tax people's assets twice regardless of your status. It's a fairness issue. It's an issue of principle, not politics." About affirmative action: "[I favor a] policy that rejects quotas. I don't like quotas. Quotas tend to pit one group of people against another. Quotas are bad for America. It's not the way America is all about . . . I think we can do that in a way that represents what America is all about, which is equal opportunity and opportunity for people to realize their potential." Gore speaks a different sort of language in regard to affirmative action: "I believe in this goal with all of my heart . . . How do you do it? Well, you establish respect for differences. You don't ignore differences. It's all too easy for somebody in the majority in the population to say, oh we're just the same, without an understanding of the different life experiences that you've had, that others have had." Bush's response: "If affirmative action means quotas, I'm against it."

Even when the two agree on an issue, they express it in different language. On the death penalty they seem to agree, but in another sense they do not; both are in favor, but in different ways. When asked whether he were "proud of the fact that Texas is number one in executions," Bush responded, "I was sworn to uphold the laws of my state. Some of the hardest moments since I've been the governor of the state of Texas is to deal with those cases. But my job is to ask two questions, sir. Is the person guilty of the crime? And did the person have full access to the courts of law? . . . I'm proud of the fact that we hold people accountable." In Bush's rhetoric, the question is simply the requirements of the job, enforcing the bounds set by the people of his state. The standards of doing so are relatively simple. Gore, however, takes a different view: "I support the death penalty. I think it has to be administered not only fairly with attention to things like DNA evidence, which I think should be used in all capital cases, but also with very careful attention. If, for example, somebody confesses to the crime and somebody is waiting on death row, there has to be alertness to say wait a minute, have we got the wrong guy? If the wrong guy is put to death, then that's a double tragedy." He is in favor of capital punishment, but immediately points to its problems and limitations; he emphasizes its flaws, not its virtues. The standard is neither simple nor fully endorsed. It is instead a consequentialist endorsement, limited by its effects, not a full endorsement grounded in the values it promotes or boundaries it sets.

Sacred Domains: Abortion and Guns

The term *sacred* is employed three times in the 2000 debates, each time by Bush. And each is in regard to the moral issues that inspire some of the most clear examples of sacred rhetoric. On same-sex marriage: "I'm not for gay marriage. I think marriage is a *sacred* institution between a man and a woman. And I appreciated the way the administration signed the Defense of Marriage Act. I presume the vice president supported it when the president signed that bill and supports it now. But I think marriage is a *sacred* institution." On abortion: "I believe that the judges ought not to take the place of the legislative branch of government. That they're appointed for life and that they ought to look at the Constitution as *sacred*." Bush's boundary setting and citation of authority in regard to abortion are matched by his clear invocation of values: "I think what the next president ought to do is to promote a culture of life in America. Life of the elderly and life of those women all across the country. Life of the unborn . . . Surely this nation can come together to promote the value of life."

In regard to this issue, however, there is boundary setting on both sides. Gore responds: "I support a woman's right to choose. My opponent does not . . . Here is the difference. He trusts government to order a woman to do what it thinks she ought to do. I trust women to make the decisions that affect their lives, their destinies, and their bodies. And I think a woman's right to choose ought to be protected and defended." In the single exchange devoted solely to abortion, both candidates made arguments that are more sacred than negotiable. Gore's rhetoric employs two of the elements of sacredness (protected status, boundary citation), but Bush's rhetoric is more expansively sacred, employing four different facets (protected status, nonconsequentialism, boundary citation, and citation of authority).

That both sides employ sacred rhetoric in regard to abortion fits with our understanding of this issue as a double-sided sacred domain. The issue of gun rights, however, is generally a single-sided sacred domain, and in the two exchanges devoted to this issue, the Republican rhetoric is decidedly sacred, while the Democratic rhetoric is clearly not. Gore emphasizes the consequences of gun ownership: "The problem I see is that there are too many guns getting into the hands of children, and criminals, and people who, for whatever reason, some kind of history of stalking or domestic abuse really should not be able to get guns"; "All of my proposals are focused on that problem, gun safety . . . Let's have a three-day waiting period, cooling off, so we can have a background check to make sure that criminals and people who really shouldn't have guns don't get them." Hence Gore spends much of his debate time advocating registration, a policy proposal to influence what he defines as the largest problem: illegal gun ownership:

> I am for licensing by states of new handgun purchases.
>
> A photo license I.D. like a driver's license for new handguns . . . I think states should do that for new handguns, because too many criminals are getting guns . . . Look, this is the year, this is in the aftermath of Columbine, and Paducah, and all the places in our country where the nation has been shocked by these weapons in the hands of the wrong people. The woman who bought the guns for the two boys who did that killing at Columbine said that if she had had to give her name and fill out a form there, she would not have bought those guns. That conceivably could have prevented that tragedy.

Bush takes a different approach. However, he does not offer the more strident sacrednesses of the gun rights position. He does not cite the Second Amendment as an absolute or dismiss the costs of gun violence. He employs the more subtle approach of shifting the argument to national values and the boundaries of clear punishment for infractions:

> I believe law-abiding citizens ought to be allowed to protect themselves and their families.
>
> Well, it starts with enforcing law. When you say loud and clear to somebody if you're going to carry a gun illegally, we're going to arrest you. If you're going to sell a gun illegally, you need to be arrested. If you commit a crime with a gun, there needs to be absolute certainty in the law.
>
> I'm not for photo licensing. Let me say something about Columbine . . . Columbine spoke to a larger issue. It's really a matter of culture. It's

a culture that somewhere along the line we've begun to disrespect life. Where a child can walk in and have their heart turned dark as a result of being on the Internet and walk in and decide to take somebody else's life. So gun laws are important, no question about it, but so is loving children, and character education classes, and faith-based programs being a part of after-school programs. Some desperate child needs to have somebody put their arm around them and say, we love you. So there's a, this is a society that, of ours that's got to do a better job of teaching children right from wrong. And we can enforce law . . . But there's a larger law. Love your neighbor like you would like to be loved yourself. And that's where our society must head if we're going to be a peaceful and prosperous society.

In this language it is boundaries that count, but bounds of law enforcement, punishment for gun violence, and "absolute certainty in the law." The problem is not gun ownership, but a lack of other important values, traditional family structures, and the appropriate teaching of right and wrong.

The Role of Explicit Religion

In understanding these partisan differences, we should avoid a conflation between sacred rhetoric and references to religion. Citations of religious authority may be an important subset of sacred rhetoric, which could make it appear that Republicans employ more sacred rhetoric simply because they employ more references to God. But the first invocation of God by either party is not until the second debate; it is by the Republican, but only in the traditional "God bless" at the end of his closing statement, a variation of which appears in Bush's final sentences in the third debate as well. By contrast, Gore did not employ the traditional invocation of God's blessing—a mainstay of presidential rhetoric—in any of his three closing remarks.

What about religious references in the main body of the debates? They appear in the predictable areas, but by both men. In response to a question in the third debate about public morality and Hollywood, Bush mentions faith-based schooling: "I think that after-school money ought to be available for faith-based programs and charitable programs." On this topic, however, Gore was not to be outdone, especially given the history of his wife Tipper's efforts to encourage parental warning labels: "Tipper and I have four children. And God bless them, every one of them decided on their own to come here this evening." This religious reference was not even directly related to the topic, but it is unlikely a coincidence that God was invoked in the exchange on this particular topic, even if just in passing. This was Gore's only specific mention of God in the debates.

Religious references also came up regarding some less predictable topics, specifically guns and the environment. Responding to a gun control question in the second debate, Bush argues that "gun laws are important, no question about it, but so is loving children, and character education classes, and faith-based programs being a part of after-school programs." Invocations of religion in regard to the environment may be more predictable given the biblical foundations of American environmentalism. In this case the reference was from Gore: "In my faith tradition, it is, it's written in the book of Matthew, 'Where your heart is, there is your treasure also.' And I believe that, that we ought to recognize the value to our children and grandchildren of taking steps that preserve the environment in a way that's good for them."

Invocations of religion, however, are somewhat limited. In all three debates, the total number of explicit mentions of God is four, of faith is three, of the Bible is two, and of Jesus is zero (some of these overlap; the total number of explicit religious references is seven, five from Bush and two from Gore).[4] This is clearly not the religion-soaked rhetoric of much of American politics, especially compared to previous eras. The word *Bible* appears only once, only one biblical quote is offered, and Jesus is ignored. This is an unusual paucity of God compared to the rhetoric of the Founders, the abolitionists (and the entire Civil War era), or the civil rights movement, not to mention the contemporary rhetoric of many social movements. It is worth noting that this may be different in the context of intraparty debates. Democratic candidates may well place less emphasis on religion, and it is plausible that Republicans would speak in more religious terms while attempting to appeal to their own base. Bush's most famous religious reference took place during the primary contest in the December 1999 Iowa debate against John McCain, when in answer to the question, "What political philosopher or thinker do you most identify with and why?" Bush responded, "Christ, because he changed my heart." But in the presidential debates both mainstream party candidates avoided much more than perfunctory references and traditional formulations.[5] The Republican candidate holds the lead in citing religious authority, but Republican sacred rhetoric is in no way limited to or dominated by religious rhetoric.

Partisan Reversals: The Environment and Nation Building

While it is clear that Bush is more prone to sacred rhetoric, it is also the case that Democrats seem to have their own sacred domains. The first of these is the environment. In the two exchanges devoted to this issue, it is clearly Gore who is the more sacred speaker and Bush the more consequentialist. One of Gore's only invocations of religion, and the only biblical quote of the debates, is in regard to the environment (from the book of Mathew, quoted earlier). Although Gore does cite the consequences of further pollution and global warming, he also speaks of fundamental values, boundaries, and authorities:

> Now, another big difference is Governor Bush is proposing to open up some of our most precious environmental treasures, like the Arctic National Wildlife Refuge, for the big oil companies to go in and start producing oil there. I think that is the wrong choice. It would only give us a few months' worth of oil and the oil wouldn't start flowing for many years into the future. I don't think it's a fair price to pay to destroy precious parts of America's environment.
>
> Domestic exploration yes, but not in the environmental treasures of our country. We don't have to do that. That's the wrong choice. I know the oil companies have been itching to do that, but it is not the right thing to do.

In regard to this issue Bush is essentially consequentialist, arguing that we simply need the oil reserves from the Arctic Refuge and that environmental issues should be seen as simple trade-offs. But even in an area where his arguments are more instrumental, he turns his rhetoric to a value or principle, in this case the opposition to centralized authority and economic regulation: "Well, I don't believe in command and control out of Washington, D.C."

The clearest reversal of the normal pattern of the debates is in regard to the use of American military force and the dispute over nation building. Bush argues for American self-interest and a more instrumental approach. When questioned about whether he has formulated guiding principles for the use of force, his first lines are, "I have, I have. First question is what's in the best interests of the United States? What's in the best interests of our people?" Gore's opening words to the same question are, "I've thought a lot about that particular question, and I see our greatest national strength coming from what we stand for in the world. I see it as a question of values."

Later in the debate, Gore repeats his focus on values over instrumental security interests, directly questioning Bush about interventions in genocides:

Now, I did want to pick up on one of the statements earlier, and maybe I have heard, maybe I have heard the previous statements wrong, Governor. In some of the discussions we've had about when it's appropriate for the U.S. to use force around the world, at times the standards that you've laid down have given me the impression that if it's something like a genocide taking place or what they called ethnic cleansing in Bosnia, that that alone would not be, that that wouldn't be the kind of situation that would cause you to think that the U.S. ought to get involved with troops. Now, have to be other factors involved for me to want to be involved. But by itself, that to me can bring into play a fundamental American strategic interest because I think it's based on our values. Now, have I got that wrong?

Bush's response is pure instrumentalism: "If I think it's in our nation's strategic interest, I'll commit troops."

This is part of Bush's well-known antagonism toward nation building (though this position changed dramatically following 9/11). In regard to Somalia, his criticism was that it "started off as a humanitarian mission and it changed into a nation-building mission, and that's where the mission went wrong. The mission changed. And as a result, our nation paid a price. And so I don't think our troops ought to be used for what's called nation building. I think our troops ought to be used to fight and win war. I think our troops ought to be used to help overthrow the dictator when it's in our best interests." The contrast between Kosovo and Rwanda is clear in Bush's mind: "There's got to be priorities, and Middle East is a priority for a lot of reasons, as is Europe and the Far East, our own hemisphere. And those are my four top priorities should I be the president."

Gore disagrees about nation building as a concept, taking the more value-laden position:

> I don't think we agree on that. I would certainly also be judicious in evaluating any potential use of American troops overseas. I think we have to be very reticent about that. But look, Jim, the world is changing so rapidly. The way I see it, the world is getting much closer together. Like it or not, we are now, the United States is now the natural leader of the world. All these other countries are looking to us. Now, just because we cannot be involved everywhere, and shouldn't be, doesn't mean that we should shy away from going in anywhere.

Bush's response is that this just isn't possible. American forces are overextended, and we must limit military commitments—a strong statement not of values but of consequentialism. The same applies to foreign aid, which is not for principle or for show, but only for specific results, without which it should be restricted: "I believe we ought to have foreign aid, but I don't think we ought to just have foreign aid for the sake of foreign aid. I think foreign aid needs to be used to encourage markets and reform. I think a lot of times we just spend aid and say we feel better about it and it ends up being spent the wrong way, and there's some pretty egregious examples recently . . . So I'll look at every place where we're investing money. I just want to make sure the return is good." Gore sees the whole question as one of values and leadership: "We have a fundamental choice to make. Are we going to step up to the plate as a nation the way we did after World War II, the way that generation of heroes said okay, the United States is going to be the leader." When Bush does invoke a value—freedom—it is framed not as America promoting liberty abroad, as in the post-9/11 approach, but freedom for individual nations to chart their own course:

> I think one way for us to end up being viewed as the ugly American is for us to go around the world saying, we do it this way, so should you. Now, we trust freedom. We know freedom is a powerful, powerful, powerful force, much bigger than the United States of America, as we saw recently in the Balkans. But maybe I misunderstand where you're coming from, Mr. Vice President, but I think the United States must be humble and must be proud and confident of our values, but humble in how we treat nations that are figuring out how to chart their own course.

We should bear in mind that these exchanges took place before 9/11 and the dramatic change in Bush's foreign policy approach. By the time of the 2004 debates, Bush was no longer arguing a narrow version of American self-interest, but a grander vision of spreading democracy and the role of America in a free world, a rhetorical approach much closer to Gore's. This suggests that one of the two partisan reversals evident in 2000 is likely not still the case for the current parties. The environment may be the sole remaining domain with a Democratic sacred advantage.

The evidence from the Bush-Gore debates seems to indicate that with the exception of a few political domains, Republicans employ a greater degree of sacred rhetoric. But in addition to this general observation, there are a few subtler notes about how sacredness operates within presidential rhetoric. Three brief topics bear mentioning: the use of stories and narrative; the perceived role of a democratic leader; and the place of fluid versus flawed language.

Winifred Skinner versus Michael Feinberg: The Rhetorical Meaning of Political Narrative

It has become an expected element of presidential debates (and State of the Union addresses) to introduce short narratives about specific Americans, often ones in attendance. Both candidates in 2000 employed such devices, but with different rhetorical styles and meaning. Winifred Skinner and Michael Feinberg seemed to have very different stories to tell, which is to say that Gore and Bush employed the narratives to different ends, grounded in their competing rhetorical styles. Gore mentions Winifred Skinner for the first time in the middle of the first debate: "Now, I think that it's very important to understand that cutting benefits under Social Security means that people like Winifred Skinner from Des Moines, Iowa, who is here, would really have a much harder time. Because there are millions of seniors who are living almost hand to mouth." But her full story comes out in the closing statement:

> There is a woman named Winifred Skinner here tonight from Iowa. I mentioned her earlier. She's seventy-nine years old. She has Social Security. I'm not going to cut her benefits or support any proposal that would. She gets a small pension, but in order to pay for her prescription drug benefits, she has to go out seven days a week several hours a day picking up cans. She came all the way from Iowa in a Winnebago with her poodle in order [to] attend here tonight. I want to tell her, I'll fight for a prescription drug benefit for all seniors and fight for the people of this country for a prosperity that benefits all.

Taken as a whole this narrative is a consequentialist, instrumental appeal. It is her circumstances and the effects of a change in Social Security that are at issue. Moreover, it is meant to appeal to many Americans in a similar position of relying on government aid, who should vote based on their own self-interest in regard to Social Security.[6]

Bush's narrative appeal is more a series of boundary citations, proposing acceptable limits and appropriate roles:

> Let me give you a story about public education, if I might. It's about Kipp Academy in Houston, Texas. A charter school run by some people from Teach for America. Young folks saying I'm going to do something good for my country. I want to teach. A guy named Michael runs the school . . . It's one of the best schools in Houston. Here are the key ingredients. High expectations, strong accountability. What Michael says, don't put all

these rules on us, just let us teach and hold us accountable for every grade. That's what we do. And as a result, these mainly Hispanic youngsters are some of the best learners in Houston, Texas. That's my vision for public education all around America . . . We have to consolidate the system to free the schools and encourage innovators. Let them reach out beyond the confines of the current structure to recruit teach-for-the-children type teachers . . . We're going to say if you receive federal money, measure third, fourth, fifth, sixth, seventh, and eighth grade. Show us if they are learning to read, write, add, and subtract there will be bonus plans. If not, instead of continuing to subsidize failure, the money will go to, the federal money will go to the parents for public school or charter school or tutorial or Catholic school. What I care about is children. And so does Michael Feinberg.

This is clearly a different use of narrative. Gore's story illustrates the causes and consequences of a problem, implicitly making an argument about how you should see your self-interest (if the story fits your situation), or what consequences you should care about (if the story does not fit your situation). Bush's story illustrates the appropriate values one should uphold, implicitly making an argument about how you should feel (if it fits your situation), or about what you should admire in others (if it does not fit your situation). Even in their choice of narrative, the sacred versus consequential distinction is evident.

Numbers, Details, and Plans:
Leaders as Educators versus Priority Setters

The partisan distinction in regard to sacredness appears to be connected to competing views of the role of a democratic politician. Is it the place of the president to lead a discussion of policy consequences in order to educate the public, or is it to set national value priorities? Implicit in the first view is an emphasis on numbers, details, and plans, as opposed to values, symbols, and bounds. Bush tends to state broad principles: "It's a difference between government making decisions for you and you getting more of your money to make decisions for yourself"; "I am pro-life"; "I just don't think its fair to tax people's assets twice regardless of your status. It's a fairness issue"; "I trust people, I don't trust the federal government. It's going to be one of the themes you hear tonight"; "I wish we could spend an hour talking about trusting people. It's just the right position to take"; "I don't believe, like the vice president does, in huge government. I believe in limited government." He generally avoids discussing numbers and offers few explicit details.

Gore, in contrast, grounds his answer to the opening question of the first debate in a series of policy proposals: "If I'm entrusted with the presidency, here are the choices that I will make. I will balance the budget every year. I will pay down the national debt. I will put Medicare and Social Security in a lockbox and protect them. And I will cut taxes for middle-class families . . . I will make sure that we invest in our country and our families. And I mean investing in education, health care, the environment, and middle-class tax cuts and retirement security. That is my agenda." Throughout the debates, Gore continues to cite numbers, details, and plans, but especially numbers: "I've a plan in my budget to recruit 100,000 new, highly qualified teachers"; "[I will add] a $10,000 college tuition tax deduction per child per year"; "I have been in charge of this reinventing government streamlining project that's reduced the size of government by more than 300,000 people in the last several years"; "My proposal gives $10,000 hiring bonuses for those teachers who are, who get certified to teach in the areas where they're most needed"; "I believe there are 1.4 million children in Texas who do not have health insurance, 600,000 of whom . . . were actually eligible for it but they couldn't sign up"; "If you make less than $60,000 a year and you decide to invest $1,000 in a savings account, you'll get a tax credit, which means in essence that the federal government will match your $1,000 with another $1,000. If you make less than $30,000 a year and you put $500 in a savings account, the federal government will match it with $1,500. If you make more than $60,000 and up to 100 you'll still get a match, but not as generous." This propensity led directly to the famous "fuzzy math" exchange.

The Meaning of Fuzzy Math

One of the most discussed features of the first Bush–Gore debate was their numbers squabble, or the accusation of "fuzzy math." While this may have appeared to be a simple ploy by Bush to discredit Gore's criticisms of his proposed tax changes, it takes on a different meaning in the context of our discussion of sacredness. The phrase comes up in the very first exchange between the candidates. Bush's second comment of the debates begins, "Let me just say that obviously tonight we're going to hear some phony numbers about what I think and what we ought to do." And later in the first debate he says, "Look, this is a man who has great numbers. He talks about numbers. I'm beginning to think not only did he invent the Internet, but he invented the calculator. It's fuzzy math." Then Bush immediately argues for an easily understood boundary: "I set one-third. The federal government should take no more than a third of anybody's paycheck." Why one-third? Why not a quarter or a half? A justification for the boundary is never made, but it is also not necessarily relevant; the psychological point is that a boundary has been established.

It is also a clear statement of principle over consequence: don't count up the effects with your intellect, but feel what is right with your values. One-third is not the right standard because there are data to refer to, but because it *feels* right. Gore employs a different rhetorical style. His next statement following Bush's Internet jibe is, "It's clear you can go to the website and look. If you make more than $25,000 a year you don't get a penny of help under the Bush prescription drug proposal for at least four to five years, and then you're pushed into Medicare." Bush goes on to mention fuzzy math three more times: "The man is practicing fuzzy math again"; "This man has been disparaging my plan with all this Washington fuzzy math"; "I can't let the man continue with fuzzy math." The meaning of the phrase emerges as not merely incorrect calculation, but unimportant, irrelevant consequences. It is a statement about what counts and what does not. For Bush it is values and boundaries, not consequences and instrumental calculation.

"I've Been Known to Mangle a Syllable or Two": Sacred Language and Clarity

In the second debate, when Bush said, "I've been known to mangle a syllable or two myself, you know, if you know what I mean," he may have been making more than an empirical observation. In a sense he was addressing a common misconception about rhetoric: that flowing language is clear language. Or that more grammatical language is more easily understood. Another way of phrasing this misconception is that more polished arguments are more persuasive. On the contrary, I would argue that persuasion is often grounded less in impressing the audience with a display of knowledge, and more in making the audience feel that the speaker is similar to themselves and shares their values. Overly polished language could operate much like Samuel Popkin's famous tamale example.[7] President Gerald Ford's failure to know how to eat ethnic food, demonstrated by biting into the husk of a tamale, offers the same message as speaking too well: clearly he is not like us. Political analysts may make a grave mistake by assuming a correlation between the language that they respect and admire, and the language respected and admired by most voters. In this sense the homespun approach may have great traction. Moreover, it may have a natural affinity with sacred rhetoric.

Sacred language is not necessarily flowing language; sacred rhetoric may be no more grammatically correct than it is politically correct. It is true that "Here I stand, I can do no other" has a certain ring to it. But the ring is not in its complexity; it is in its boiled-down simplicity. This same effect may be achieved by rougher language, as long as the sentiment is equally clear. The connection between sacredness and simple talk may be grounded in the more uncomplicated and symbolic nature of sacred rhetoric. Boundaries and authorities are most clearly invoked by short statements. Further elaboration is not an improvement, but a detriment to communication. Details do not clarify, but simply muddy the argument. If an authority is authoritative, it is because it needs no introduction; a boundary is rhetorically effective because it is clear immediately. Values are expressed most clearly by symbols and sweeping generalizations. In this sense sacred rhetoric lacks nuance by design, not through failure. Consequentialism, in contrast, takes longer to invoke. It requires chains of logic that connect a demonstrated situation to its likely effects, and then to a reason we should care. At any point in the chain of argument, agreement could be lost or counterarguments raised. Moreover, to accomplish the needed combination of steps requires a more untroubled form of language. Halting verse will not take you there. If the devil is in the details, then the details must get across.

If "I've been known to mangle a syllable or two" is Bush's self-revealing statement about his rhetorical style, Gore's counterpart would be: "Getting a detail wrong interfered several times with the point that I was trying to make." Interestingly, the two statements were made within moments of each other, at the end of the second debate. Gore is referring to his admission that in the previous debate he mischaracterized Bush's tax proposals, "getting a detail wrong." But Gore's statement is less self-aware than Bush's. One gets the impression that Bush knows that he makes grammatical mistakes, but also knows that in the end it doesn't make him less persuasive. (Bush never in eight years corrected his pronunciation of "nuclear," regardless of countless jibes, perhaps because to have done so would have been to admit that it was relevant, or that it would be a good thing to be less like normal citizens.) Gore seems to take his flaw seriously but thinks that his misstep was in getting the details wrong. He seems sincere in his statement, "I got some of the details wrong last week in some examples that I used, Jim, and I'm sorry about that. And I'm going to try to do better . . . I can't promise that I will never get another detail wrong. I can promise you that I will try not to, and hard." If only he had gotten the details right. A better way to understand the debates may be that he would have been better served by not emphasizing the details at all. It wasn't so much getting the details wrong as it was discussing them in the first place that interfered with the points he was trying to make.

THE 2004 BUSH–KERRY DEBATES

The Bush–Gore debates in 2000 offer an illustrative snapshot of the partisan differences in sacred rhetoric. But is the evidence limited to that specific time, or did the trends continue in the 2004 election and beyond? A crucial question is whether the domains in which Democrats held the sacred advantage—the environment and the use of force—continued after the 2000 debates. Are sacred appeals about the environment associated with the Democratic Party, or only with Al Gore himself? And in the post-9/11 era, has the discussion of military force gone in the other direction? To address these questions and expand our view of the partisan differences in rhetoric, we can conduct an examination of the 2004 debates between George W. Bush and John Kerry.

Unlike the debates in 2000, in the first 2004 debate the candidates focused entirely on foreign policy. This highlights one of the clearest changes from 2000 to 2004: the discussion of the use of military force reversed dramatically. Kerry employed none of Gore's emphasis on values as a justification for American intervention, but spoke in consequentialist terms about the war in Iraq, emphasizing policy outcomes, mistakes made, and better plans. Bush, on the other hand, abandoned his previous instrumentalism in foreign policy for a decided emphasis on protected values, calls for sacrifice, and the necessity of holding the line in the face of adverse circumstances. The president even made reference to his change of heart: "I understand how hard it is to commit troops. Never wanted to commit troops. When I was running—when we had the debate in 2000, never dreamt I'd be doing that." But he makes it clear that 9/11 changed everything, so this is not an example of flip-flopping or being wishy-washy. It is important to note that Bush's emphasis on sacred rhetoric in foreign policy applies to both the Iraq War and to Islamist terrorism. The Republican advantage in sacred rhetoric applies to exchanges on Osama bin Laden as well as on Iraq, and also includes other areas such as North Korean proliferation and antidemocratic movements in Russia.

An exchange on Iraq in the first debate illustrates the rhetorical divide. Bush invokes freedom as a value with protected status: "A free Iraq will set a powerful example in that part of the world that is desperate for freedom. A free Iraq will help secure Israel. A free Iraq will enforce the hopes and aspirations of the reformers in places like Iran. A free Iraq is essential for the security of this country . . . We have a duty to our country and to future generations of Americans to achieve a free Iraq, a free Afghanistan." The trope of a free Iraq is repeated not just within these sentences but throughout the debates. Bush was asked whether the casualties of the conflict were worth it, a difficult question to answer well. But he invokes the values that make the sacrifices worthwhile, in one of the more sacred responses of the debates: "You know, every life is precious. Every life matters . . . That's what distinguishes us from the enemy. Everybody matters. But I think it's worth it, Jim. I think it's worth it because I think—I know in the long term a free Iraq, a free Afghanistan, will set such a powerful example in a part of the world that is desperate for freedom. It will help change the world; that we can look back and say we did our duty." In his rebuttal, Kerry immediately moves from values to plans:

> Now, we have a choice here. I've laid out a plan by which I think we can be successful in Iraq: by doing better training, faster, by cutting—by doing what we need to do with respect to the UN and the elections. There's only 25% of the people in there. They can't have an election right now. The president's not getting the job done. So the choice for America is, you can have a plan that I've laid out in four points, each of which I can tell you more about, or you can go to johnkerry.com and see more of it; or you have the president's plan, which is four words: more of the same. I think my plan is better.

Later in the debate, Bush argues that "the way to make sure that we succeed is to send consistent, sound messages to the Iraqi people that when we give our word, we will keep our word, that we stand with you, that we believe you want to be free. And I do. I believe that twenty-five million people, the vast majority, long to have elections . . . I reject the notion that some say that if you're a Muslim you can't be free, you don't desire freedom. I disagree, strongly disagree with that." Kerry's response is, "I couldn't agree more that the Iraqis want to be free and they could be free. But I think the president, again, still hasn't shown that he's going about it the right way." He moves immediately from values to policy once again. Bush's focus was the value—freedom—while Kerry's response centered on better tactics and

Bush's failure to secure the Iraqi borders. Bush counters with the key values at stake: "The reason why Prime Minister [Ayad] Allawi said they're coming across the border is because he recognizes that this is a central part of the war on terror. They're fighting us because they're fighting freedom. They understand that a free Afghanistan or a free Iraq will be a major defeat for them. And those are the stakes. And that's why it is essential we not leave. That's why it's essential we hold the line. That's why it's essential we win. And we will win."

The focus of the 2004 debates was clearly foreign policy (55% of the questions asked), and Bush's sacredness in this realm was a dramatic change from 2000. The rhetoric on the environment also shifted in Republicans' favor, although this was a much smaller part of the debates. Kerry displayed none of Gore's sacredness about environmental protection. In the single exchange on the environment, Bush had a slight advantage by claiming to protect natural resources, while Kerry focused on criticizing the environmental achievements of the Bush administration but stated no protected values, bounds, or authorities as Gore did. The sacred advantage on the environment in 2000 may indeed have been held by Gore himself rather than Democrats in general.

The two Democratic reversals of 2000 no longer seemed to hold in 2004. But the central pattern of 2000 was still present, a substantial sacred advantage to the Republican candidate (table 6.2). Although the domains shifted, the degree of sacred language remained, with Bush employing on average 1.4 more facets of sacredness than Kerry in each response, and 2.3 in the closing statements (compared to 1.5 and 3.7, respectively, in 2000). This is the case even though the debate also shifted away from the domestic topics where Bush had the sacred advantage in the previous debates. Questions on morals, guns, taxes, and school constituted 39% of the total questions in 2000, and only 29% in 2004. But Bush remains effective at setting nonnegotiable bounds in several arenas. When asked about a potential draft, he says in his second sentence, "We're not going to have a draft, period," and in his closing sentences, "Now, forget all this talk about a draft. We're not going to have a draft so long as I am president." Kerry, however, continues Gore's dislike of clear boundaries. In the second debate, the candidates were asked about government funding of abortions. When Kerry gives a nuanced answer about whether he would approve or disapprove of state funding, Bush responds, "I'm trying to decipher that. My answer is, we're not going to spend taxpayers' money on abortion."

128 ∾ The Politics of Sacred Rhetoric

It is not the case, however, that Kerry employs no sacred rhetoric or does not understand how. In a few instances during the debates he surpasses Bush and engages in particularly effective exchanges. The two most prominent ones both revolve around moral issues in which Bush usually has the advantage. Kerry pulls off an unusual reversal of sacred positions in the third debate when asked about reports of Catholic bishops telling church members that it would be a sin to vote for him because of his views on

Table 6.2
Sacred Rhetoric in the 2004 Presidential Debates

Topic	Bush	Kerry	Difference	Reversals
DEBATE 1 (Foreign Policy)				
How to Prevent Terror	2	0	2	
Who Would Prevent Terror	2	0	2	
Bush Administration Misjudgments	3	1	2	
Osama or Hussein the Priority	3	1	2	
How to Increase Homeland Security	0	1	-1	x
Criteria to Bring Home Troops	5	0	5	
Was Iraq War a Mistake	2	0	2	
Miscalculation of Post-war Iraq	3	0	3	
Lying about Iraq War	3	1	2	
Has War Been Worth the Casualties	4	0	4	
Plan for Ending War	4	1	3	
Pre-emptive Military Action	3	0	3	
Nuclear Proliferation in Iraq and North Korea	2	0	2	
Intervention in Darfur	0	1	-1	x
Character as Commander in Chief	2	0	2	
Greatest Threat to National Security / Proliferation	0	1	-1	x
Putin Moving away from Democracy	4	0	4	
Closing Statements	3	0	3	
AVERAGE	2.5	0.4	2.1	

TABLE 6.2 (CONT.)

Topic	Bush	Kerry	Difference	Reversals
DEBATE 2 (*Town Hall Format*)				
Kerry Wishy-Washy	1	0	1	
Without WMD, Should We Have Invaded Iraq	2	0	2	
Future of Iraqi Government	2	0	2	
International Opinion of U.S.	4	0	4	
Iran Nuclear Weapons	0	0	0	
Reinstituting the Draft	3	1	2	
Post-9/11 Security	2	0	2	
Canadian Drug Imports	1	1	0	
Lawsuits and Medical Costs	0	0	0	
Deficit Spending	3	1	2	
Will Kerry Raise Taxes	0	1	-1	x
Environmental Protection	1	0	1	
U.S. Competitiveness in Manufacturing	0	0	0	
Patriot Act	2	2	0	
Stem-Cell Research	2	0	2	
Supreme Court Nominations	2	0	2	
Abortion	3	1	2	
Examples of Wrong Decisions	2	0	2	
Closing Statements	3	1	2	
AVERAGE	1.7	0.4	1.3	
DEBATE 3 (*Domestic Policy*)				
Domestic Security	3	1	2	
Flu Vaccine Shortage	1	0	1	
Taxes and Deficits	0	0	0	
Outsourcing	1	0	1	
Federal Government Role in Job Creation	1	0	1	

cont. on next page

Table 6.2 (cont.)

Topic	Bush	Kerry	Difference	Reversals
DEBATE 3 (Domestic Policy) (cont.)				
Gay Marriage	2	1	1	
Catholic Church Opposing Kerry over Abortion	1	2	-1	x
Health Insurance Costs	0	0	0	
Taxes for New Health Care Spending	0	0	0	
Social Security Privatization	1	0	1	
Social Security Retirement Age	1	0	1	
Immigration	1	0	1	
Minimum Wage	2	1	1	
Overturning *Roe v. Wade*	1	3	-2	x
Back-door Draft	3	0	3	
Assault Weapons Ban	2	1	1	
Affirmative Action	0	0	0	
Faith and Public Policy	3	0	3	
Political Polarization	0	0	0	
Closing Statements	3	1	2	
AVERAGE	1.4	.5	0.9	
TOTAL AVERAGE	1.8	0.4	1.4	
Average Difference of Closing Statements			2.3	

Topics in bold indicate especially noteworthy differentials in sacred rhetoric.

abortion and stem-cell research. He cites boundaries and authorities in an unusual display of facets of sacredness, reminding us that he is a Catholic three times, citing President Kennedy twice, and quoting the Bible:

> Now, I will not allow somebody to come in and change *Roe v. Wade*. The president has never said whether or not he would do that. But we know from the people he's tried to appoint to the Court he wants to. I will not. I will defend the right of *Roe v. Wade*.

Now, with respect to religion, you know, as I said, I grew up a Catholic. I was an altar boy. I know that throughout my life this has made a difference to me. And as President Kennedy said when he ran for president, he said, "I'm not running to be a Catholic president. I'm running to be a president who happens to be Catholic."

My faith affects everything that I do, in truth. There's a great passage of the Bible that says, "What does it mean, my brother, to say you have faith if there are no deeds? Faith without works is dead." And I think that everything you do in public life has to be guided by your faith, affected by your faith, but without transferring it in any official way to other people. That's why I fight against poverty. That's why I fight to clean up the environment and protect this earth. That's why I fight for equality and justice. All of those things come out of that fundamental teaching and belief of faith. But I know this, that President Kennedy in his inaugural address told all of us that here on earth, God's work must truly be our own. And that's what we have to—I think that's the test of public service.

The other important reversal also centers on *Roe v. Wade*, when President Bush is asked whether he would like the ruling to be overturned. In his response, Kerry argues for nonnegotiable bounds and the authority of the Constitution: "I'm not going to appoint a judge to the Court who's going to undo a constitutional right, whether it's the First Amendment, or the Fifth Amendment, or some other right that's given under our courts today under the Constitution. And I believe that the right of choice is a constitutional right. So I don't intend to see it undone." This is a remarkable use of sacred rhetoric for Kerry, indicating that it is possible, even if unusual.

The Party of Numbers and Plans

In the 2004 exchanges, Democrats continued to be the party of numbers. In the two debates on domestic policy, Kerry cites figures 149 times, compared to Bush's 88 times. (In the first debate on foreign policy, the language was not as heavily numerical, Kerry citing numbers 44 times to Bush's 33.) Kerry mentions numbers on average twice per answer in the foreign policy debate, moving to three times in the first domestic debate, and four times each answer in the final debate. But this is not as striking as the disparity in the final 2000 Bush-Gore debate on domestic policy, when Gore cites numbers 47 times to Bush's 17.

Democrats also continue to be the party of plans. Kerry said, "I have a plan" (or a close variant such as "I have a better plan") 26 times, while Bush used the phrase twice. In the first debate on Iraq, Kerry insists, "I have a plan to do it. He doesn't." In Bush's response, the phrase in his lexicon is not that he has a plan, but instead, "I have a solemn duty." Later in the first debate, Kerry argues, "I couldn't agree more that the Iraqis want to be free and that they could be free. But I think the president, again, still hasn't shown how he's going to go about it the right way." It is not about having the right goals, but having the best plans; not about proper ends, but efficient means. Kerry seems convinced that a good plan is a selling point: in the second debate he insists that "labels don't mean anything. What means something is, do you have a plan?"

In the second debate on domestic policy Kerry exceeds even Gore's predilection to plan:

> *I have a plan. I have a plan* to lower the cost of health care for you. *I have a plan* to cover all children. *I have a plan* to let you buy into the same health care senators and congressmen give themselves. *I have a plan* that's going to allow people fifty-five to sixty-four to buy into Medicare early. And *I have a plan* that will take the catastrophic cases out of the system, off your backs, pay for it out of a federal fund, which lowers the premiums for everybody in America, makes American business more competitive and makes health care more affordable.

The plan becomes a trope of Kerry's, and while repetition can be a powerful tool of persuasion, repetition of the wrong thing is a different story. Again in his closing statement of the second debate he makes it clear that in his mind the test for voters should be who has a plan:

> *I have a plan* that will help us go out and kill and find the terrorists. And I will not stop in our efforts to hunt down and kill the terrorists. But *I'll also have a better plan* of how we're going to deal with Iraq: training the Iraqi forces more rapidly, getting our allies back to the table with a fresh start, with new credibility, with a president whose judgment the rest of the world trusts. In addition to that, I believe we have a crisis here at home, a crisis of the middle class that is increasingly squeezed, health care costs going up. *I have a plan* to provide health care to all Americans. *I have a plan* to provide for our schools so we keep the standards but we help our teachers teach and elevate our schools by funding No Child Left Behind. *I have a plan* to protect the environment so that we leave this place in better shape to our children than we were handed it by our parents. That's the test.

Mixed Signals and Flip-Flopping

While Kerry's signature repetition of the debates is either having or not having a plan, for Bush it is the accusation of sending mixed signals. When Bush says in the first debate, "I know we won't achieve if we send mixed signals," this has an interesting double meaning, like many of his statements. "Mixed signals" is Bush's accusation that Kerry does not possess the nonnegotiability necessary for leadership in wartime. The charge of mixed signals invokes the nonnegotiable boundaries in Bush's stances and the implicit accusation that Kerry would be weak in foreign relations, or as Margaret Thatcher once said to his father George H. W. Bush during the First Gulf War, "This is no time to go wobbly." But on a second level Bush is arguing that a leader cannot achieve *politically* if he sends mixed messages; it is a statement about domestic rhetoric as well as foreign relations, as much about Bush's own prospects as about the war's outcome.

To quote just a few of Bush's repeated accusations (in the same order they appear in the first debate):

> I don't see how you can lead this country and succeed in Iraq if you say "wrong war, wrong time, wrong place." What message does that send our troops? What message does that send to our allies? What message does it send to the Iraqis?

> My opponent says help is on the way, but what kind of message does it say to our troops in harm's way, "wrong war, wrong place, wrong time"? Not a message a commander in chief gives, or this is a "great diversion."

> I sit down with the world leaders frequently and talk to them on the phone frequently. They're not going to follow somebody who says, "This is the wrong war at the wrong place at the wrong time." They're not going to follow somebody whose core convictions keep changing because of politics in America.

> I think what is misleading is to say you can lead and succeed in Iraq if you keep changing your positions on this war. And he has. As the politics change, his positions change. And that's not how a commander in chief acts.

> The only consistent about my opponent's position is that he's been inconsistent. He changes positions.

The mixed signals accusation became a major campaign message, most clearly articulated in the charge that Kerry was a "flip-flopper." This interpretation of Kerry gained such currency that the very first question addressed to him in the town hall debate was whether he was too "wishy-washy": "Senator Kerry, after talking with several coworkers and family and friends, I asked the ones who said they were not voting for you, 'Why?' They said that you were too wishy-washy. Do you have a reply for them?" Later in the debate Bush brings up one of Kerry's most noted campaign statements: "He complains about the fact our troops don't have adequate equipment, yet he voted against the $87 billion supplemental I sent to the Congress and then issued one of the most amazing quotes in political history: 'I actually did vote for the $87 billion before I voted against it.'" Kerry's most famous remark of the campaign was said at a campus rally in March, and in September on *Good Morning America* he described it as "one of those inarticulate moments." In the debates he explained the comment (twice) by saying, "I made a mistake in how I talk about the war. But the president made a mistake in invading Iraq. Which is worse?" A reasonable answer, but not one that erases the fundamental lack of clarity, invocation of negotiability, and hint of political calculation inherent in the famous remark.

Near the end of the first debate, Bush and Kerry engaged in a discussion of character, but the exchange focused on the conflict over mixed messages. The candidates were asked about leadership traits but moved immediately to accusations of too much negotiability versus Kerry's counterchange of too much certainty:[8]

> *Bush:* My concerns about the senator is that, in the course of this campaign, I've been listening very carefully to what he says, and he changes positions on the war in Iraq. He changes positions on something as fundamental as what you believe in your core, your heart of hearts, is right on Iraq. You cannot lead if you send mixed messages. Mixed messages send the wrong signals to our troops. Mixed messages send the wrong signals to our allies. Mixed messages send the wrong signals to the Iraqi citizens. Of course, we change tactics when we need to, but we never change our beliefs.
>
> *Kerry:* Let me talk about something the president just sort of finished up with. Maybe someone would call it a character trait, maybe somebody wouldn't. But this issue of certainty. It's one thing to be certain, but you can be certain and be wrong. It's another to be certain and be right, or to be certain and be moving in the right direction or be certain about

a principle and then learn new facts and take those new facts and put them to use in order to change and get your policy right.

Kerry's interpretation about the role of additional facts in making judgments, about the negative potential of certainty, and about the primacy of getting your policy right, is the opposite of Bush's view that the most important thing is that "I won't change my core values." In Kerry's view, "Judgment is what we look for in the president of the United States of America." This is the opposite of Bush's take on politics, that what voters look for is clarity and certainty, principle and predictability, or in a word, sacredness.

The Valorization Effect

The experimental evidence presented in previous chapters demonstrates that sacred rhetoric inspires absolutist reasoning and motivates political engagement. If Republicans gain the activation advantages of sacred appeals, this provides a significant electoral advantage. But another effect specific to political campaigns also adds to the absolutist advantage. In addition to increasing citizens' political engagement, leaders who employ sacred rhetoric rise in citizens' estimations of their character. This could be termed a valorization effect, or an enhanced impression of the speaker's virtue. When an object or idea is imbued with sacred status, it is to be respected and treated differently. To show disrespect is profane, and to defend the sacred object is a valorous act. Citizens who defend the sacred realm gain esteem in others' eyes as well as their own. And leaders who defend the sacred are seen as more valorous. When voters evaluate candidates, their gut appraisal is grounded in their sense not only of candidates' values but also of perceived character traits and the clues they provide. Considerable empirical evidence indicates that citizens are swayed by their assessment of candidates' personal qualities above and beyond evaluations of political values or policies. Some of the central qualities that influence voters are whether a candidate appears to be principled and determined, exactly the traits that sacred rhetoric emphasizes.[9]

To test the hypothesis that sacred rhetoric valorizes the speaker, another experiment was conducted, in which participants were exposed to a set of statements attributed to a single hypothetical political candidate. Participants were randomly assigned to hear either sacred or nonsacred appeals expressing the same policy opinions. They were then asked to evaluate the character traits of the candidate. After reading all four statements on gun rights, the environment, gay marriage, and the death penalty, participants rated the speaker along a scale from 1 (Not at all) to 4 (Extremely) for being caring, competent, determined, intelligent, principled, and virtuous—traits that have been shown to influence citizens' vote choice. As illustrated in table 6.3, citizens perceived the leader employing sacred language to be distinctly more principled, virtuous, and determined than the one employing nonsacred language. The average increase for the sacred speaker was 0.8 along the four-point scale for principled, 0.6 for virtuous, and 0.4 for determined, representing a distinct difference in perception.

TABLE 6.3
Valorization Effect Experimental Results

Character Trait	Effect
Principled	F = 20.92 (p = .001) (3.46, 2.71)
Virtuous	F = 16.83 (p = .001) (2.62, 2.00)
Determined	F = 7.68 (p = .01) (3.46, 3.07)
Caring	F = 2.31 (p = .13) (2.46, 2.25)
Competent	F = 1.44 (p = .23) (2.62, 2.79)
Intelligent	F = 0.68 (p = .41) (2.65, 2.79)

Results are F statistics derived from a one-way analysis of variance (ANOVA), comparing the sacred rhetoric treatment to the negotiable rhetoric treatment. All statistically significant results are in bold ($p < .05$). The numbers reported below the F statistics are the means of the dependent variable for the sacred and negotiable groups respectively. Participants read either sacred or mundane appeals for all four domains and then were asked their impressions of the speaker. N = 108.

However, a possible concern in employing sacred appeals is that while increasing citizens' perceptions of a candidate's determination and principle, they could simultaneously decrease perceptions of caring or intelligence. This concern fits with the Democratic insistence on not simplifying arguments or dumbing down the quality of political discourse—by appealing to simple principles that lack nuance, candidates could appear to be less intelligent and competent. But citizens' perceptions of caring, competence, and intelligence did not vary between the sacred and nonsacred conditions. The sacred group displayed only small and statistically insignificant differences from the mundane rhetoric group: 0.2 higher in caring, 0.2 lower in competence, and 0.1 lower in intelligence, all of which were in the range of random variations, unlike the strong effects on principle, virtue, and determination. This indicates that sacred rhetoric influences perceptions of the specific character traits that reflect the valorization of the speaker, but does not influence other traits. The benefits gained by employing sacred rhetoric are expansive, increasing not only political intensity and engagement but also the positive image of a candidate.

The Absolutist Advantage

Following his victory in 2004, Bush began to outline his domestic agenda, especially the introduction of Social Security private accounts. When pressed by reporters for details, he responded that he refused to "negotiate with myself in public."[10] Like many of his phrases, this one may be more strategic than it appears. To not negotiate with oneself is to remain absolute, uncompromising, sacred. To refuse to do so in public is to privilege sacred rhetoric. The Republican form of sacred rhetoric is only marginally grounded in explicit references to religion, but is instead a matter of a secular sacred style, emphasizing boundaries, protected values, nonconsequentialism, and sources of authority such as the Constitution. Democrats, in contrast, seem to prefer the logic of consequences and the instrumentality of policy effects. Rather than the simplicity of values, symbols, and bounds, Democratic rhetoric offers the greater complexity of numbers, details, and plans. Democrats are more wedded to the view that things are complicated. We cannot, and should not, reduce them. The goal of political rhetoric should not be to dumb the message down; instead it should be to bring the public up. The role of a politician is to educate. Some evidence indicates that within certain specific domains, it is the Democrats who are the more rhetorically sacred party. On the whole, though, Republicans employ a decidedly more sacred form of discourse. If this distinction holds, what does it mean for the electoral prospects of the two parties?

Paired with our evidence of the influence of sacred rhetoric, a Republican sacred propensity suggests not only a meaningful difference between the two parties but also a substantial electoral advantage. Sacred rhetoric has a strong activation effect, leading listeners to see the political meaning of their personal values. The greater discussion and engagement that this inspires is an important political advantage. The experimental evidence indicates that sacred rhetoric is not more effective at changing minds, but it is clearly more effective at increasing absolutist reasoning, encouraging a more strident and intransigent form of citizen engagement. Employing sacred rhetoric also valorizes candidates, leading citizens to see them as more principled, determined, and virtuous. In the current climate of a divided electorate and potentially close margins in presidential campaigns, the activation, intensity, and valorization that are associated with sacred over negotiable appeals create a significant electoral advantage. It may be the marginal edge required in a marginal political environment.

Whether Democrats would desire to employ a more sacred approach if they recognized its effects, or be able to do so given their other commitments, is an open set of questions. That Democrats do employ sacred rhetoric in regard to some issues suggests that it is not entirely outside of their realm. Republicans, however, seem much more comfortable with sacred appeals. As long as this difference remains, Republicans are likely to enjoy the absolutist advantage.

Chapter Seven

SACRED RHETORIC FROM CARTER TO CLINTON

The 1976–1996 Presidential Debates

While the 2000 and 2004 elections are powerful examples of the role of sacred rhetoric, we may learn more by examining the influence of sacred appeals across a broader scope. In this chapter I examine the rhetoric of presidential hopefuls in the decades prior to the George W. Bush years, and in the following chapter the evidence from the 2008 contest. In the decades from Richard Nixon to George W. Bush, Republicans gained the presidency in seven out of ten electoral contests, even though during the entire period Democrats had the greater number of registered voters. In the forty years following Lyndon Johnson in 1964, only Jimmy Carter, who ran as a Washington outsider with strong religious beliefs, and Bill Clinton, whose program was grounded in a move to the center and his own remarkable charisma, ran successful Democratic campaigns. During the same period, four different Republicans were elected. The Republican dominance during this era is a thing to be explained, and the more strategic use of language may be one of the crucial factors.

A Republican advantage in sacred rhetoric was a general but not absolute trend in the presidential campaigns of this period. As illustrated in figure 7.1, during the three successful Democratic campaigns of 1976, 1992, and 1996, the absolutist advantage for Republicans does not appear. With one important exception, this was not the result of the Democratic candidates displaying unusual sacredness, but instead the Republican candidates falling to levels similar to their Democratic counterparts. Democrats have varied less across time, while Republicans have ranged considerably in their use of sacred appeals. The noteworthy exception is Jimmy Carter in 1976, who spoke of moral leadership, public trust in Washington following

Watergate, and a value-based foreign policy. In that race, Gerald Ford preferred to concentrate on policy debates regarding taxation and foreign affairs, creating the only contemporary race in which the Democrat held a substantial advantage in sacred language. In Bill Clinton's two successes, he also faced Republicans who did not emphasize sacred rhetoric. Both George H. W. Bush and Bob Dole stuck more to policy debates rather than staking out sacred boundaries. Bush is famous for his boundary statement "Read my lips, no new taxes," which likely helped him in 1988 and then hurt him in 1992 after he became infamous for violating it, losing his nonnegotiable credentials. Although several factors contributed to the Democratic victories in 1976, 1992, and 1996, including scandal in the incumbent party, poor economic performance, and third-party candidates, these campaigns

FIGURE 7.1
Sacred Rhetoric in Presidential Debate, 1976–2004

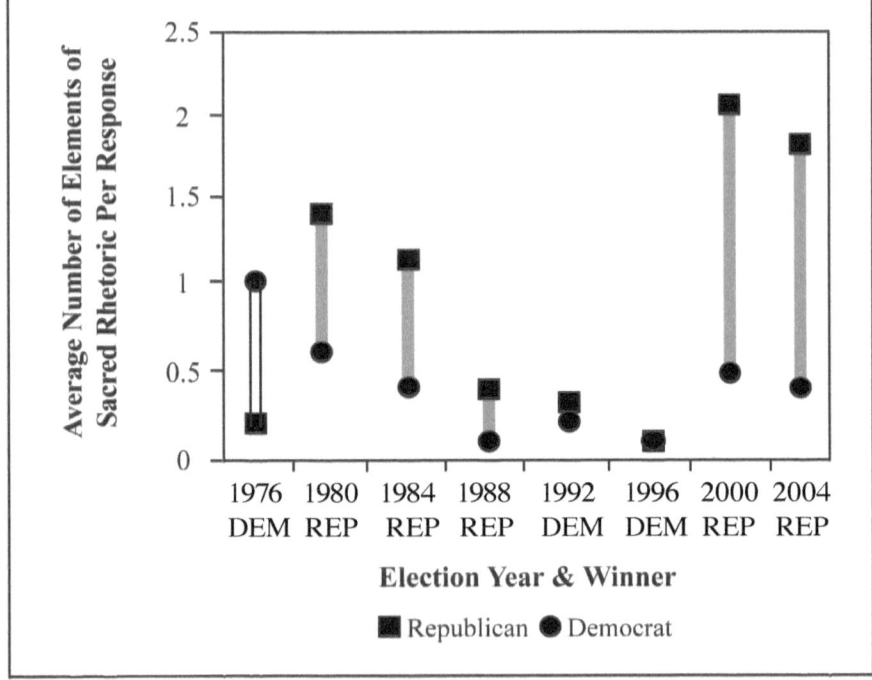

Data points represent the average number of elements of sacred rhetoric in each response by the competing candidates. The candidates are, for 1976: Carter–Ford; 1980: Carter–Reagan; 1984: Mondale–Reagan; 1988: Dukakis–Bush; 1992: Clinton–Bush; 1996: Clinton–Dole; 2000: Gore–Bush; 2004 Kerry–Bush

were also the only three occasions when the absolutist advantage for Republicans was not present.

The 1976 Carter-Ford Debates

The presidential debates have varied widely in the prevalence of sacred rhetoric as well as the avoidance of sacred violations. The televised debate format first appeared with the famous Kennedy-Nixon debates in 1960, but it was distrusted by candidates and did not take place in 1964 between Johnson and Barry Goldwater, nor in the Nixon campaigns of 1968 and 1972. The contemporary institutionalized debates began in 1976 between Gerald Ford and Jimmy Carter.[1] In his challenge to President Ford, Carter was the most sacred speaker among contemporary Democrats. He emphasized government decency following the Watergate years, a principled vision of foreign policy, and moral outrage at the failures of the Ford administration. Carter was openly devout, but his Evangelical roots did not emerge in distinct invocations of God and faith; instead they emerged in a secular sacred style of language. God is rarely mentioned in his arguments, but moral outrage and nonnegotiable boundaries are central themes.[2] Ford, in contrast, is one of the least sacred speakers among Republicans, creating the only case of a Democratic advantage in sacred rhetoric in the contemporary races.

More than any other facet of sacredness, Carter invoked moral outrage. When Ford attempts to defend his administration's economic record, Carter responds, "With all due respect to President Ford, I think he ought to be ashamed of mentioning that statement, because we have the highest unemployment rate now than we had at any time between the Great Depression caused by Herbert Hoover and the time President Ford took office . . . And I think this shows a callous indifference to the families that have suffered so much . . . This is a very serious indictment of this administration. It's probably the worst one of all." The level of taxation and economic redistribution was a central issue of the campaign, and Carter discusses this in openly moral terms: "The present tax structure is a disgrace to this country; it's just a welfare program for the rich"; "Now we have such a grossly unbalanced tax system—as I said earlier, that it is a disgrace . . . And when those rich corporations don't pay that tax, the average American taxpayer pays it for them. Another one that's very important is the business deductions—jet airplanes, first-class travel, the fifty-dollar martini lunch. The average working person can't take advantage of that, but the wealthier people can . . . You can't hire a lobbyist out of unemployment checks."

Carter's Moral Foreign Policy

Carter's expressions of moral disgust are even more pronounced in the second debate on foreign policy.[3] In Carter's language, our recent failings in dealing with other nations have meant that "sometimes we've been embarrassed and sometimes we've been ashamed." When asked about the Arab boycott of Israeli and Jewish companies, Carter responds with one of his most striking examples of sacred rhetoric (particularly illustrative language is in italics):

> I believe that the boycott of American businesses by the Arab countries because those businesses trade with Israel or because they have American Jews who are owners or directors in the company is *an absolute disgrace*. This is the first time that I've, remember in the history of our country when we've let a foreign country circumvent or change our *Bill of Rights*. I'll do everything I can as president to stop the boycott of American businesses by the Arab countries. It's not a matter of diplomacy or trade with me. *It's a matter of morality*. And I don't believe that Arab countries will pursue it when we have a strong president who will protect the integrity of our country, the commitment of our *Constitution and Bill of Rights* and protect people in this country who happen to be Jews. It may later be Catholics; it may be, later be Baptists who are threatened by some foreign country. *But we ought to stand staunch*. And I think *it's a disgrace* that so far Mr. Ford's administration has blocked the passage of legislation that would've revealed by law every instance of the boycott and it would've prevented the boycott from continuing.

This passage is a clear example of moral outrage, citation of authority (the Bill of Rights and Constitution), and taking a nonnegotiable stance. On average across the three debates, Carter employed 1.0 facets of sacred rhetoric in each exchange (compared to Ford's negligible 0.2). But this figure masks a meaningful difference between domestic policy discussions, which average 0.6, and the foreign policy exchanges, which average 1.6. Carter approaches George W. Bush's levels when discussing foreign policy, but only in that realm.

In addition to moral outrage, Carter's discussion of foreign policy focuses on two other sacred aspects: the protected status of government openness, and Ford's failure to be nonnegotiable when moral issues are at stake. Carter connects his criticisms of government secrecy during Watergate to a similar secrecy in foreign diplomacy. He is especially critical of Secretary of State Henry Kissinger's approach to private negotiations:

> First of all, I would quit conducting the decision-making process in secret, as has been a characteristic of Mr. Kissinger and Mr. Ford.
>
> Mr. Ford, Mr. Kissinger have continued on with the policies and failures of Richard Nixon. Even the Republican platform has criticized the lack of leadership in Mr. Ford and they've criticized the foreign policy of this administration. This is one instance where I agree with, with the Republican platform. I might say this in closing, and that is that as far as foreign policy goes, Mr. Kissinger has been the president of this country. Mr. Ford has shown an absence of leadership, and an absence of a grasp of what this country is and what it ought to be. That's got to be changed. And that's one of the major issues in this campaign of 1976.

The value that Carter believes should be protected is openness or the inclusion of the public in decision making:

> What we were formerly so proud of, the strength of our country, its moral integrity, the representation in foreign affairs of what our people are, what our Constitution stands for, has been gone. And in the secrecy that has surrounded our foreign policy in the last few years, the American people, the Congress have been excluded . . . Every time we've made a serious mistake in foreign affairs, it's been because the American people have been excluded from the process . . . Every time Mr. Ford speaks from a position of secrecy in negotiations, in secret, in secret treaties that've been pursued and achieved, in supporting dictatorships, in ignoring human rights, we are weak and the rest of the world knows it.

Carter goes on to accuse Ford of being too negotiable and not upholding absolute boundaries across a number of foreign policy dimensions, including failing to enforce treaties with the Soviets, allowing Radio Free Europe to be jammed, going along with the Arab boycott of Jewish-owned businesses, and yielding to Arab pressure to sell them arms: "This is a deviation from idealism; it's a yielding to economic pressure on the part of the Arabs on the oil issue . . . It's a matter of being tough. It's a matter of being strong. It's a matter of being consistent"; "He's also shown a weakness in yielding to pressure. The Soviet Union, for instance, put pressure on Mr. Ford and he refused to see a symbol of human freedom recognized around the world, Alexander Solzhenitsyn." Instead, Carter would take a nonnegotiable position against our adversaries and in support of our allies: "If the Arab countries ever again declare an embargo against our nation on oil, I would consider that not a military but an economic declaration of war, and I would respond instantly and in kind. I would not ship that Arab country anything—no weapons, no spare parts for weapons, no oil-drilling rigs, no oil pipe, no nothing"; "Our allies feel that we've neglected them . . . They have felt neglected. And using that base of strength, and using the idealism, the honesty, the predictability, the commitment, the integrity of our own country, that's where our strength lies." In Carter's rhetoric, it is not military strength but moral strength that counts the most:

> I think that militarily we are as strong as any nation on earth . . . But as far as strength derived from commitment to principles, as far as strength derived from the unity within our country, as far as strength derived from the people, the Congress, the secretary of state, the president sharing in the evolution and carrying out of a foreign policy, as far as strength derived from the respect of our own allies and friends, their assurance that we will be staunch in our commitment, that we will not deviate and that we'll give them adequate attention, as far as strength derived from doing what's right, caring for the poor, providing food, becoming the breadbasket of the world instead of the arms merchant of the world—in those respects we're not strong.

Ford's Failure to Communicate

In response to Carter's attacks on the morality of his administration (as well as his personal valor in refusing to face a press conference and turning over critical decisions to the secretary of state), Ford sticks to discussions of policy. His essential argument is that the consequences of his decisions have been positive—he has kept the peace and maintained the economy. In his response to Carter's statement about the immorality of his acquiescence to the Arab boycott, President Ford elides the moral issues and defends his policy actions:

> Again Governor Carter is inaccurate. The Arab boycott action was first taken in 1952. And in November of 1975 I was the first president to order the executive branch to take action, affirmative action, through the Department of Commerce and other cabinet departments, to make certain that no American businessman or business organization should discriminate against Jews because of an Arab boycott . . . Just on Monday of this week I signed a tax bill that included an amendment that would

prevent companies in the United States from taking a tax deduction if they have in any way whatsoever cooperated with the Arab boycott. And last week when we were trying to get the Export Administration Act through the Congress—necessary legislation—my administration went to Capitol Hill and tried to convince the House and the Senate that we should have an amendment on that legislation which would take strong and effective action against those who participate or cooperate with the Arab boycott.

Ford defends himself on consequentialist grounds but fails to identify the values at issue or the bounds that he wants to uphold. In this sense he fails to communicate at critical junctures. The most damaging inarticulate moment occurred in his famous statements about Eastern Europe not being under the domination of the Soviet Union, comments that were perhaps the largest gaff of the 1976 campaign. Asked whether the Soviets were getting the best of us in recent international events, Ford ended his response by stating that "there is no Soviet domination of Eastern Europe and there never will be under a Ford administration." When asked in a follow-up question whether he meant to say that the Russians were not using Eastern Europe as their own sphere of influence, Ford said he did not believe that the Yugoslavians, Romanians, or Poles "consider themselves to be dominated by the Soviet Union. Each of those countries is independent, autonomous. It has its own territorial integrity and the United States does not concede that those countries are under the domination of the Soviet Union. As a matter of fact, I visited Poland, Yugoslavia, and Romania to make certain that the people of those countries understood that the president of the United States and the people of the United States are dedicated to their independence, their autonomy, and their freedom." In the context of his entire response, Ford likely intended to convey that the *people* of the region had not been dominated, were continuing to resist, and would be supported by the United States. What he actually said, however, was taken by many commentators and viewers to imply either a lack of understanding of the region or a foolish denial of reality. It also provides an important lesson regarding the use of sacred rhetoric.

In one sense Ford was invoking a nonnegotiable boundary: he would not tolerate Soviet domination of the region, and "it never will happen under a Ford administration." But this was clearly not a successful use of sacred rhetoric and was perhaps the most damaging statement he made during the campaign. This occurred because his statement invoked a *violated sacred value*. He appealed to a sacred boundary—that free countries should not be allowed to fall to Soviet domination—but it was all too clear that the boundary had already been violated, as Soviet domination of Eastern Europe was an established fact. To invoke a sacred value and your abrogation of it simultaneously has the effect of pointing out your own sacrilege; it is worse than your opponent accusing you of such a violation. If a politician argues that he is upholding a sacredness when the audience clearly thinks this is not the case, it is more likely to remind the audience of the violation and have an unintended negative effect.

At the close of the foreign policy debate, Carter returns to the values that he expressed throughout the discussion—the protected status of government openness and human rights as American principles. He invokes the authority of God and the Constitution. To Carter, "the purpose of this debate and the outcome of the election will determine three things: leadership, upholding the principles of our country, and proper priorities and commitments for the future." He discusses the future and sacred values, not the past and instrumental concerns:

> This election will also determine what kind of world we leave our children . . . Will we have *a government of secrecy that excludes the American people* from participation in making basic decisions and therefore covers up mistakes and makes it possible for our government, our government to depart from the *principles of our Constitution and Bill of Rights?* . . . We ought to be a beacon for nations who search for peace and *who search for freedom, who search for individual liberty, who search for basic human rights.* We haven't been lately . . . We can have that strength if we return to the basic principles. It ought not to be a strength of bombast and threats. It ought to be a quiet strength based on the integrity of our people, *the vision of the Constitution*, an innate strong will and *purpose that God's given us in the greatest nation on earth*, the United States.

Ford's final words invoke none of this emphasis on values, but instead argue that experience and policy knowledge are what count:

> As we have seen tonight, foreign policy and defense policy are *difficult and complex issues*. We can debate methods, we can debate one decision or another, but there are two things which cannot be debated: *experience and results*. In the last two years, I have made policy decisions involving long-range difficulties and policies and made day-to-day judgments not only as president of the United States but as the leader of the free world. *What is the result of that leadership?* America is strong. America is free. America is respected. Not a single young American today is fighting or dying on

any foreign battlefield. America is at peace and with freedom. Thank you, and good night.

Ford's emphasis on complexity mirrors the language of recent Democratic candidates. Foreign policy is subtle and contingent, not transparent or principled. Carter, on the other hand, sees its more clear aspects that can be communicated in sacred language. The combination of Ford's failings and Carter's moral language resulted in the single case from 1976 to 2004 of the absolutist advantage accruing to the Democratic candidate. Carter prevailed in a close contest, with 50.1% of the popular vote to Ford's 48.0%, and 297 electoral votes to 240.

RONALD REAGAN AND THE CARTER REVERSAL IN 1980

The first question in the 1980 debate was from Marvin Stone of *U.S. News & World Report*, about the candidates' differences regarding the use of military force.[4] Carter responds, "Mr. Stone, I've had to make thousands of decisions since I've been president, serving in the Oval Office. And with each one of those decisions that affect the future of my country, I have learned in the process. I think I'm a much wiser and more experienced man than I was when I debated four years ago against President Ford. I've also learned that there are no simple answers to complicated questions." He employs the same complexity language that Ford emphasized four years earlier. Throughout this debate, Carter abandons his previous insistence on moral standards in foreign policy in favor of defending the consequences of his policies and the need for negotiable standards. Later in the same answer he says, "I and my predecessors, both Democrats and Republicans, have advocated resolving those troubles in those difficult areas of the world peacefully, diplomatically, and through negotiation." Reagan emphasizes this difference in their worldview, accusing Carter of being too negotiable, and therefore too easily out-negotiated, when a hard line with the Soviet Union is the better principle: "I believe that we must have a consistent foreign policy, a strong America, a strong economy . . . We went back into negotiations on their terms . . . The Soviet Union sat at the table knowing that we had gone forward with unilateral concessions without any reciprocation from them whatsoever." Because of Carter's lack of resolve, "we've been out-negotiated for quite a long time." But more important, because of the lingering failure of the Iran hostage crisis, Carter had lost his ability to invoke bounds, limits, and moral absolutes. He cannot say, as Reagan does, "I believe it is high time that the civilized countries of the world made it plain that there is no room worldwide for terrorism. There will be no negotiations with terrorists of any kind."

In this debate Carter suffered a dramatic reversal of his previous advantage. This is the first instance of a fall in sacred rhetoric in a president's reelection campaign, a trend that continues for each of the second-term presidents. It stands to reason that incumbents are more likely to be positioned to defend their record, often in consequentialist rather than principled terms. It is easier to speculate on the bounds they would uphold rather than to justify the violations they have allowed. But Carter also faced an additional problem as an incumbent. His moral outrage in 1976 was directed against people more than policy. His targets were the legacy of Nixon in regard to Watergate, and Kissinger regarding government secrecy. Without these living examples on which to cast aspersions, Carter had less opportunity to establish moral boundaries. In his second campaign Carter fell from his previous average of 1.0 facets of sacred rhetoric in each debate response (and 1.6 in foreign affairs) to 0.6, with no distinction between his domestic and foreign policy rhetoric. Reagan had the distinct advantage at 1.4 overall, and 1.8 when discussing foreign affairs.

Reagan does not employ sacred language only in regard to nonnegotiable bounds in foreign policy, but also in regard to protected values in domestic politics. He clearly communicates the protected status of individual freedom, especially economic freedom: "I would like to see us a little more free, as we once were"; "I happen to believe that the federal government has usurped powers of autonomy and authority that belong back at the state and local level. It has imposed on individual freedoms of the people." Reagan's closing words emphasize that during his governorship of California, "we did give back authority and autonomy to the people. I would like to have a crusade today, and I would like to lead that crusade with your help. And it would be one to take government off the back of the great people of this country, and turn you loose again to do those things that I know you can do so well, because you did them and made this country great. Thank you." Carter begins the debate by invoking complexity; Reagan ends it with a simple value statement. The incumbent fails to employ his previous rhetoric and is eclipsed by Reagan's sacred claims.

Reagan's Second-Term Debates

In his 1984 challenge to Reagan, Walter Mondale proved to be more similar to Al Gore and John Kerry than to Carter. He invoked little of his former running mate's moral outrage or protection of key values, preferring more negotiable positions in both domestic and foreign affairs. Of the few elements of sacred language he employs, three citations of boundaries stand out: to Social Security cuts, to the interweaving of church and state, and to the militarizing of space with the Strategic Defense Initiative. One of his best concluding sentences of any response in the debates is, "Why don't we stop this madness now and draw a line and keep the heavens free from war?" He also employs a very interesting invocation of noninstrumental sacrifice in his closing statement of the first debate: "I would rather lose a campaign about decency than win a campaign about self-interest. I don't think this nation is composed of people who care only for themselves. And when we sought to assault Social Security and Medicare, as the record shows we did, I think that was mean spirited. When we terminated four hundred thousand desperate, hopeless, defenseless Americans who were on disability, confused and unable to defend themselves, and just laid them out on the street, as we did for years, I don't think that's what America is all about." But these examples are exceptions; the overwhelming tenor of Mondale's rhetoric is policy oriented and consequentialist. He gives Reagan credit for inspirational rhetoric, "raising the sense of spirit, morale, good feeling in this country," but believes "what we need . . . is not just that, but to move forward, not just congratulating ourselves but challenging ourselves to get on with the business of dealing with America's problems." Again it is the consequences that count. In his final closing statement he says, "I think strength must also require wisdom and smarts in its exercise." As Gore argued, getting it right is paramount.

In contrast to Mondale's approach, Reagan describes policy decisions as nonconsequentialist. In one of the more revealing statements of the debates, he describes the centrality of values to his style of governance: "When I became Governor of California I started this, and I continue it in this office, that any issue that comes before me, I have instructed Cabinet members and staff they are not to bring up any of the potential ramifications that might surround the issue. I don't want to hear them. I want to hear only arguments as to whether it is good or bad for people, is it morally right? And on that basis and that basis alone, we make a decision on every issue." Reagan continues in his second round of debates with a more value-laden and less specific but also less negotiable rhetoric than Mondale. Again he emphasizes the protected status of freedom, as in the 1980 debates: "First of all, I think you must have some principles you believe in. In mine, I happen to believe in the people and believe that the people are supposed to be dominant in our society—that they, not government, are to have control of their own affairs to the greatest extent possible, with an orderly society." He repeatedly advocates "a program of returning authority and autonomy to the local and state governments that has been unjustly seized by the federal government."

Reagan establishes bounds not only to what the federal government ought to do but to what he will do as president. Even in a policy area such as Social Security, which seems to allow Mondale to state clear boundaries for the protection of senior citizens and forces Reagan to argue the monetary consequences of this approach, Reagan turns the rhetoric to his advantage: "A president should never say 'never,' but I'm going to violate that rule and say 'never.' I will never stand for a reduction of the Social Security benefits to people that are now getting them." This is a clear boundary statement, though one more nuanced than it might at first appear. Reagan was defending himself against Mondale's accusations that he would cut Social Security payments—that he was "constantly picking on our senior citizens and the most vulnerable in American life." Even where Reagan was vulnerable to criticism given his views on limiting government spending, he was able to create sacred language that fit. The bound is limited to *current recipients*, not to a reduction of benefits to future retirees, a policy that he still had in mind. By choosing the bound that fit his views, Reagan was able to speak the language of limits regardless of the inhospitable context.

Reagan's boundaries applied to foreign as well as domestic politics. When asked about the withdrawal from Lebanon after the attack on the Marine barracks, an issue on which he was accused of being too weak and negotiable, Reagan turns this into another form of boundary: "I will never send troops anywhere on a mission of that kind without telling them that if somebody shoots at them, they can darn well shoot back . . . But we went in in the interest of peace and to keep Israel and Syria from getting into their sixth war between them. And I have no apologies for our going on a peace mission." Reagan also emphasizes the need for strength and nonnegotiability with the Soviet Union, whose government he had not hesitated to frame in moral terms as the Evil Empire: "I believe that many of the things they have done are evil in any concept of morality that we have." In regard to dealing with the Soviets, he says, "The question that comes down to you is this: Do you want to see America return to the policies of weakness of the last four years? Or do we want to go forward, marching together, as a nation of strength and that's going to continue to be strong?"

Much has been said about Reagan's communication skills as the foundation of his politics. In his influential book *The Rhetorical Presidency*, Jeffrey Tulis concludes that Reagan is the exemplar of the new form of executive leadership—the twentieth-century shift to direct appeals to the people in a continual moral campaign.[5] This style of rhetorical leadership may indeed have reached its peak with Reagan. Nevertheless, it may be instructive to compare him with George W. Bush, who is perhaps a strong example as well, even more so because he does not possess Reagan's natural oratorical gifts. Bush's advantage is that he employs an even more sacred style. As Tulis describes the Reagan era, "At the time of the midterm elections in 1986, Reagan could boast of major legislative victories (budget cuts, tax reform, militarization), foreign policy victories (Grenada, the Philippines), substantial changes in the management of the bureaucracy (more centralized control, regulatory reform), a reinspiriting of the population, and a landslide re-election."[6] In Bush's case, if you substitute, "at the time of the midterm elections in 2006, Bush could boast of major legislative victories (*education reform, tax reform, the Patriot Act*), foreign policy victories (*leading wars in Afghanistan and Iraq*), substantial changes in the management of the bureaucracy (*creation of the Department of Homeland Security*—a historic increase and reorganization of the federal bureaucracy), and a *clear* re-election," it becomes apparent that Bush achieved much of his political agenda as well, regardless of the questionable circumstances of his first election and the divisive politics of his era. In politicians' definition of success—whether they achieved their agenda and gained reelection—Bush was remarkably successful in his first term, regardless of his lack of legislative achievements and plummeting popularity during his second term (which also befell, in different ways, both Reagan and Clinton).

In Tulis' view, Reagan understood himself as a salesman of policy rather than a planner or researcher.[7] The same could be said of Bush. Without detracting from the Great Communicator, whose influence was partly grounded in his use of sacred appeals, Bush is the more interesting case because he relies on such appeals even more heavily. As we saw in previous chapters, this has both positive and negative effects on the polity as a whole, increasing political participation at the same time that it degrades meaningful deliberation among more absolutist citizens. But it was effective in promoting Bush's agenda. Even more than Reagan, Bush may be the instructive case, as a president with less oratorical skill but in an important sense more effective language.

The Republican Doldrums and the Emergence of Clinton

The rhetorical contests from 1988 to 1996 reveal a different story. Among George H. W. Bush, Michael Dukakis, Clinton, and Dole, none stands out as a sacred speaker. Their styles were more akin to Ford than to Reagan, centering on policy discussions and assertions of greater expertise rather than higher principles. Nonetheless, important differences in language separated the candidates, in particular when one appeared especially antisacred, which happened to Dukakis in 1988 and Bush in 1992. In these two contests it was not the sacred character of one antagonist but the powerfully antisacred impression created by the other that may have been influential.

1988: The Kinder, Gentler Republican and the "Smartest Clerk in the World"

In the first 1988 debate, Peter Jennings of ABC News described Dukakis as, "passionless, technocratic, the smartest clerk in the world." He continued, "Your critics maintain that in the 1960s your public passion was not the war in Vietnam or civil rights, but no-fault auto insurance." This characterization is supported by Dukakis' language in the debate, which is the least sacred among the contemporary presidential candidates. Moreover, while other unsuccessful candidates such as Ford may have been nonsacred, Dukakis ventured into the antisacred, violating expected boundaries of presidential bearing, especially in his response to the famous Kitty Dukakis question on the death penalty.

George H. W. Bush, in contrast, could be described as a kinder, gentler absolutist, not of the same mold as Reagan, but still having a slight advantage over the anemic Dukakis. Bush begins and ends the first debate discussing values: "I think we've seen a deterioration of values . . . And then it gets down to a question of values. We've had a chance to spell out our differences on the Pledge of Allegiance here tonight and on tough sentencing of drug kingpins and this kind of thing. And I do favor the death penalty. And we've got a wide array of differences on those. But in the final analysis, the person goes into that voting booth, they're going to say, 'Who has the values I believe in?'" Bush opens the second debate in similar fashion: "Well, a lot of what this campaign is about, it seems to me, Bernie, goes to the question of values." In his response to the third question he returns to this theme: "I think it's whether you share the broad dreams of the American people . . . You see, I think it's a question of values." For Bush, the central topics that represent these value distinctions are the death penalty, abortion, small government, and national defense. Like Reagan, he argued for a nonnegotiable posture toward the Soviets. Although he did not use the phrase in the debates, his most repeated boundary statement of the campaign was his pledge against any tax increase: "Read my lips, no new taxes." But the issue that allowed Bush to establish definitive boundaries, and to plague Dukakis with his violations of them, was law enforcement and the death penalty.

In this realm Dukakis made what were perhaps his most damaging statements of the debates. Two points in particular illustrated his lack of sacred standing and became remembered aspects of the campaign. The first was his refusal to take an absolutist position regarding capital punishment, even in regard to attacks on his own family, and the second was his association with the decision to release Willie Horton, representing a failure of boundary setting. Like Gore and Kerry, Dukakis preferred to dwell on concrete proposals and plans: "Senator Bensen and I have a plan for the 1990s and beyond. Mr. Bush and Mr. Quayle do not." Also like Gore and Kerry, he downplayed expressions of broad principle or patriotism in favor of policy discussion: "If we can just put away the flag factories and the balloons and those kinds of things and get on to a real discussion of these issues, I think we will have a good success." But unlike the later candidates, even when the context cried out for a more absolute position, Dukakis remained committed to a measured response.

The most noted case is the Kitty Dukakis question. In the first question of the second debate (from Bernard Shaw of CNN), Dukakis was asked, "Governor, if Kitty Dukakis were raped and murdered, would you favor an irrevocable death penalty for the killer?" If it seems to be out of appropriate bounds to discuss a candidate's wife in this fashion, this is all the more reason that Dukakis could not respond in the way he did without losing ground. The first part of his response (84 words) is a reiteration of his position against capital punishment: "No, I don't, Bernard. And I think you know that I've opposed the death penalty during all of my life. I don't see any evidence that it's a deterrent, and I think there are better and more effective ways to deal with violent crime. We've done so in my own state. And it's one of the reasons why we have had the biggest drop in crime of any industrial state in America and why we have the lowest murder rate of any industrial state." An absolutist position against the death penalty—emphasizing its moral failings or inherent brutality—would have provided a moral counterpart, but Dukakis focused on the consequentialism of whether capital punishment is a deterrent to crime, as if this political issue were solely about cause and effect rather than morals and feelings. The longer second part of his response (269 words) deals with his proposals for the war on drugs. No part of the response deals with his wife, or his reaction to such a personal question, or what his own desires for retribution would be as opposed to what the rule of law ought to be. But a necessary part of a response to that question was to defend his family, not resort immediately to policy considerations. The question created a distinct dynamic by framing it in a personal way, and Dukakis failed to perceive the downfall of a pure policy response. Some statement of moral outrage, some sense that personal boundaries would not be crossed, some expression of a desire for revenge, even lashing out at the questioner for his inappropriate question, before launching into the policy response was demanded by the situation. To do so had little cost; to do otherwise appeared weak, unfeeling, and lacking valor.

The second aspect of Dukakis' failure to protect appropriate boundaries was his association with the furlough of Willie Horton. Whether this was an accurate or fair association is a different question, but Dukakis clearly became linked with this story. Bush's response to the death penalty question in the first debate included the following statement: "When a narcotics-wrapped-up guy goes in and murders a police officer, I think they ought to pay with their life. And I do believe it would be inhibiting. And so I am not going to furlough men like Willie Horton, and I would meet with their, the victims of his last escapade, the rape and brutalization of the family down there in Maryland. Maryland would not extradite Willie Horton, the man who was furloughed, the murderer, because they didn't want him to be furloughed again." The Willie Horton discussion provided a subtext to the Kitty Dukakis question, though Horton was only mentioned by name during the first debate in the passage just quoted, and not at all in the second. But the infamous television ad had aired in the days leading up to the debate, linking Dukakis' support for prison furloughs with the violent crimes committed by Horton while on furlough from a life sentence for murder in Massachusetts.[8]

The Willie Horton ad had become a popular topic of media and pundit discussion before the second debate. In a follow-up ad, the Bush campaign played part of Dukakis' response to the death penalty question during the first debate: "I'm opposed to the death penalty. I think everybody knows that. I'm also very tough on violent crime," followed by the scattered laughter from the debate audience.[9] By invoking a boundary that members of the audience likely believed had been violated, Dukakis was put in a position similar to President Ford when he tried to uphold the boundary against Soviet domination of Eastern Europe, only calling attention to its violation.

Like Ford and Mondale in the previous campaigns, Dukakis avoided sacred rhetoric in favor of policy discussion. But he also allowed himself to appear to violate expected norms and boundaries in a dramatic fashion that was remembered by pundits and voters. Even though George H. W. Bush was no match in sacred rhetoric for Reagan, or for George W. Bush in 2000, he still had a meaningful advantage (and victory) over Dukakis. It was not until the 1992 and 1996 races that the absolutist advantage was erased entirely, leveling the field for the Democratic contender.

The Clinton Era

In Clinton's first statement of the 1992 debates, he frames the differences between himself and Bush in consequentialist terms: "The most important distinction in this campaign is that I represent real hope for change, a departure from trickle-down economics, a departure from tax-and-spend economics, to invest in growth." In his follow-up response he says, "I've worked hard to create good jobs and educate people. My state now ranks first in the country in job growth this year, fourth in income growth, fourth in reduction of poverty, third in overall economic performance . . . I think the American people deserve better than they're getting. We have gone from first to thirteenth in the world in the last twelve years, since Mr. Bush and Mr. Reagan have been in. Personal income has dropped while people have worked harder." Clinton continues throughout the debates with the economy as his dominant theme—by nature a consequentialist concern about government policy. Another clear summary of Clinton's central argument came in the third debate: "The real problem in this country is that most people are working hard and falling further behind. My passion is to pass a jobs program and get incomes up with an investment incentive program to grow jobs in the private sector, to waste less public money and invest more, to control health care costs and provide affordable health care for all Americans, and to make sure we've got the best-trained workforce in the world. That is my passion." In another crucial passage he says, "I think it's important to elect a president who is committed to getting this economy going again, and who realizes we have to abandon trickle-down economics and put the American people first again, and who will send programs to the Congress in the first hundred days to deal with the critical issues that

America is crying out for leadership on—jobs, incomes, the health care crisis, the need to control the economy."

Clinton's emphasis was policy, consequences, and political expertise; the Clinton victory was clearly not the product of sacred appeals. His use of sacred rhetoric was as sparse as that of the other Democratic contenders, and lower than Gore's or Kerry's. This demonstrates that sacred language is not the only way to be successful in American politics, if the circumstances are right. But it raises the question of whether Clinton would have been successful against more formidable and sacred-speaking Republicans. Clinton had an advantage that Carter, Mondale, Gore, and Kerry did not—his Republican opponents were equally low in sacred language. With no absolutist advantage to either side, Clinton's other rhetorical virtues were influential, including his remarkable charisma, his ability to project empathy, and his refusal to remain on the defensive.

An important facet of Clinton's success was avoiding the wholeheartedly antisacred messages of Dukakis. When Clinton was criticized, he struck back rather than agreeing to simply defend his position. An important example occurred early in the first debate, when Bush criticized him for demonstrating overseas against the Vietnam War: "I think it's wrong to demonstrate against your own country or organize demonstrations against your own country in foreign soil. I just think it's wrong . . . I couldn't do that. And I don't think most Americans could do that." In response to this boundary statement from Bush, Clinton did not remain defensive and allow Bush to gain the advantage, but instead displayed moral outrage at Bush's attack, expressing his own perspective on clear lines of right and wrong: "You have questioned my patriotism. You even brought some right-wing congressman into the White House to plot how to attack me for going to Russia in 1969 to '70, when over fifty thousand other Americans did . . . But when Joe McCarthy went around this country attacking people's patriotism he was wrong. He was wrong. And a senator from Connecticut stood up to him named Prescott Bush. Your father was right to stand up to Joe McCarthy, you were wrong to attack my patriotism." Clinton's reaction was categorically different from Dukakis' more passive approach. Clinton was also able to make a virtue out of compromise, a difficult thing to manage with Bush accusing him of turning "the White House into the Waffle House." But in return, Clinton criticized the president for taking absolutist positions: "That's what's wrong with Mr. Bush. His whole deal is you've got to be for it or against it, you can't make it better. I believe we can be better.

I think the American people are sick and tired of either/or solutions, people being pushed in the corner, polarized to extremes."

Clinton was also able to capitalize on Bush's greatest rhetorical success-turned-failure: the "Read my lips" pledge against new taxes. Once broken, this vow became a symbol of the loss of his nonnegotiable credentials. In the second exchange of the first debate, Bush admitted his mistake in raising taxes during his first term, but the damage was done: "They get on me, Bill's gotten on me about 'Read my lips.' When I make a mistake I'll admit it." When asked in the third debate about his broken pledge, he again argued, "So I made a mistake, and I, you know, the difference, I think, is that I knew at the time I was going to take a lot of political flak. I knew we'd have somebody out there yelling, 'Read my lips,' and I did it because I thought it was right." But Clinton did not let him off the hook: "The mistake that was made was making the 'Read my lips' promise in the first place just to get elected, knowing what the size of the deficit was . . . You just can't promise something like that just to get elected if you know there's a good chance that circumstances may overtake you."

Clinton went on to mention the broken vow at least four more times:

> So I don't want you to read my lips, and I sure don't want you to read his. I do hope you will read our plans.

> And as far as what Mr. Bush says, he is the person who raised taxes on the middle class after saying he wouldn't.

> Now, furthermore, I am not gonna tell you "Read my lips" on anything because I cannot foresee what emergencies might develop in this country. And the president said never, never, never would he raise taxes in New Jersey, and within a day Marlin Fitzwater, his spokesman, said "Now, that's not a promise." So I think even he has learned that you can't say "Read my lips" because you can't know what emergencies might come up. But I can tell you this. I'm not gonna raise taxes on middle-class Americans to pay for programs I've recommended. Read my plan.

> I really can't believe Mr. Bush is still trying to make trust an issue after "Read my lips" and fifteen million new jobs and embracing what he called voodoo economics.

Bush declined in his sacred appeals from 1988 to 1992 (as each of the second-term presidents did), and in addition suffered the reversal of his most remembered boundary statement; however, the Republican candidate who employed the least sacred rhetoric in the contemporary campaigns was Bob Dole in 1996. As a long-time legislator, Dole was steeped in the compromise and negotiation of the Senate. He rarely spoke in absolutes, limits, or nonnegotiables. As much as Dole disagreed with Clinton on ideology, they agreed on a basic premise about governance—that it centers on policy debate. Dole readily agreed to focus on the state of the economy and the question of who would be a more effective governor. Toward the end of the first debate Dole argues, "This is important business. This is about getting the economy moving again. This is about American jobs and opportunities." The conclusion of Dole's final statement of the debates were the words, "And I'll just make you one promise, my word is good. Democrats and Republicans said Bob Dole's word is good. I keep my word. I promise you the economy is going to get better. We're going to have a good economic plan. We're going into the next century a better America." These statements, focusing on consequentialist views of policy management, could just as easily have been made by Clinton in 1992, Gore in 2000, or Kerry in 2004.

Clinton's remarkable political skills and personal charisma often mask another aspect of his electoral success, which was unusually favorable conditions. Clinton ran against two weak opponents under positive circumstances (especially the poor economic performance in 1992, and likely the intervention of Ross Perot as a third-party candidate). George H. W. Bush in 1992 and Dole in 1996 employed some of the least sacred rhetoric among contemporary Republicans, comparable only to Ford's losing performance in 1976. An attempt to emulate Clinton's style of rhetoric under less favorable conditions and facing a more formidable opponent may be an unwise approach.

Sacred Rhetoric in Historical Perspective

Candidates have varied widely in their emphasis on sacred appeals in the past thirty-five years of campaign rhetoric. However, a clear pattern emerges when we look across these races. The candidates with a substantial absolutist advantage have been successful (Carter in 1976, Reagan and George W. Bush twice each, and to a lesser extent George H. W. Bush in 1988). In the two races in which the absolutist advantage was erased—1992 and 1996—the Democratic candidate emerged with the victories. This is a powerful historical trend, but no doubt not an absolute one given the many factors that influence national elections. It is important to note that employing sacred rhetoric is an aid to electoral victory rather than a guarantee of it. But in a close contest, any one of several factors could turn an election. In a marginal electoral environment, even small advantages can matter a great deal. This is not to say that candidates cannot win while employing nonsacred rhetoric, bolstered by other factors such as the state of the economy, scandal, policy failure among the opposition, or fatigue with the incumbent party. But they are disadvantaged, especially in close races.

In addition to this central observation about the role of sacred rhetoric, a few other patterns stand out from the historical record. One is the second-term decline. All five incumbent presidents have employed fewer sacred appeals in the second round of debates, with an average decline of 0.2 facets of sacred rhetoric per response. The largest decline occurred for Carter (0.4) and the smallest for George H. W. Bush and Clinton (0.1), perhaps because the numbers of their appeals were low to begin with. The reason for this decline may simply be that the incumbent candidate is cast on the defensive. A challenger has an easier time stating bounds that they haven't yet faced. In this sense sacred rhetoric may be a particularly effective tool against incumbent presidents or parties, as it was for Carter against Ford, and for Reagan against Carter.

Another observation is the powerful reverse effect of invoking a sacred boundary that the audience believes has been violated. This is one way of understanding the remarkably negative reaction to Ford's assertion that the people of Eastern Europe were not being dominated by the Soviets. Stating that Poland or Romania were not and would not be allowed to be under Soviet control, when listeners knew that they were, made Ford appear not only foolish or out of touch but also weak and invalorous. A similar effect damaged George H. W. Bush in 1992, after the violation of his well-known pledge against taxes created the impression of negotiability, calculation, and lack of principle. Even though Clinton's party favored the tax increase, he consistently criticized Bush on this score, not for the policy action, but for the broken pledge. What was an effective campaign tool for Bush in 1988—as a humorous, easily understood, and often-repeated sound bite that established a clear boundary—became an equally well-understood violation in 1992 that established a form of bankruptcy.

One key to recent Republican success is not that the candidates spoke more about religion, but that they did not miss many opportunities to talk about other things as if they were religion. Democrats, in contrast, have taken fewer opportunities to frame secular domains in sacred terms. The trends in the historical record and the accumulated psychological evidence allow us to make informed speculations about the future prospects of these partisan differences, which the next chapter addresses in the context of the 2008 election and beyond.

Chapter Eight

SACRED RHETORIC, THE 2008 CAMPAIGNS, AND THE DEMOCRATIC PARTY

Given the evidence for an absolutist advantage, our discussion ends with two questions of some importance to citizens and leaders on the left: can Democrats also gain the advantages of sacred rhetoric, and what impediments do they face? In this chapter I focus on the 2008 campaigns as an important test, not only because of the Democratic victory, but also because the unusually open primary season allows us to examine a broad range of language that illustrates the role of sacred rhetoric within the two parties.

THE PARTY OF CONSEQUENTIALISM?

Are Democrats wedded to the language of calculated consequences? Will they continue to see policy outcomes as primary, and values as relative rather than set aside from secular trade-offs? Will leaders on the left persist in projecting negotiability rather than setting hard boundaries or citing unbending sources of authority? Republicans gain a meaningful advantage by being the party of values, symbols, and bounds, and Democrats pay a cost for being the party of numbers, details, and plans. However, many strategists on the left deny the value of sacred positions. A well-known article appeared in the *New York Times Magazine* just before the 2004 election, discussing the role of faith and certainty in the Bush presidency. Ron Suskind quoted a senior Bush aide as deriding "the reality-based community," a phrase that represented for Suskind and many others the Republican disavowal of empiricism and consequentialism in favor of a false certainty in the power of faith. The full quote is that liberals were "in what we call the reality-based community," or people who "believe that solutions emerged from your judicious study of discernible reality. That's not the way the world really works anymore ... When we act, we create our own reality. And while you're studying that reality—judiciously, as you will—we'll act again, creating new realities."[1] This was widely misunderstood as an admission of ignoring empirical evidence and flouting the logic of consequences. But perhaps a more accurate reading of the argument is an invocation of the power of social construction. The Bush aide was emphasizing that it is not the current reality that counts, but instead the possibilities of future realities. And those depend on our own belief, or our political will to construct the world as we envision it. Social constructionists in the tradition of Peter Berger and Thomas Luckmann would understand this argument quite well. The Bush administration was speaking the language of academic sociologists and rhetorical theorists, perhaps something so unexpected that it was not recognized.

A more generous interpretation of the phrase "reality-based community" would have been people who accept the current reality and do not recognize the possibilities of a different future. They are reasonable people, in the sense that only *un*reasonable people attempt to change the world. This is the case because reasonable people accept the world the way they find it—one of the very definitions of being reasonable—so it is usually unreasonable people who bring about significant changes, either positive or negative. It is also people who speak of unreasonable or sacred commitments who inspire others to support and join them, transcending the normal apathy of democratic politics. An excess of public consequentialism has hurt Democrats in gaining supporters, just as sacred rhetoric has aided Republicans. It is one thing to evaluate policies in terms of consequences, but it is another to employ this language when communicating with the voting public.

The 2008 Primary Campaign:
The Neglect or Emergence of Sacred Appeals?

Given the advantages of sacred rhetoric, will Democratic candidates begin to employ sacred appeals? The 2008 primary campaign was an important test, as the long primary season allowed candidates to hone their rhetoric. Moreover, this campaign was unique in the history of the modern presidential primary system (first begun in 1972), in the sense that it was an open race for both parties. Neither side had an incumbent or clear party favorite going into the campaign, which had never occurred on both sides simultaneously. Both fields were heavy at the beginning of the campaign season, with eight declared candidates participating in the debates on the Democratic side, and ten for the Republicans. Three candidates could make a claim to being a leading Democratic hopeful: Hillary Clinton, John Edwards, and Barack Obama.[2] While Clinton led in the early polls, Obama was ahead in fundraising, and Edwards had a strong base of support and name recognition from his 2004 vice presidential run. Republicans were in a similar position, with a large field led by three clear frontrunners: Rudy Giuliani, John McCain, and Mitt Romney.[3] Unencumbered by a dominant early candidate, both parties were exposed to a broad range of rhetoric.

Did the 2008 Democratic candidates employ sacred appeals or did they follow the pattern of 2000 and 2004? Table 8.1 illustrates the analysis of the first three Democratic debates of the primary campaign. The first took place in April 2007 in South Carolina, the second in early June in New Hampshire, and the third in late June at Howard University in Washington, D.C. Concentrating on the early debates allows us to capture the full range of candidates and rhetorical styles. Comparing the 2008 Democrats to their Republican counterparts, the pattern of Republican sacred advantage continues to be clear. The average number of facets of sacred rhetoric employed in each debate by the Democratic leaders is 2.0, while for the Republican leaders it is 9.6 (table 8.2).[4] Democrats also display a marked difference between their leaders and fringe candidates, who employ sacred rhetoric at almost twice the rate of the leading candidates (3.5 to 2.0). This is the case even though the leaders tended to draw more questioning than the others (only in the third debate did all candidates receive equal time). This is further evidence that Democratic candidates could employ sacred appeals, but that the leading candidates choose not to do so.

Other trends from 2000 and 2004 also continued in the 2008 campaign. Democrats continued to be the party of plans. As discussed earlier, Martin Luther King Jr. did not say, "I have a plan," but the 2008 Democrats did so *eleven* times in the first three debates, compared to twice by the Republicans. King's dream was not to be efficient; it was to see right be done. He understood that plans—consequentialist appeals to chains of cause and effect—do not stir people. Visions may, if they invoke a protected value for which we are willing to sacrifice. This distinction can be seen not only in effective social movements, but also between mainstream Democrats and Republicans. The Democratic candidates tended to provide plans, while the Republicans tended to express values.

The Republican use of sacred rhetoric was more consistent across the leading and following candidates, with no meaningful front-runner/fringe

TABLE 8.1
Sacred Rhetoric in the 2008 Democratic Primary Debates

Topic	Clinton	Edwards	Obama	Biden	Dodd	Gravel	Kuc.	Rich.
DEBATE 1								
Iraq War	1					1, 3	1, 1	1
Abortion							1	
Gun Rights								1
Energy		1						1
War on Terror							1	
Impeach Cheney							4	
Moral Leadership		1						
TOTAL	1	2	0	0	0	4	8	3
DEBATE 2								
War on Terror / Civil Liberties		2					3	
Iraq War Funding		1		2		2	1	
Immigration						1		
Universal Health Care		1			1		1	
Gays in Military	1					2		
Veterans' Hospitals			2					2

SACRED RHETORIC, THE 2008 CAMPAIGNS, AND THE DEMOCRATIC PARTY 165

Topic	Clinton	Edwards	Obama	Biden	Dodd	Gravel	Kucinich	Richardson
Pakistan / Killing Osama	1						1	
Darfur Genocide				3				1
Universal Military Service							1	
TOTAL	1	5	2	5	1	5	7	2
DEBATE 3								
Racial Inequality		1			1		2	
Black Unemployment	1				1		1	1
HIV among African Americans							1	1
Taxes on Wealthy	1	2	1	1			2	
Black Prison Rates								1
New Orleans Reconstruction				1			1	
Darfur and Moral Leadership		2		2	1		1	
TOTAL	2	3	1	2	1	4	8	3
AVERAGE PER DEBATE	1	3	1		1		8	3
	Average for Leaders: 2.0			Average for Others: 3.5				

The three leaders are Hillary Clinton, John Edwards, and Barack Obama; the other candidates in alphabetical order are Joe Biden, Chris Dodd, Mike Gravel, Dennis Kucinich, and Bill Richardson.

Tables 8.1 and 8.2 are not comprehensive tallies of all questions as in the previous tables, but only indicate the exchanges in which facets of sacred rhetoric emerged. When topics are repeated in the debate, a candidate may have two sets of figures such as 1, 2.

TABLE 8.2.
Sacred Rhetoric in the 2008 Republican Primary Debates

Topic	Giuliani	McCain	Romney	Bro.	Gil.	Huc.	Hun.	Paul	Tan.	Tho.
DEBATE 1										
Reagan's Leadership	2									
Iraq War		1	2	2				1		1, 2
Replacing Sec. Rumsfeld						1				
Iran		1			2		1		2	
Osama		2	1							
Dislikes About America			2							
Environment						2				
Organ Shortages									1	
Roe v. Wade			1	2, 3	1	3	1		3, 1	1
Unity of Purpose for GOP		2					1	1		
Religion			1							
GOP Platform		2		1	1	1	1		2	2
Racism								1		1
Presidential Decisions					1					
Prison Population								1		
Stem Cell Research	1		2	1	1	1			1	

SACRED RHETORIC, THE 2008 CAMPAIGNS, AND THE DEMOCRATIC PARTY — 167

Taxes	1									
Cabinet Appointments	1		1							
Conservative Credentials					2					
Internet Regulation								2		
Foreign Policy			1							
Weaknesses and Mistakes	1		1	1						
National ID Card		1						2	1	
Schiavo Case			1	2			1			
Bill Clinton in White House			1	1				1		
Distinctions from Bush		2	1			1			2	1
TOTAL	**6**	**11**	**13**	**14**	**9**	**8**	**4**	**9**	**13**	**8**
DEBATE 2										
Iraq War	3, 1	2	2	1	1	1		1, 2	1	
Taxes	1		1			1				
Gas Prices				1						
Gov. Spending / Soc. Sec.					1			1		
Conservative Credentials		2		1					2	
Stem Cells										1
Abortion			1	4		4				

cont. on next page

168 ❧ The Politics of Sacred Rhetoric

Table 8.2 (cont.)

Topic	Giuliani	McCain	Romney	Bro.	Gil.	Huc.	Hun.	Paul	Tan.	Tho.
DEBATE 2 (cont.)										
Immigration		1	1					2	2	
Confederate Flag		1					2			
Torture, Response to Terror		3		3		1			2	1
Education			1							
TOTAL	5	7	8	10	2	8	2	6	7	2
DEBATE 3										
Iraq War	2, 2	1, 2, 2	1	1		2	2	2	1, 2, 1	
Iran	1		2		1		2			1
Immigration	1, 2	1, 2	1		1				3	1
Conservative Credentials			1			2				
Abortion	1									
Evolution and Religion		1	3	1		2		2		
Energy	1	1						2		
Don't Ask, Don't Tell										
Bush Role in New Admin.				1					1	
Scooter Libby Pardon							2			

Environment					1				1	
Greatest Moral Problem	2			3	1	3		2		
Bush Mistakes		1	1		2		1			1
Moderate Voters	1	2	2		1					
TOTAL	13	13	10	10	6	7	7	8	9	3
AVERAGE PER DEBATE	8	10	10	10	6	8	4	8	10	4
	Average for Leaders: 9.6			Average for Others: 7.0						

The three leaders are Rudy Giuliani, John McCain, and Mitt Romney; the other candidates in alphabetical order are Sam Brownback, James Gilmore, Mike Huckabee, Duncan Hunter, Ron Paul, Tom Tancredo, and Tommy Thompson.

distinction as among the Democrats. If anything, the leading candidates employed slightly more sacred rhetoric than the rest of the field, the opposite of the pattern among Democrats. The 2008 GOP candidates were comfortable invoking sacred values, and even appear conscious of it, as when Senator Brownback argued, "We lose when we walk away from our principles. That's when we have trouble. And that's what the country wants us to do, is to stand for principles." Governor Huckabee invoked probably the most telling statement of a sacred bound, when asked about his faith and its influence on his policies: "In the words of Martin Luther, 'Here I stand, I can do no other.' And I will not take that back."

Aside from issues of faith, a prominent set of Republican sacred commitments focused on the war in Iraq and Islamist terror:[5]

> *McCain:* It's long, it's hard, it's tough, it's difficult. Americans are frustrated because of the mishandling of this war. But our national interests—the United States' national interests are at stake. I believe the Maliki government has got to improve. They've got to pass certain laws that we all know about. But we must succeed, and we cannot fail, and I will be the last man standing if necessary.
>
> My friends, this is a transcendent struggle between good and evil. Everything we stand for and believe in is at stake here. We can win. We will never surrender. They will. I am prepared to lead. My life and my experience and my background and my heroes inspire me and qualify me to lead in this titanic struggle, which will not be over soon. But we will prevail.
>
> *Brownback:* I think we win the war by standing up for our values . . . We've got to be very confrontational and very aggressive there . . . You've got to confront. You've got to confront those that are coming after us. And they've been doing this for over a decade—coming at us—from before 9/11. We cannot be weak on this whatsoever.

But it is Giuliani who seems most sacred about terrorism. Michael Powell in the *New York Times* describes his rhetoric as "taut three-step progressions that end with a pleasing verbal whap." One of Powell's examples took place when Giuliani was challenged by a middle-aged woman during a meeting at Oglethorpe University, about whether jihad really had a peaceful meaning: "They hate you. They don't want you to be in this college . . . This is reality, ma'am. You've got to clear your head." And at another talk: "Right now, as we sit here enjoying breakfast, they are planning on coming here to kill us. I don't blame people for not getting it before 9/11. But I do blame people who don't get it now."⁶ During the debates he is clear that the Iraq War and a campaign against Islamism are not things he sees as negotiable:

> I was talking about the timetable for retreat that the Democrats passed in Congress, in which they did something extraordinary and that I've never heard of in the history of war, which is to give your enemy a schedule of how a retreating army is going to retreat. That was irresponsible, highly irresponsible . . .
>
> I think Senator McCain is correct, these people do want to follow us here and they have followed us here. Fort Dix happened a week ago. That was a situation in which six Islamic terrorists, who were not directed by Al Qaeda but claimed to have been inspired by them, were going to kill our military in cold blood at Fort Dix. It was a sixteen-month investigation done by the FBI and the United States Attorney's Office, and thank God they caught them. But we have to remind ourselves that we are facing an enemy that is planning all over this world, and it turns out planning inside our country, to come here and kill us. And the worst thing to do in the face of that is to show them weakness.

Giuliani's language underscores the important distinction between religious and secular sacredness. His rhetoric regarding Islamism may be the most sacred, but his political stances are the most secular among the leading Republicans, opposing the Christian right on abortion and stem-cell research. One of the memorable moments of the debates occurred when lightning crackled repeatedly through the speakers when Giuliani responded to a question about criticism of him by a Catholic bishop. McCain, who was standing beside him, backed away from his podium, and Giuliani said, "I guess I'm here by myself. Look, for someone who went to parochial schools all his life, this is a very frightening thing that's happening right now." The audience laughed, but it underscored a serious point about Giuliani's irreligious resolve, or sacredness without religion.

But the Republican sacred rhetoric goes far beyond the Islamist movement and the Iraq War. On Iran gaining nuclear capacity:

> *McCain:* At the end of the day we cannot allow Iran to acquire nuclear weapons.
>
> *Giuliani:* [President Mahmoud] Ahmadinejad is clearly irrational. He has to understand it's not an option; he cannot have nuclear weapons. And he has to look at an American president and he has to see Ronald Reagan. Remember, they looked in Ronald Reagan's eyes, and in two minutes, they released the hostages.

On immigration:

> *Tancredo:* We're talking about something that goes to the very heart of this nation: whether or not we will actually survive as a nation. And here's what I mean by that. What we're doing here in this immigration battle is testing our willingness to actually hold together as a nation or split apart into a lot of balkanized pieces. We are testing our willingness to actually hold on to something called the English language, something that is the glue that is supposed to hold us together as a nation. We are becoming a bilingual nation. And that is not good. And that is the fearful part of this. The ramifications are much, much more significant than any that we've been discussing so far. And so, yes, I have said dramatic things. And, yes, I am willing to do whatever is necessary to try to stop this piece of legislation.

On abortion, when the candidates were asked, "Would the day that *Roe v. Wade* is repealed be a good day for America?":

> *Romney:* Absolutely.
> *Brownback:* It would be a glorious day of human liberty and freedom.
> *Huckabee:* Most certainly.
> *Tancredo:* After forty million dead because we have aborted them in this country, I would say that that would be the greatest day in this country's history when that, in fact, is overturned.

One of the striking things about the use of sacred rhetoric by the Republican candidates is the diversity of domains to which it applies. While each candidate stakes out slightly different issue space to distinguish their candidacy, the same form of rhetoric is applied to many domains. A clear illustration of this came when the candidates were asked about the "most pressing moral issue facing this country today." For Huckabee it was life, for Giuliani, the struggle with Islamism, and for Paul it was preemptive warfare. With each respondent the focus shifted (and even contradicted previous speakers), but the sacred rhetoric remained constant:

> *Huckabee:* I really believe that, if you define it as a moral issue, it is our respect, our sanctity, and our understanding of the value of every single human life. Because that is what makes America a unique place on this planet: we value every life of an individual as if it represents the life of us all ... It should never be acceptable to us that people are treated as expendable—any people. But the unique part of our country is that we

elevate and we celebrate human life. And if you look at us with a contrast to the Islamic jihadists, who would strap a bomb to the belly of their own child, march him into a crowded room, set the detonator, and kill innocent people, they celebrate death; we celebrate life. It's the fundamental thing that makes us unique, and it keeps us free. I pray we never, ever abandon that basic principle.

Giuliani: I think the governor is correct. I would put it in maybe a slightly different way. We have great gifts in this country that come to us from God. We have a country in which we have freedom of religion, freedom of press, freedom for the individual, the right to elect our own officials. And the reality is that in some of the world, much of the world, that doesn't exist. And I think the challenge for our generation is going to be, are we able to share those gifts in an appropriate way with the rest of the world? If we can bring along the Middle East, if we can bring along those countries that are presently our enemies, and get them to see the values of these ideals, if we have the moral strength to be able to explain it to them in the way Ronald Reagan was able to do with communism, then we can end up having the peace that we want . . . We have great resources in this country. And watching the strength of America when we believe in the essential ideals that we have—they're not just American ideals; they come from God. And I think it's our moral obligation to find the right way to share that with the rest of the world.

Paul: I think it is the acceptance just recently that we now promote preemptive war. I do not believe that's part of the American tradition. We, in the past, have always declared war in defense of our liberties or to go aid somebody. But now we have accepted the principle of preemptive war. We have rejected the just war theory of Christianity. And now, tonight, we hear that we're not even willing to remove from the table a preemptive nuclear strike against a country that has done no harm to us directly and is no threat to our national security. I mean, we have to come to our senses about this issue of war and preemption and go back to traditions and our Constitution and defend our liberties and defend our rights, but not to think that we can change the world by force of arms and to start wars.

The 2008 Republicans far surpassed the Democratic candidates in sacred rhetoric. But how did the 2008 Democrats compare to each other? The following sections analyze Democratic rhetoric by political domain, facets of sacredness, and candidate.

Political Domains

Of the political domains that lend themselves to sacred rhetoric, some were employed by the 2008 Democratic contenders but most were neglected. The environment and civil liberties attracted little sacred language, while the war in Iraq emerged as the leading example, though only by the fringe candidates. Equal opportunity and fairness, particularly in regard to health care and education, claimed some attention, but only in a limited fashion.

While Gore in 2000 emphasized the environment as a sacred treasure, boundaries toward natural resources did not emerge as a significant discussion in the 2008 debates. Interestingly, one of the Republican candidates was the leading proponent of a sacred approach to nature, reflecting the growth of evangelical environmentalism. In the first GOP debate, Huckabee argued, "I believe that even our responsibility to God means that we have to be good stewards of this earth, be good caretakers of the natural resources that don't belong to us, we just get to use them. We have no right to abuse them." This is a reference to the Noadic Covenant to husband the earth, which many Christians interpret as a boundary to despoiling nature. As a political authority this is both old and new. The two founding constituencies of early conservationism were outdoorsmen and churchgoers—the first wanted to preserve animals so they could hunt them, and the second wanted to respect God's treasures. Many of each group were Republicans, famously including Teddy Roosevelt and Gifford Pinchot, founder of the national park system. The conservation movement of the Progressive Era was later eclipsed by the ecology approach of Earth Day, making the hunting and religious foundations of environmentalism sound odd to many contemporary Americans.[7] But even today one of the prime protectors of wetlands is the environmental group Ducks Unlimited—in other words, duck hunters. And Evangelicals, who sit firmly on the right on most issues, are increasingly concerned with environmental protection. The old religious approach to the environment is new again, encapsulated in the ad campaign begun in 2002, "What Would Jesus Drive?" But among the Democratic candidates, sacred language regarding the environment appeared only twice: the first was by Bill Richardson and the second was perhaps Edwards' most notable line of the debates:

> *Richardson*: I would plan a huge initiative on making America energy independent, with an Apollo-like program to become more reliant on renewable fuels. I'd ask the American people to sacrifice in so doing.

Edwards: We ought to ask Americans to be patriotic about something other than war. To be willing to conserve.

Another potentially sacred domain that is mentioned but not emphasized is civil liberties. This area could be discussed in terms of inviolable boundaries, the authority of the Constitution, and protected values of liberty or tolerance. The civil liberties domain taps into the consensus sacred value of constitutionalism, perhaps one of the strongest consensus values in American culture. This can serve as a master frame or overarching principle to bring discussions of civil liberties, limited war powers, reproductive rights, and rights to health or education under one umbrella value. The public discussion of torture is an area that is especially suited to the invocation of boundaries, although Republican rhetoric in this domain is unusually consequentialist. The GOP candidates argued most often that extreme interrogation is allowable because of the importance of the outcome, eliding concerns about justice, fairness, or other values in play. Even Republicans on the opposing side who advocate banning the torture of captives, such as John McCain, employ equally consequentialist rather than sacred grounds—if we do not ban the practice, our enemies will be more likely to torture American captives.

When John Kerry discussed the Patriot Act in the 2004 debates, this was one of his most sacred exchanges:

> People's rights have been abused. I met a man who spent eight months in prison, wasn't even allowed to call his lawyer, wasn't allowed to get—finally, Senator Dick Durbin of Illinois intervened and was able to get him out. This is in our country, folks, the United States of America. They've got sneak-and-peek searches that are allowed. They've got people allowed to go into churches now and political meetings without any showing of potential criminal activity or otherwise . . . We need to be stronger on terrorism. But you know what we also need to do as Americans is never let the terrorists change the Constitution of the United States in a way that disadvantages our rights.

In 2008 Kucinich and Edwards were the only candidates who took similar positions:

> *Kucinich:* The Patriot Act has undermined civil rights in this country. And as President of the United States, one of my first acts in office will be to move forward to have the Justice Department overturn the Patriot Act as unconstitutional.

Edwards: Guantanamo, Abu Ghraib, spying on Americans, torture. None of those things are okay. They are not the United States of America.

Another domain that lends itself to sacred rhetoric but was not fully developed in the 2008 primary campaign is government truthfulness. Charges of lying by the Bush administration were hinted at more than addressed as a bound that should not be crossed in democratic politics. Even the popular phrase "[Bush, Cheney, etc.] lied and people died" is oddly consequentialist, as if it would have been acceptable if the lying simply had not had the wrong outcome. While it is accurate that deaths and hence the implied sacred value of lives are invoked, the value consideration arrives only at the end, rather than being put up front as an inviolable regardless of the outcome. To be offended by the argument of the slogan, the listener has to believe two things—the lying occurred and it led to deaths—but in the sacred formulation the offense only requires convincing the hearer of one thing, the simple act of lying itself.

Kerry addressed the charge of government deceit to a degree in the 2004 debates, but he argued that lying is counterproductive, not that it is wrong and unacceptable: "So what I am trying to do is just talk the truth to the American people and to the world. The truth is what good policy is based on. It's what leadership is based on." One of the questions from Jim Lehrer was, "Senator Kerry . . . you've repeatedly accused President Bush—not here tonight, but elsewhere before—of not telling the truth about Iraq, essentially of lying to the American people about Iraq. Give us some examples of what you consider to be his not telling the truth." Kerry downplays the accusation of lying, soft-peddling the charge rather than accusing Bush of violating a sacred boundary: "Well, I've never, ever used the harshest word, as you did just then. And I try not to." It is an instructive failure that in this exchange, Bush employed more sacred language than Kerry did, by quoting Kerry's previous statements in favor of the invasion of Iraq and shifting the discussion toward the importance of nonnegotiability and taking clear positions.

In the 2008 debates, the lying charge was addressed twice each by Biden, Edwards, and Kucinich, and once by Gravel, but not in a sacred fashion in any of these mentions.

Biden: We've not been told the truth about this war from the beginning by this president. And the fact is, we got to tell the truth now.

Edwards: I think one of the things we desperately need in our next president is someone who can restore the trust bond between the American people and the president of the United States. Because I think that trust has been devastated over the last six years. And I think, beyond that, it's important for the president of the United States to restore trust between the president and the rest of the world. It is impossible for the United States of America to provide the stabilization and the leadership in the world that the world desperately needs from us unless, first, the American people trust their president, believe he's an open, honest, decent human being, and the rest of the world has faith in the president of the United States.

Kucinich: This war has been based on lies.

Perhaps the strongest use of sacred language in the Democratic debates was on ending the Iraq War and invoking boundaries against war in general. When asked whether a candidate who voted to authorize the war should become president, Gravel responds, "Not at all, because it's a moral criteria . . . That disqualifies them for president. It doesn't mean they're bad people. It just means that they don't have moral judgment." It is important to note that all of these examples come from fringe candidates, some of whom take positions on military force far to the left of mainstream Democrats:

> *Kucinich*: Just say no money. The war is over. You want to end it? Bring them home. Stop the funding.
>
> I opposed the war from the start, but I opposed the idea of using war as a matter of policy. I don't think it reflects America's greatness.
>
> Dr. King recognized that when there's a war, people of two countries suffer, because what he was talking about was the link between war and fear and poverty, as opposed to peace and security and prosperity.
>
> I want to see the end of war as an instrument of policy.
>
> *Richardson*: No. Let me be very clear about my position. This war is a disaster. We must end this war.
>
> *Gravel*: I got to tell you, we should just plain get out—just plain get out.
>
> I'm president of the United States, there will be no preemptive wars with nuclear devices. To my mind, it's immoral, and it's been immoral for the last fifty years as part of American foreign policy.

Facets of Sacredness

Because there are several different facets of sacred rhetoric, it may be instructive to examine the elements employed and neglected by the 2008 candidates. Table 8.3 displays the breakdown by each Democratic candidate. Moral outrage is the most commonly employed aspect of sacredness, focused most often on the Iraq War, civil liberties violations, health care, and the genocide in Darfur. When the protected status of a value was invoked, it was across a range of domains, but most often civil liberties, fairness, and equal opportunity. Republicans, in contrast, focused on the single protected value of liberty. When boundaries were cited or nonnegotiability invoked by Democrats, half the time it was in regard to the war in Iraq, with the other leading domain being violations of civil liberties. Nonconsequentialism and noninstrumentalism were even more rarely invoked, the candidates instead focusing on policy consequences and voters' self-interest.

The final facet of sacredness is the citation of authority, where Democrats displayed a noteworthy distinction from the Republican candidates. Of the nine authorities cited for their positions, only one was repeated and the other eight showed no clear pattern (table 8.4). The Constitution was invoked twice (both times by Kucinich), and the other authorities often represent party figures such as John F. Kennedy and Franklin D. Roosevelt, but also included more surprising references such as Ben Franklin and Barry Goldwater. Republicans, however, focused their sixty-one invocations of authority (often several in the same response, totaling six times as many as the Democrats) on three objects: Reagan, God, and the Constitution, in that order. These account for three quarters of all authorities cited. Whereas the Democratic use of authorities was scant and haphazard, the Republican employment was frequent and focused, clearly representing the party worldview.

While Republicans invoked the Constitution four times as often as their competitors, the sacred document was still the leading authority for Democrats. Kucinich centers one of his strongest statements around the role of the Constitution, invoking boundaries and his outrage at their violation by the vice president:

> This is a pocket copy of the Constitution, which I carry with me, because I took an oath to defend the Constitution. We've spent a lot of time talking about Iraq here tonight and America's role in the world. This country was taken into war based on lies. This country was taken into war

TABLE 8.3
Facets of Sacred Rhetoric Employed by Democrats in 2008

Facet	Clinton	Edwards	Obama	B	D	G	K	R	Total	%	Object
Protected Status		3	2		1		5	2	13	19%	Civil Liberties (3)
Nonconsequentialism			1				1	2	4	6%	Health Care (2)
Noninstrumentalism	1	1		2				1	5	7%	Environment (2)
Nonnegotiability	1	1		1		3	3	1	10	14%	Iraq War (5)
Citation of boundaries		1		2		3	6		12	17%	War in General (6)
Citation of authority	1	1	1			2	5		10	14%	Constitution (2)
Moral outrage	1	3		2	1	3	2	2	14	22%	Iraq War (3)
TOTAL	4	10	4	7	2	11	22	8	68		

Figures represent the numbers of times candidates employed each facet of sacred rhetoric.

The "Object" column lists the single most frequent object of the rhetoric, with the number of times discussed in parentheses.

B = Joe Biden, D = Chris Dodd, M = Mike Gravel, K = Dennis Kucinich, and R = Bill Richardson.

TABLE 8.4
Authorities Cited in the 2008 Presidential Primary Debates

Authority	Democrats			Republicans	
	Candidate	#	%	#	%
Reagan*				25	41%
Constitution	Kucinich	2	20%	9	15%
God/Bible	Edwards	1	10%	12	20%
Ben Franklin	Kucinich	1	10%	2	3%
JFK	Kucinich	1	10%	2	3%
FDR	Gravel	1	10%		
Goldwater	Clinton	1	10%		
MLK	Kucinich	1	10%		
Thurgood Marshall	Obama	1	10%		
Truman	Gravel	1	10%		
Eisenhower				2	3%
Nixon				2	3%
LBJ				1	2%
Lincoln				1	2%
Martin Luther				1	2%
Teddy Roosevelt				1	2%
Separation of Church and State				1	2%
Sen. Robert Taft				1	2%
Woodrow Wilson				1	2%
TOTAL		10		61	

* Of the 25 citations of Reagan, 14 took place in the first debate, which was held in the Reagan library and attended by Nancy Reagan. For this reason, citations to Reagan are somewhat inflated.

based on lies about weapons of mass destruction and Al Qaeda's role with respect to Iraq, which there wasn't one at the time we went in. I want to state that Mr. Cheney must be held accountable. He is already ginning up a cause for war against Iran. Now, we have to stand for this Constitution. We have to protect and defend this Constitution. And this vice president violated this Constitution.

The Constitution can serve as an overarching authority for several of the domains the Democratic candidates emphasized—civil liberties, limited war powers, and health or education as fundamental rights. An interesting note on the memorable nature of sacred rhetoric is that another of Kucinich's citations is to President Kennedy, from what is perhaps his best-known example of sacred rhetoric: "I would take the approach that John F. Kennedy took when he said, 'Ask not what your country can do for you. Ask what you can do for your country,' and inspire young people to want to serve." It is sacred language that is often remembered and quoted.

Candidates

The sacred rhetoric that did occur in the 2008 Democratic debates was clearly more fringe than front-runner. Kucinich is the only candidate who was in the Republicans' league, employing on average eight facets of sacred rhetoric per debate. He was followed by Biden, Edwards, Gravel, and Richardson, each employing a few examples, and then Clinton, Obama, and Dodd as the least sacred. Kucinich frequently invoked boundaries of appropriate standards, including bounds to employing military force or violating civil liberties. He emphasized the protected status of fairness as applied to education, health care, and taxes. And he was the Democratic leader in citing authorities, including the Constitution, President Kennedy, and Martin Luther King Jr. Gravel was the next most sacred Democratic candidate, centering on expressions of moral outrage, boundaries, and nonnegotiability regarding the war and its moral dimensions, even attacking the other candidates for their lack of concern: "We have to have a president who has moral judgment. Most of the people on this stage with me do not have that judgment, and have proven it by the simple fact of what they've done." Biden employed sacred rhetoric almost exclusively about the genocide in Darfur, an issue on which the rest of the field was slow to commit to a clear answer about their boundaries.

You know, we have to stop talking about it. A lot of talk goes on about it. The United Nations has already said they're prepared to put in a twenty-one thousand force, including the African Union. In fact, you have in the capital of Sudan the government saying, "We're not going to allow that to happen." They have forfeited their sovereignty by engaging in genocide. We should impose a no-fly zone if the UN will not move now . . . You could take out the Janjaweed tomorrow. I went there. I sat in the borders. I went in those camps. They're going to have thousands and thousands and thousands of people die. We've got to stop talking and act.

I have been calling for three years to stop talking and start acting. We don't have to wait to get out of Iraq to regain our moral authority. We've lost part of our moral authority because we stood by and watched this carnage.

What is perhaps more interesting, however, is the lack of sacred expressions by the leading candidates. For Clinton the use of sacred language was negligible, with only four instances, including a reference to nonnegotiability regarding the war and a reference to noninstrumentality regarding taxes on the wealthy. When discussing gays in the military she cited an authority, but this was an unusual reference to Barry Goldwater: "And I just want to end by saying Barry Goldwater once said you don't have to be straight to shoot straight. And I think he was right." What was likely her most effective example, prompting cheers and applause, was the invocation of moral outrage when addressing the high rates of HIV among African Americans: "You know, it is hard to disagree with anything that has been said, but let me just put this in perspective. If HIV/AIDS were the leading cause of death of white women between the ages of twenty-five and thirty-four, there would be an outraged outcry in this country."

Obama's use of sacred appeals was equally low. His four instances included citing Thurgood Marshall as an authority in regard to racial justice and invoking both nonconsequentialism and protected status regarding veterans' care. In the second debate he argued that members of the Bush administration "have been trying to keep the costs down of this war and have not fully factored in the sacred obligation that I think we have to make sure that every single veteran has the services that they need." In the final debate he invoked the protected status of fairness: "But I think this goes to a broader question, and that is, are we willing to make the investments in genuine equal opportunity in this country? People aren't looking for charity, and one of the distressing things sometimes when we have a conversation about race in America is that we talk about welfare and we talk about poverty, but what people really want is fairness."

Among the leading candidates, only Edwards stood out as employing any meaningful degree of sacred rhetoric, though still not in the same range as the Republican candidates. He seemed somewhat aware of his own distinction, in the second debate criticizing Clinton and Obama for not taking clear positions against funding the war. When discussing leadership regarding Iraq, he accused Obama and Clinton of acting like politicians rather than leaders, following winds rather than making stands: "There is a difference between making clear, speaking to your followers, speaking to the American people about what you believe needs to be done. And I think that all of us have a responsibility to lead on these issues, not just on Iraq, but on health care, on energy, on all the other issues."

Edwards' campaign focused on a more populist approach to social inequality, best encapsulated in his "two Americas" theme. Perhaps for this reason he was more prone than his leading competitors to invoke moral outrage and the protected status of the value of fairness: "These two Americas that I've talked about in the past—man, they are out there thriving every single day. We have two public school systems in America—one for the wealthy, one for everybody else." But perhaps his most notable phrase from the debates was his previously quoted remark about the environment: "We ought to ask Americans to be patriotic about something other than war. To be willing to conserve." The same line (without the reference to conservation) also appeared as the closing statement of one of Edwards' early campaign ads. Two other television spots carried similar rhetoric invoking nonnegotiability and setting boundaries: "President Bush isn't listening to Iowans . . . We, the people, want Congress to stand firm. Don't back down. Send him the same bill that you sent him before. Iowans support our troops, and we have a responsibility to bring them home. Because stopping a president who believes he can do no wrong takes people with the courage to do what's right"; "We're gonna build an America where we say no to kids going to bed hungry, no to kids not having the clothes to keep them warm. And no forever."

That Democrats are capable of employing sacred rhetoric was illustrated more clearly in the third debate, which differed substantially from the first two. This debate took place at Howard University in front of a mostly African American audience. It was also broadcast on PBS rather than the normal commercial channels, at a later time slot (9:00 p.m. rather than 7:00 p.m.), and was expected to draw a smaller audience. It was the shortest of the debates (only three-quarters of the average of debates 1 and 2), but it contained just as many uses of sacred rhetoric.[8] All of the references to fairness and equal opportunity as a protected value took place in this debate. When combining all three debates, equal access to health care and education appears to be the largest single domain in which Democrats employ sacred rhetoric, but of the twelve times that elements of sacred rhetoric are employed in this domain, eleven are in the third debate.[9] The inclusion of this unusual debate in the analysis both inflates the appearance of a Democratic emphasis on equal opportunity and demonstrates that such language is possible even if not usually employed.

Two of the most noteworthy statements by the leading candidates quoted earlier—Clinton's reference to moral outrage at the HIV epidemic among young African Americans, and Obama's invocation of the protected status of fairness—took place in this debate. Other examples of sacred rhetoric in regard to equal opportunity came from Biden, Dodd, Kucinich, Richardson, and Edwards:

> *Biden*: Warren Buffett is right. I would eliminate the tax cut for the wealthy. They didn't ask for it, as someone earlier said. They don't need it. They're as patriotic as anyone else if you ask them, and we've asked nothing of them.
>
> *Dodd*: There's nothing that will be a higher priority to me as president of the United States than to see to it that America's children, from the earliest days of their arrival, certainly through the upper education branches of our educational system, have the equal opportunity. None of us here can guarantee success, but we have an obligation to guarantee an opportunity to that success. The key to that door is the education of the American child.
>
> *Kucinich*: We need to have a policy in education which first of all is guided by certain fundamental right. Jesse Jackson Jr. has a bill that makes having an equal opportunity for education a matter of a constitutional privilege. And with this Supreme Court ruling [referring to the recent decision in *Community Schools v. Seattle*, which ruled against race-based criteria in assigning children to public schools], it is imperative that we have a constitutional amendment guaranteeing educational opportunity equality.
>
> But there's another dimension here, too, and that is we have a nation of such wealth, yet we have forty-six million Americans without any health insurance, another fifty million underinsured. It's time for us to make

every American know that they should have access. It is a basic right in a Democratic society.

Richardson: You know, sometimes when I talk about education, and this is the first time we have talked about it in any debate, the first thing you hear is, how are you going to pay for it? Nobody asks how we're going to pay for the war. *(Applause)* But it's important to state that improving our schools, improving education, access to education to all Americans, should be America's foremost priority.

Edwards: I also want to thank you for hosting this debate where finally we can talk about inequality in America, which is at the heart and soul of why I'm running for president of the United States. The truth is that slavery followed by segregation followed by discrimination has had an impact that still is alive and well in America, and it goes through every single part of American life. We still have two public school systems in America.

What we want to do, I think, is live in an America where, no matter who your family is or what the color of your skin or where you're born, everybody gets the same chance to do well. And people who have done well ought to have more responsibility to pay back to the country and to the community and those around them . . . That's not right. There is a moral disconnect. We ought to honor work in this country, not just wealth.

One way to interpret this collective evidence is that the Democratic candidates *could* employ more sacred rhetoric, as demonstrated by some examples, *but generally do not*, especially among the leading candidates.

THE 2008 PRESIDENTIAL CAMPAIGN

The historically open primary campaign of 2008—with no party favorite on either side, eight or more candidates on the debate stage, and a likely pathbreaking result on the Democratic ticket regarding either gender or race—resulted in a Republican who was perhaps the most secular and least favored by the party establishment in recent times, against the most openly religious Democratic candidate since Jimmy Carter. McCain's primary campaign had been declared dead by many commentators going into fall 2007, and Obama won a close victory for the nomination against a strong candidate who was more heavily favored by the party leadership in the early days of the campaign. So what role did sacred rhetoric play in the contest between these two unusual products of a remarkable primary season?

By most scholarly expectations in summer 2008, the Democratic Party should have won the fall election, and won easily. Every established predictor of presidential contests favored a Democratic victory. The incumbent party had been in power for eight years and was led by a historically unpopular president. A long and divisive war was supported by the Republican Party. The economic crisis emerging in the late summer and early fall further cemented Democratic prospects. But what of the rhetorical factors? Would the Republican assert an absolutist advantage that could counterbalance some of the strengths of the Democrat, or would the unusually secular and antiestablishment Republican fail to capitalize on his possible assets against the unusually religious Democrat known for his skills as an orator?

One of the first tests came in an unofficial debate known as the Saddleback Forum, hosted by Pastor Rick Warren on August 16, 2008, even before the Republican convention. The Saddleback Forum was an unusual event, somewhat like the presidential debates to come, but hosted by a prominent megachurch and its well-known pastor.[10] Rather than a traditional debate forum, the format was more akin to two solo interviews with identical questions, one devoted to the senator from Illinois and another to the senator from Arizona. A few examples of their competing answers illustrate McCain's potential (important passages are higlighted in italics):

> *Warren:* Does evil exist? And if it does, do we ignore it? Do we negotiate with it? Do we contain it? Do we defeat it?
> *McCain: Defeat it.* A couple of points. One, if I'm president of the United States, my friends, *if I have to follow him to the gates of Hell,* I will get bin Laden and bring him to justice. I will do that. And I know how to do that. I will get that done. *(Applause)* No one, no one should be allowed to take thousands of American—innocent American lives. Of course, *evil must be defeated.* My friends, we are facing the transcendent challenge of the twenty-first century—radical Islamic extremism. Not long ago in Baghdad, Al Qaeda took two young women who were mentally disabled, and put suicide vests on them, sent them into a marketplace, and by remote control, detonated those suicide vests. If that isn't evil, you have to tell me what is. And *we're going to defeat this evil.* And the central battleground according to David Petraeus and Osama bin Laden is the battle, is Baghdad, Mosul, Basra, and Iraq, and we are winning and succeeding and our troops will come home with honor and with victory and not in defeat. And that's what's happening. And we have—and we faced this threat throughout the world. It's not just in Iraq. It's not just in Afghanistan. Our intelligence people tell us Al Qaeda continues to try to establish cells here in the United States of America. My friends,

we must face this challenge. We can face this challenge. And we must totally defeat it, and we're in a long struggle. But when I'm around the young men and women who are serving this nation in uniform, I have no doubt, none.

Obama: *Evil does exist.* I mean, I think we see evil all the time. We see evil in Darfur. We see evil, sadly, on the streets of our cities. We see evil in parents who viciously abuse their children. I think *it has to be confronted. It has to be confronted squarely,* and one of the things that I strongly believe is that, now, we are not going to, as individuals, be able to erase evil from the world. That is God's task, but we can be soldiers in that process, and *we can confront it when we see it.* Now, the one thing that I think is very important is for to us have some humility in how we approach the issue of confronting evil, because a lot of evil's been perpetrated based on the claim that we were trying to confront evil.

Warren: At what point is a baby entitled to human rights?

McCain: *At the moment of conception.* I have a twenty-five-year pro-life record in the Congress, in the Senate. And as president of the United States, I will be a pro-life president. And this presidency will have pro-life policies. *That's my commitment.* That's my commitment to you.

Obama: Well, you know, I think that whether you're looking at it from a theological perspective or a scientific perspective, *answering that question with specificity, you know, is above my pay grade.* But let me just speak more generally about the issue of abortion, because this is something obviously the country wrestles with. One thing that *I'm absolutely convinced of is that there is a moral and ethical element to this issue.* And so I think anybody who tries to deny the moral difficulties and gravity of the abortion issue, I think, is not paying attention. So that would be point number one. But point number two, I am pro-choice. I believe in *Roe v. Wade,* and I come to that conclusion not because I'm pro-abortion, but because, ultimately, I don't think women make these decisions casually. I think they, they wrestle with these things in profound ways, in consultation with their pastors or their spouses or their doctors or their family members. And so, for me, the goal right now should be—and this is where I think we can find common ground, and by the way, I've now inserted this into the Democratic Party platform—is how do we reduce the number of abortions? The fact is that although we have had a president who is opposed to abortion over the last eight years, abortions have not gone down and that is something we have to address.

Warren: Define marriage.

McCain: A union, a union between man and woman, between one man and one woman. That's my definition of marriage.

> *Obama*: I believe that marriage is the union between a man and a woman. Now, for me as a Christian—for me—for me as a Christian, *it is also a sacred union*. God's in the mix.

In each case, McCain's answer was simple and concise, often emphasizing protected values, boundaries, and nonnegotiability. But Obama also invoked clear boundaries and standards. Unlike Gore or Kerry, he was comfortable discussing values as well as policy proposals. When questioned about evil in the world, he was clear that "it has to be confronted. It has to be confronted squarely." He was also clear about not supporting gay marriage. He described marriage as a "sacred union" and abortion as a moral question. The one rhetorical error was in his response to the question on abortion. The statement that such knowledge was "above my pay grade" drew extensive commentary in mainstream media as well as from conservative pundits.[11] The response evoked uncertainty and evasiveness rather than clear boundaries. In a subsequent interview on ABC's *This Week*, Obama tried to correct the comment: "What I intended to say is that, as a Christian, I have a lot of humility about understanding when does the soul enter into—it's a pretty tough question. And so, all I meant to communicate was that I don't presume to be able to answer these kinds of theological questions." Obama's correction indicated that he was aware of how such uncommitted statements could be perceived. Unlike his predecessors, it would be one of Obama's few antisacred gaffes.

McCain: Sacred by Half

When John McCain addressed foreign policy he was the most sacred speaker among contemporary presidential candidates. As a firm supporter of both the Iraq invasion in 2003 and the troop surge in 2007, McCain spoke of the need for nonnegotiable positions, noninstrumental sacrifice, and absolute victory rather than negotiated withdrawal:

> And I want to tell you that now that we will succeed and our troops will come home, and not in defeat, that we will see a stable ally in the region and a fledgling democracy . . . And we are winning in Iraq, and we will come home. And we will come home as we have when we have won other wars and not in defeat.
>
> Two Fourths of July ago I was in Baghdad. General Petraeus invited Senator Lindsey Graham and me to attend a ceremony where 688 brave young Americans, whose enlistment had expired, were reenlisting to stay and

fight for Iraqi freedom and American freedom. I was honored to be there. I was honored to speak to those troops. And you know, afterwards, we spent a lot of time with them. And you know what they said to us? They said, let us win. They said, let us win. We don't want our kids coming back here. And this strategy, and this general, they are winning. Senator Obama refuses to acknowledge that we are winning in Iraq.

And I'll tell you, I had a town hall meeting in Wolfeboro, New Hampshire, and a woman stood up and she said, "Senator McCain, I want you to do me the honor of wearing a bracelet with my son's name on it." He was twenty-two years old and he was killed in combat outside of Baghdad, Matthew Stanley, before Christmas last year. This was August, a year ago. And I said, "I will. I will wear his bracelet with honor."

McCain spoke clearly on the war in Iraq, but he also applied sacred language to other aspects of foreign policy. On Iran acquiring nuclear weapons:

My reading of the threat from Iran is that if Iran acquires nuclear weapons, it is an existential threat to the State of Israel and to other countries in the region because the other countries in the region will feel compelling requirement to acquire nuclear weapons as well. Now we cannot have a second Holocaust. Let's just make that very clear.

On talks with the Iranian government:

The point is that throughout history, whether it be Ronald Reagan, who wouldn't sit down with Brezhnev, Andropov, or Chernenko until Gorbachev was ready with glasnost and perestroika. Or whether it be Nixon's trip to China, which was preceded by Henry Kissinger, many times before he went. Look, I'll sit down with anybody, but there's got to be preconditions.

And we ought to go back to a little bit of Ronald Reagan's "trust, but verify," and certainly not sit down across the table from, without precondition, as Senator Obama said he did twice, I mean, it's just dangerous.

And on Russian aggression in Georgia:

Well, I was interested in Senator Obama's reaction to the Russian aggression against Georgia. His first statement was, "Both sides ought to show restraint." Again, a little bit of naïveté there. He doesn't understand that Russia committed serious aggression against Georgia. And Russia has now become a nation fueled by petrodollars that is basically a KGB apparatchik-run government. I looked into Mr. Putin's eyes, and I saw three letters, a K, a G, and a B. And their aggression in Georgia is not acceptable behavior.

But have no doubt that Russia's behavior is certainly outside of the norms of behavior that we would expect for nations which are very wealthy, as Russia has become because of their petrodollars.

We've got to show moral support for Georgia. We've got to show moral support for Ukraine. We've got to advocate for their membership in NATO. We have to make the Russians understand that there are penalties for this kind of behavior . . . The Russians must understand that these kinds of actions and activities are not acceptable.

If we were to examine only the first debate, the comparison between McCain and Obama would appear to be similar to the contests in 2000 and 2004, with a substantial dominance of sacred language by the Republican. But this distinction evaporated when the debates moved away from the foreign policy focus of the first exchange. While the opening debate centered on foreign affairs, the second was a town hall format in which only a third of the questions were on national security, and the final debate concentrated solely on domestic policy. Table 8.5 details the rhetorical analysis of each debate, and also breaks down the results by domestic and foreign affairs. When speaking of national security and foreign relations, McCain employed on average 2.3 elements of sacred rhetoric in each exchange, comparable to George W. Bush's level of absolutist language. He was substantially higher than Obama's average of 0.6, creating a differential even slightly larger than Bush's advantage over Gore or Kerry. However, in the discussion of domestic affairs that dominated the debates (twenty questions compared to nine on foreign policy), McCain did not employ a substantial degree of sacred appeals, creating no distinction between his and Obama's language. The average use of sacred rhetoric in each response for the entire debates was 1.1 for McCain and 0.5 for Obama, but in domestic affairs it was 0.6 to 0.5, levels comparable to most contemporary Democrats.

In the final analysis, McCain was half sacred. In his signature realm he spoke of absolute requirements, hard boundaries for the behavior of adversaries, and nonnegotiable positions. But in terms of domestic policy, he had no such predilections. McCain had never been a true social conservative and did not share the same morally driven domestic policies of the previous administration. He was not defined by boundaries and authorities in

TABLE 8.5
Sacred Rhetoric in the 2008 Presidential Debates

Topic	McCain	Obama	Difference	Reversals
DEBATE 1 (Foreign Policy)*				
Financial Recovery Plan	1	0	1	
Differences over Financial Crisis	1	0	2	
Spending Programs Reduced Due to Bailout Costs	1	1	0	
Lessons of Iraq	2	0	2	
Troop Levels in Afghanistan	3	0	3	
Threat from Iran	3	1	2	
Relationship with Russia	2	2	0	
Likelihood of Future Terrorist Attacks	2	0	2	
AVERAGE	1.9	.5	1.4	
Domestic Affairs Average	1.0	.3	0.7	
Foreign Affairs Average	2.4	.6	1.8	
DEBATE 2 (Town Hall Format)				
Solution to Economic Crisis	0	1	-1	*
How Will the Bank Bailout Help Citizens	0	0	0	
Are Both Parties to Blame for the Financial Crisis	0	1	-1	*
What Sacrifices Will Be Asked of Americans	0	1	0	
Social Security and Medicare Reform	1	1	0	
Environment, Climate Change, and Green Jobs	0	0	0	
Should Health Care Be Treated as a Commodity	0	1	-1	*
Influence of Financial Crisis on National Security	3	1	2	
Pakistani Sovereignty in War on Terror	2	0	2	

* The first debate was scheduled to focus on foreign policy, but the financial collapse in the preceding weeks led the moderator to shift focus in the opening portion of the debate.

cont. on next page

TABLE 8.5 (CONT.)

Topic	McCain	Obama	Difference	Reversals
DEBATE 2 (Town Hall Format) (cont.)				
How to Influence Russians without New Cold War	2	0	2	
Will U.S. Defend Israel if Iran Attacks	2	1	1	
What Don't You Know and Where Will You Learn It	1	0	1	
AVERAGE	.9	.6	.3	
Domestic Affairs Average	.3	.6	-.3	
Foreign Affairs Average	2.3	.5	1.8	
DEBATE 3 (Domestic Policy)				
Financial Recovery Plans	2	0	2	
Deficit Spending	0	0	0	
Negative Campaigning	1	1	0	
Vice Presidential Selection	1	0	1	
Foreign Oil Imports	0	0	0	
Health Care	0	0	0	
Roe v. Wade	1	2	-1	*
Education in Math and Science	0	0	0	
Closing Statements	1	1	0	
AVERAGE	.7	.4	.3	
Domestic Affairs Average	.7	.4	.3	
Foreign Affairs Average	-	-	-	
TOTAL AVERAGE	1.1	.5	.6	
Domestic Affairs Average	.6	.5	.1	
Foreign Affairs Average	2.3	.6	1.7	

Foreign policy questions are displayed in italics.

the social realm, but only when national security was invoked. In regard to the financial crisis and the economy, which became a central focus of the debates, McCain was policy driven and did not distinguish himself rhetorically from Obama. McCain's sacred half was likely an asset, but it was perhaps the wrong half, focusing on an unpopular war in a campaign increasingly defined by a growing financial crisis.

Obama: Neither Sacred Nor Antisacred

While McCain's rhetoric was divided, Obama displayed a consistent tone across foreign and domestic affairs. In the debates of the primary campaign, he and Hillary Clinton had some of the lowest tallies among the Democratic candidates, behind Edwards and distinctly below Gravel and Kucinich. But Obama's rhetoric reflected greater absolutist sentiment as he moved into the general election. For example, on Russian aggression in Georgia:

> Their actions in Georgia were unacceptable. They were unwarranted. And at this point, it is absolutely critical for the next president to make clear that we have to follow through on our six-party—or the six-point cease-fire. They have to remove themselves from South Ossetia and Abkhazia. It is absolutely important that we have a unified alliance and that we explain to the Russians that you cannot be a twenty-first-century superpower, or power, and act like a twentieth-century dictatorship.

On Iran:

> Senator McCain is absolutely right. We cannot tolerate a nuclear Iran.

> We cannot allow Iran to get a nuclear weapon . . . And so it's unacceptable. And I will do everything that's required to prevent it.

On health care:

> One of the things I have said from the start of this campaign is that we have a moral commitment as well as an economic imperative to do something about the health care crisis that so many families are facing.

McCain often discusses service and noninstrumental sacrifice, but so does Obama:

> President Bush did some smart things at the outset, but one of the opportunities that was missed was when he spoke to the American people, he

said, "Go out and shop." That wasn't the kind of call to service that I think the American people were looking for . . . There is going to be the need for each and every one of us to start thinking about how we use energy . . . But each and every one of us can start thinking about how we can save energy in our homes, in our buildings . . . And that's going to require effort from each and every one of us. And the last point I want to make. I think the young people of America are especially interested in how they can serve, and that's one of the reasons why I'm interested in doubling the Peace Corps, making sure that we are creating a volunteer corps all across this country that can be involved in their community, involved in military service, so that military families and our troops are not the only ones bearing the burden of renewing America.

And that's why I think it is important for the president to set a tone that says all of us are going to contribute, all of us are going to make sacrifices.

It's not going to be easy. It's not going to be quick. It's going to be requiring all of us, Democrats, Republicans, independents, to come together and to renew a spirit of sacrifice and service and responsibility.

Obama's rhetoric is neither strenuously nor frequently sacred. He displays an even and moderate degree of absolutist rhetoric, comparable to the overall levels of Gore and Kerry. But he also avoids the antisacred errors of his predecessors. Perhaps even more memorable than sacred stances are antisacred gaffes. But Obama avoided the explicit violations of sacred boundaries committed by Dukakis and Kerry. He also avoided the mind-numbing devotion to numbers offered by Gore. In the end he is not meaningfully more sacred than they were, but he is importantly less antisacred.

Figure 8.1 compares the rhetoric of 2008 to the previous campaigns. In the aggregate, the closest comparison is Reagan's second term in 1984. McCain was not as sacred as Reagan in his first campaign of 1980, but equal to Reagan's second performance after the usual incumbent decline. Obama seems to be comparable to Reagan's second-term opponent, Walter Mondale, though slightly higher. However, this may be a deceptive comparison, as aggregate figures sometimes are. In terms of foreign policy discussion, the closest comparison is the 2000 debate. McCain was even slightly higher than Bush's average, while Obama was marginally higher than Gore, creating a distinct advantage for the Republican. In the domestic realm, however, the most comparable election is 1992, when George H. W. Bush lost to Bill Clinton. Like 1992, it is an even contest, with only a 0.1 differential

Figure 8.1
Sacred Rhetoric from 1976 to 2008

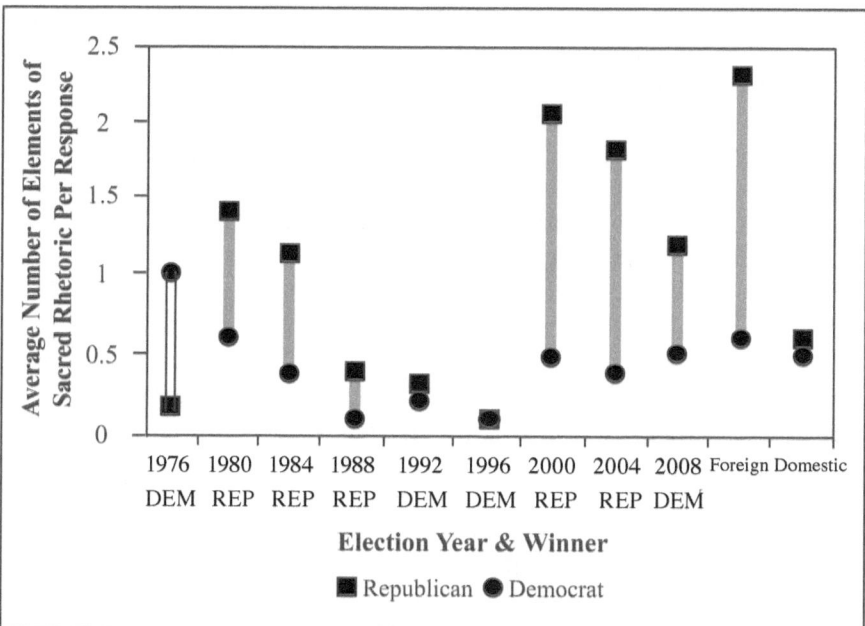

between the candidates. McCain's advantage in the foreign policy realm alone is borne out in the reported reactions to the first debate. CNN sponsored a random survey of citizens directly after the broadcast.[12] Of those who watched the debate, 51% believed that Obama had won, while only 38% saw McCain as the victor. This may not reflect an accurate reporting of citizen perceptions, as the sample comprised 41% Democrats to only 27% Republicans, a 14-percentage-point gap similar to the 13-percentage-point difference in perceived victory. But for our purposes the important figures are the differences in perception regarding the economy as opposed to the war. Respondents saw Obama as prevailing on economic matters by 21 percentage points (58% to 37%). But on the war, McCain was perceived as the victor in the debate by 4 percentage points (49% to 45%). Even while supporting an unpopular war, McCain had the advantage, but only in this realm in which he spoke in sacred terms.

Given that the 2008 election focused on domestic issues, especially the economy, this lessened the significance of McCain's advantage in foreign policy. In the domestic aspect of the rhetorical contest, it is a draw. And in the contemporary elections that reflected a draw, the Democrat has won. From 1976 to 2004 there were five contests in which the Republican had a clear absolutist advantage; in all five that candidate won. There was one case, 1976, in which the Democrat had the advantage, and he won. In two cases there was no absolutist advantage to either side because neither candidate spoke in sacred terms; in both of these cases the Democrat won. The potential exception to the pattern is 2008. The seeming Republican advantage did not lead to victory. This could be because of the prevailing circumstances that favored the Democratic Party regardless of the candidates themselves. It could also be in part because the Republican advantage appears in the aggregate, but there is no advantage in the domestic policy debates that dominated the campaign. In this realm, both candidates were low in absolutist rhetoric, putting the 2008 contest in the category of an even contest rather than a Republican advantage.

Given the structural circumstances of the 2008 campaign season—eight years of Republican rule, an unpopular incumbent, and a decreasingly popular war—political science scholars would predict a Democratic victory in a hypothetical matchup with unknown candidates. Once the financial crisis and economic downturn hit in the late summer, it became a Democratic victory to lose. For the Republican to prevail would require an exceptional campaigner against a weak Democratic candidate. This combination has occurred before, but not this year. McCain was not in the upper leagues of Republican presidential hopefuls, and Obama was an unusually charismatic and strategic Democrat. Moreover, McCain did not seize the absolutist advantage in the full scope of his rhetoric. Half sacred was not sacred enough. The electoral outcome in 2008 illustrates an important facet of rhetorical influence: it is not a silver bullet that can overcome other limitations. It is clearly not the case that the more sacred speaker will always prevail, which would be to argue that of all the factors that determine elections, this one overrides all of the others. Moreover, the theory offered here is one of rhetoric—that absolutist language provides distinct advantages—rather than a theory of elections. Social science scholars see presidential election outcomes as driven by a combination of structural factors (the state of the economy, the popularity of the incumbent) and campaign influences (personal qualities and avoidance of gaffes). But they have not been able to identify one single factor that alone determines the winner. Nonetheless, as a theory of influential rhetoric, absolutist appeals have a surprisingly strong connection to presidential victory in contemporary contests, though not an absolute one.

The larger lesson to be drawn from this analysis of partisan language across the recent presidential campaigns is about the broad distinction in rhetoric. When responding to questions on the central political debates of a campaign season, do Democrats and Republicans tend to speak differently? The evidence from the debates, both historically and from the most recent campaigns, is that they do.

Democratic Impediments and the Problem of Authenticity

Is the Democratic failure to employ sacred rhetoric in the manner of their Republican counterparts a matter of simple neglect or a preference for an alternative strategy? In the wake of the 2000 election, there was much public discussion of the lack of a clear Democratic message that could compete with the unified Republican vision. (The GOP worldview can be understood easily as "You Keep What You Earn," "God Is Great," and "It's a Dangerous World," the three essential messages of economic, social, and national defense conservatives, grounded in the sacred values of liberty, faith, and patriotism, respectively.) In both the 2004 and 2006 elections, some Democratic leaders attempted to frame an articulated worldview rather than a list of policy initiatives, but failed to do so.[13] Their failure to speak in a clear and value-laden fashion that was bounded and nonnegotiable is tied to two commitments that block Democrats from seizing the advantages of sacred rhetoric: complexity and policy.

Complexity

Many leaders and thinkers on the American left are wedded to the view that things are complex, that they cannot be reduced to simple statements or notions of right and wrong.[14] Social conditions and world events are multicausal, so we must seek expertise as the prime virtue of government. This leads Democrats to argue that they should not reduce issues to simplistic views or dumb things down for the voting public. Instead they should educate the public, raising citizens up rather than taking the discussion down. Democrats seem convinced by H. L. Mencken's view that "for every complex problem there is a simple solution. And it's always wrong." Whether this view is accurate is a different question than whether it is persuasive. On the first question this research offers no evidence, but regarding the second it provides a clear negative answer.

If things are complex, then answers tend to be contingent, and positions are more negotiable. We cannot say for sure ahead of time, or in Hillary Clinton's phrase from the second primary debate, "We're not going to engage in these hypotheticals." We must stay flexible and not set bounds or uphold unyielding authorities. Things are dynamic and fluid, not certain or sure. We will not look to sacred values, but to reasoned consequences. However, if leaders' public commitments are only limited and contingent, then what they are asking voters to do is trust their future judgment and expertise, which may be a great deal to ask.

Can You Raise Your Hand?

An example of the Democratic embrace of complexity in the 2008 primary debates was the repeated refusal to respond to a yes-or-no question. A feature of the debates for both parties was the moderator asking the panel of candidates to respond to a specific proposition by a show of hands. During the discussion of the Darfur crisis in the second debate, Wolf Blitzer of CNN asked the candidates to indicate whether they would use force to save lives. This precipitated the most prolonged outburst of cross talk during the debate, as several candidates simultaneously tried to qualify their view or object to the question. The CNN transcript does not give the full effect of the degree and length of the reaction, but it provides important insights:

> *Blitzer*: Raise your hand if you agree with Senator Biden that the United States should use military force to stop the genocide in Darfur.
> *Clinton*: Are we talking about a no-fly zone . . .
> *Edwards*: Wolf . . .
> (*Cross talk*)
> *Blitzer*: Hold on. Hold on.
> (*Laughter*)
> (*Cross talk*)
> *Blitzer*: This is an important issue. This is an important issue.
> (*Cross talk*)
> *Clinton*: Absolutely . . .
> *Edwards*: Because you're talking about American troops . . .
> *Clinton*: . . . an apology.
> (*Cross talk*)
> *Blitzer*: . . . no-fly zone, but very often, Senator Clinton, that could move on to other operations.
> *Clinton*: Well, but, we're not going to engage in these hypotheticals. I mean, one of the jobs of a president is being very reasoned in approaching

these issues. And I don't think it's useful to be talking in these kind of abstract, hypothetical terms.

Later in the same debate, when asked about a strike against Osama bin Laden, several of the candidates reacted with a similar aversion to yes or no. Note that in both cases it is Clinton and Edwards, not Obama, who object strenuously to the absolutist format:

> *Blitzer*: I want everybody to raise their hand and tell me. If you agree that if the U.S. had intelligence that could take out Osama bin Laden and kill him, even though some innocent civilians would die in the process, would you, as president, authorize such an operation? If you would, raise your hand.
> *Biden*: It would depend on how many innocent civilians . . .
> *Clinton*: Yes, I mean, part of this is one of these hypotheticals, Wolf . . .
> *Edwards*: There's not information, not enough information.
> *Clinton*: . . . that is very difficult to answer in the abstract.

Compare this to Republican rhetoric when Osama is mentioned:

> *McCain*: On the subject of Osama bin Laden, he's responsible for the deaths of thousands of innocent Americans. He's now orchestrating other attacks on the United States of America. We will do whatever is necessary. We will track him down. We will capture him. We will bring him to justice, and I will follow him to the gates of hell.

> *Romney*: Of course we get Osama bin Laden and track him wherever he has to go, and make sure he pays for the outrage he exacted upon America . . . He is going to pay, and he will die.

Another important example of the Democratic candidates' refusal to deal in absolutes occurred in the October 30 debate moderated by Tim Russert:

> *Russert*: I want to ask each of you the same question. Senator Clinton, would you pledge to the American people that Iran will not develop a nuclear bomb while you are president?
> *Clinton*: I intend to do everything I can to prevent Iran from developing a nuclear bomb.
> *Russert*: But you won't pledge?
> *Clinton*: I am pledging I will do everything I can to prevent Iran from developing a nuclear bomb.

Russert: But they may.

Clinton: Well, you know, Tim, you asked me if I would pledge, and I have pledged that I will do everything I can to prevent Iran from developing a nuclear bomb.

(Laughter)

Clinton's first response seems to be an affirmative answer to the question, but instead it avoids the most important aspect of pledging to enforce the boundary. She uses careful language to state her intent but not commit to any absolute limit. Russert attempts to clarify the response two times, and Clinton maintains the posture that she is agreeing, refusing to admit the distinction between pledging to attempt and pledging to not accept the alternative.[15] The other Democratic candidates essentially follow suit; for example, Edwards responds, "What I will do is take all the responsible steps that can be taken to keep Iran from developing a nuclear weapon."

A difference appears with Obama and Kucinich, who challenge the entire premise of an absolutist response:

Obama: I think all of us are committed to Iran not having nuclear weapons, and so we could potentially short-circuit this.

(Laughter)

But I think there is a larger point at stake, Tim, and that is, we have been governed by fear for the last six years. And this president has used the fear of terrorism to launch a war that should never have been authorized. We are seeing the same pattern now. We are seeing the Republican nominees do the same thing . . . We haven't even talked about civil liberties and the impact of the politics of fear—what that has done to us, in terms of undermining basic civil liberties in this country, what it has done in terms of our reputation in the world.

Kucinich: With all due respect to our friends in the media here, the media itself has to be careful how you frame these questions. We don't want to be put in a position where we are taking this country to the threshold of war. The media did play a role in taking us to war in Iraq. And I'm urging the media: urge restraint upon you and our president, whose rhetoric is out of control.

Kucinich goes to the extreme of challenging the legitimacy of media questions that confront candidates with defined limits or requests for a specific pledge. Obama employs the more subtle approach of shifting focus to his concerns of civil liberties and the politics of fear. Instead of giving a half answer to the question offered, as Clinton did, he does not answer the question on its own terms and instead reframes his response to address considerations that are more favorable to his positions. This approach is in line with George Lakoff's advice to avoid frames that advantage conservatives, by reframing questions rather than answering them within their own bounds.[16] Lakoff cites Obama as an exemplar of his strategies, especially when asked to make a yes-or-no statement in the second debate:

> This led up to one of the great moments of recent political television.
> *Blitzer*: I want you to raise your hand if you believe English should be the official language of the United States.
> Barack Obama refused to take it anymore. He got up, stepped forward, and said:
> > This is the kind of question that is designed precisely to divide us. You know, you're right. Everybody is going to have to learn to speak English if they live in this country. The issue is not whether or not future generations of immigrants are going to learn English. The question is: how can we come up with a legal, sensible immigration policy? And when we get distracted by those kinds of questions, I think we do a disservice to the American people.
> I jumped up and cheered. In my living room.[17]

Lakoff argues that when clear lines are requested of candidates, they should avoid them by reframing the discussion into favorable territory. This is one of the disagreements between my perspective and Lakoff's. While the tangential rhetoric may have a more positive effect than failing to set a boundary at all, this does not alleviate the impression that the speaker has dodged the question, or that he refuses to take a clear position. This may be effective when none of the competitors on the stage is taking an absolutist stand, but when an opponent responds with an understandable boundary that they are pledged to enforce, this creates a distinct and unfavorable contrast.

Although it may seem reasonable to think that complex or nuanced answers are necessary to such questions, the insistence on complexity and nuance loses the advantage of an absolute position. To think that the world is complex is one thing; to refuse to communicate clear principles by which to navigate this complexity is another. Many voters may be convinced, as suggested by Matthew 5:37, that leaders should "let what you say be simply 'Yes' or 'No'; anything more than this comes from evil." Whether religiously inspired or not, speaking yes or no sends important signals. When the

Democratic candidates are asked whether they can raise their hand, often the answer is "No."

Policy

The assumption of complexity is connected to a second impediment for Democrats, a focus on offering the best policy. What is most important is getting it right, or in Kerry's language, "what means something is, do you have a plan?" Emphasizing complexity is in opposition to two alternative views that inhabit the far ends of the same spectrum. The first is that some things are actually simple, or at least simple enough to have an overarching principle that can clarify and unify our actions—Isaiah Berlin's hedgehogs. The second view is on the opposite side of the spectrum, that things are truly hypercomplex such that analysis or prediction exceed human abilities; in this case we should simply do what is morally right, following our core values (which is to say that if you have no confidence that you can do what's best, simply do what's right). Either end of the spectrum leads to the same response: either simplicity or hypercomplexity suggests defaulting to principle. But Democrats walk the middle path of policy expertise. Things are not so simple that we follow the obvious value, nor are they so complex that they are beyond our abilities and again we follow the obvious value, but are instead within the middle range of human knowledge. But only if we get it right.

A focus on complexity and policy means that in the end it is the consequences that count. The important thing is the public's material welfare over their emotional state or spiritual beliefs. In this sense consequentialist approaches offer bread but no circuses—physical well-being but nothing to inspire pride. Democrats are publicly committed to doing what is best, while Republicans are publicly committed to doing what is right. Both are valid ways to look at things, but the second has communication advantages that the first does not. To American voters, the Democratic approach is simply less admirable and less activating.

Democrats shy away from simple commitments, because they view people who make them as simple. But thinking and speaking can be done differently, grounded in different principles. As Ernest Hemingway phrased it, "Big men use little words," but that does not make them small thinkers. Leaders who express clear commitments are not necessarily less complex, they may simply be more strategic. And because of this, they may be more electable.

The Problem of Authenticity

A final note about sacred rhetoric revolves around the significance of authenticity. Simply employing facets of sacred rhetoric is not the same thing as expressing a genuine sacred commitment. The public may be able to distinguish on a gut level between honest feeling and calculated show. Rather than merely employing sacred rhetoric, conservative leaders often seem to have sacred commitments to match. Liberals may well *have* sacred commitments, but are uncomfortable displaying them. However, when inauthentic displays have been undertaken on the Democratic side, they have played poorly. John Kerry provides two examples that occurred at critical junctures of his 2004 campaign, regarding saluting and guns. The first was Kerry's choice of symbol for the opening moment of his acceptance speech at the Democratic National Convention. Kerry walked to the podium, and after the applause quieted he said, "I'm John Kerry, and I'm reporting for duty," while saluting to the cameras. This was clearly an attempt to raise his militarist and patriotic credentials. The image of the salute was widely disseminated and commented on, often in unfavorable or caricatured ways. It may not have made voters believe that Kerry was pro-military or increased their confidence in him as commander in chief as much as it reminded them of those concerns.

The second example occurred toward the end of the campaign, in a staged hunting trip in Ohio. Twelve days before the election, in one of the last opportunities of the campaign to influence the public, Kerry organized a brief goose-hunting trip, which produced a front-page photo in the *New York Times* of the candidate in camouflage jacket and hat, with a shotgun under his arm. Rather than an authentically revealing moment, it appeared to be what it was—a calculated media event—and was covered as such in media and pundit discussion.[18] Carrying a shotgun did not make Kerry seem to be authentically pro-gun rights, any more than saluting made him appear to be truly pro-military. Moreover, symbols that feel inauthentic can have the opposite effect. On both of these important occasions, Kerry lost opportunities to express his own sacred values, and the effect was more likely to validate the opposing view. Both statements shifted focus to fields in which Democrats cannot match Republican commitments, rather than staking out their own authentically sacred domains.

The Democratic Disadvantage, Language, and Lakoff

My argument is not that in order to win, Democrats must become Republicans, only that it would help them to speak more like Republicans. Given the party's values, Democrats are not necessarily permanently disadvantaged. Instead it is their current way of expressing those values that creates the detriment. By consciously framing appeals in the most sacred way possible they could have greater prospects. Democrats are permanently disadvantaged to the degree that they take consequentialism and material interest as central tenets. But these are not necessarily the core of liberal belief systems or language. The core Democratic value of equality is often discussed in terms of consequentialism and material interest, but it does not need to be. My point is that it would be more effective if discussed in terms of absolute requirements, boundaries, and moral imperatives, employing focusing symbols. Other Democratic core values such as civil liberties and internationalism can also be expressed in more absolutist terms. The environment and government deception are other issues that have been framed successfully in sacred rhetoric (the first by Gore and the second by Carter), but are usually not, to the Democrats' detriment.

It may be instructive to compare the perspective offered here with the prominent work of George Lakoff on political framing and metaphor.[19] Lakoff grounds his understanding of the Democratic disadvantage in Republicans' more effective usage of the government-as-family metaphor, and Democrats' refusal to believe that the repetition of facts cannot defeat the repetition of frames. Lakoff provides a succinct summary in *The Political Mind*: "Metaphorical thought is natural. We have a Nation as Family metaphor. We have two very different idealized models of the family, which are mapped by the metaphor onto two very different views of the nation. Our modes of moral and political thought are taken from these models."[20] Because Republicans frame their policies in terms of the strict-father metaphor, link their policies together into a cohesive whole under that umbrella, and repeat their message in carefully crafted language, they have been more successful than Democrats, who have not made the same metaphorical connection, linked their policies together, or employed the necessary repetition. As Lakoff explains in his 2006 book *Whose Freedom?*, "Language can be used to reframe a situation . . . In politics, whoever frames the debate tends to win the debate," and "those frames and metaphors get there, to a remarkable extent, through repetition in the media."[21]

Lakoff advises Democrats to refuse to be trapped in framings based on the strict-father metaphor, with its central value of authority, and instead to emphasize their own frame of the nurturant parent, with its central value of empathy.[22] While my own research supports important parts of Lakoff's perspective, I see two central problems with his synthesis. As a starting point, it is not clear that the central division between liberals and conservatives is the family metaphor.[23] Lakoff's argument that the family metaphor seems to fit the liberal/conservative split on almost any political issue of our time is hard to dispute.[24] But a more simple and standard view of the core distinction between liberals and conservatives is a positive versus negative view of human nature, which also leads to the same list of liberal versus conservative political positions. Other scholars see the belief or rejection of moral absolutism as the central division.

I would argue that another way to understand the core difference between liberals and conservatives is their opposing empirical assumptions about the essential fragility of our society, or whether democratic institutions are inherently stable or dangerously at risk. If our society and the achievements of the Founding are fragile, either because of a negative human nature, external enemies, or simply entropy, then we need a strong military, a unified culture, divine protection, individual gun ownership, or in short, all of the conservative political goals. The reverse is true if our democracy and society are essentially stable. We do not need to emphasize military power, can encourage multiple cultures, and do not need the stability or protection offered by religion, the respect for traditional family arrangements, or personal weapons. In the economic realm, the fragility premise leads to the conservative emphasis on individual production and economic efficiency; if things are unstable, individuals need to compete over available resources, and society needs to maximize the total economic output for national strength. If we do not need to worry about stability, then we can be concerned about fairness and equity rather than competition and efficiency. If the fragility premise is the essential division between liberals and conservatives, this may increase the significance of sacred rhetoric, as perceptions of instability may be linked to admiring invocations of sacred and hence stable values.

A second criticism of Lakoff's synthesis is that it is not clear that the strict-father metaphor and its opposite are equally effective, especially because emphasizing the nurturant-parent metaphor may cede masculinity to conservatives. Lakoff takes pains to emphasize that the opposite of a strict father is a nurturant *parent*, as the progressive worldview is gender neutral. But using the term *parent* does not eliminate the feminine connotations of nurturance, especially when paired as the opposite of the strict-father approach; as Lakoff argues persuasively, we are heavily influenced by our brains' existing metaphorical frames, such as the father/mother dichotomy. Ceding masculine ground to conservatives may be particularly ineffective if Lakoff is correct about the persuasive advantages of strict-father thinking during emergency or wartime.

The following states a direct contrast between the two perspectives on the language foundations of the Democratic disadvantage and their resulting prescriptions for effective rhetoric:

Lakoff (Metaphorical Reasoning)

- Rigorously avoid accepting the strict-father metaphor of conservative language.
- Discuss political positions in the frame of the nurturant-parent metaphor, emphasizing empathy and protection.
- Unify Democratic proposals under this approach rather than offering a laundry list of policy proposals.

Absolutist Advantage

- Employ sacred rhetoric, concentrating on authentic absolutist positions.
- Avoid consequentialist arguments about material interest, refocusing on absolute boundaries and moral requirements.
- Avoid taking negotiable or seemingly contradictory positions, especially ones that violate boundaries of personal honor or dignity.

Prospects

It is important to note that sacred rhetoric is an aid to electoral victory rather than a guarantee of it. But in a close contest, any one of several factors could turn an election. In a marginal electoral environment, even small advantages can matter a great deal. This is not to say that Democratic candidates in future elections cannot win while employing their usual rhetoric, bolstered by other factors such as the state of the economy, scandal, policy failure among the opposition, or simple fatigue with the incumbent party. But they are disadvantaged, especially in close races.

In the current environment of a closely divided electorate, a more authentically sacred Democratic Party could potentially lessen the absolutist advantage of Republicans. While some candidates, notably Carter and Obama, have employed a degree of sacred rhetoric, Democrats more often do so only rarely, even in the realms that lend themselves to this rhetoric more readily, such as the environment, civil liberties, and equal opportunity. Democratic commitments to complexity and policy create substantial impediments, while Republican rhetoric taps into the deep-seated and powerful mentality of the sacred. Democrats could make their own long-term public commitments to sacred values, but do not seem willing to do so.

Conclusion

"A Cure for Thought and the Diseases It Breeds"

Why do I spend my time with fools when I could easily invent a cure for thought and the diseases it breeds?

—Christopher Kennedy, *Trouble with the Machine*

Whether sacred rhetoric is a disease depends on your view of the groups who are gaining its political advantages, as well as your view of what constitutes a healthy democracy. One can easily come to a negative view, as sacred appeals increase discord and decrease deliberation. But this may be a limited conclusion. If democratic politics should turn on the concerns of democratic citizens, then the first threshold is that citizens care at all. Often in American politics this threshold is not met. About most issues most of the time citizens know little and care marginally, trusting in political elites to manage things for them. Sacred rhetoric increases citizen engagement, emboldening our absentee democracy. Not all political appeals activate citizens' own values and limits, bringing them into the democratic process. Sacred rhetoric increases the democratic good of participation even as it lowers the positive benefits of deliberation. In this sense our assessment of sacred rhetoric depends on which of the competing theories of democracy we find most persuasive. For sacredness there is no cure, only an appreciation of its contradictions and possibilities.

The psychological effects of sacred rhetoric are distinctive, powerful, and in a sense contradictory, with equally complex influences on the state of our democracy. The persuasive effects are distinctive because they represent a form of persuasion centered on process rather than outcome, an aspect of persuasion that has not been fully recognized by political psychologists. The initial empirical evidence indicates that the effects are strong, suggesting that sacred rhetoric is a powerful tool of the political groups that employ it. But the democratic influence is a contradiction, advantaging one aspect of democracy while disadvantaging another. Moreover, because the use of sacred rhetoric is not equally distributed among parties and interests, understanding its effects is a partisan concern as well as a normative quandary. This conclusion offers a final thought about each of these aspects of the study—the psychology of sacred rhetoric, its democratic consequences, and its influence on political power.

The Psychology of Sacred Rhetoric

> "The formation of political preferences ought to be one of the major subjects of political science... Preferences in regard to political objects are not external to political life; on the contrary, they constitute the very internal essence, the quintessence of politics: the construction and reconstruction of our lives together."[1] —Aaron Wildavsky

Persuasion is one of the earliest and most enduring interests of students of democratic politics. Is it possible to move others to our cause, and how can this best be done? The avenue examined here is not a panacea for persuasion, but rather a particular mechanism for changes in reasoning and motivation. These two effects are grounded in the psychology of the sacred, or the urge to protect what we have set aside for special reverence. The sacred shift engendered by absolutist appeals results in these particular forms of persuasion, though it gives no advantage in other significant aspects. Of the several facets of persuasion, the most obvious is attitude change, or a simple shift of opinion. In this sense sacred rhetoric is no more persuasive than its negotiable or consequentialist counterparts. Nonsacred appeals can be quite persuasive, and sacredness does not seem to change minds more effectively than reasoned consequences. But in other ways sacredness provides a powerful distinction.

About the sacred we think differently and care more. The first of these aspects of sacredness leads to the reasoning effect, or a shift toward more absolutist thinking and justification. The experimental evidence demonstrates that exposure to sacred rhetoric leads directly to an increase in absolutist justifications, concentrating on nonnegotiable and nonconsequentialist arguments, the citation of appropriate boundaries and respected authorities, and expressions of moral outrage. The value in question becomes protected, inviolable, not to be sullied by the cheap trading or power bargaining of mundane politics. This effect influences the way citizens reason and justify themselves. It is not an effect on the outcome of their opinion, but instead on the process of their thinking.

This sort of process effect has been underappreciated in studies of political psychology and political communication, perhaps because it is less visible. The most common concern of public opinion scholars is the final expressed opinion, and hence this is the most frequently measured variable. But the sacred distinction does not seem to have immediate effects on opinion, which may explain why it has come under less scrutiny. If we look again at table 3.1 describing the principal forms of persuasion studied by scholars, purely process effects have not been emphasized. Studies of framing and priming do concern the process of judgment (in the considerations at play within citizens' minds and the weights given to the different concerns), but the emphasis is still on how this alters the outcome of final opinions. The shift in considerations alone is not the focus, but instead what it does to individual judgments, or how priming and framing are employed to manipulate public opinion. A focus on process effects rather than outcome effects is a symptom of a greater psychological rather than behavioral approach to politics. As Wildavsky suggested, the origins of political beliefs are a crucial but little-understood facet of politics. And this applies with particular force to the origins of the unyielding beliefs that drive many of our political conflicts.

The importance of process alone also has to do with a shift in the concerns of political theory, or the increasing importance of the concept of deliberative democracy. Earlier studies of public opinion were framed by a background of an elite or minimalist democracy, where the essential question is how elites respond to the opinions of the mass public. In the 1970s the concern shifted toward participatory democracy, or how the public's formed opinions could motivate policy through the increased engagement of ordinary citizens. But only more recently has the development of those opinions and their public justifications become a focus of study from the perspective of a deliberative democracy. In this vein the influence of sacred rhetoric on discourse is a prime concern, because the process of how politics is conceptualized and discussed has important implications.

However, sacred rhetoric also has a powerful outcome effect in the form of activation. Sacred appeals are more effective than nonsacred rhetoric in encouraging citizens to engage in politics. The sacred shift increases citizens' level of political intensity as well as their intention to participate. In our experiments, citizens displayed greater extremity of opinions, had higher perceptions of the importance of the issue, and had lower perceptions of the legitimacy of opposing arguments. They also expressed greater intentions to engage in political discussion and to convince others of their views. Activation is a major concern for both students and practitioners of contemporary politics, not merely because of its implications for democracy, but because of its influence on elections. Parties and movements that can increase the engagement of their supporters have a distinct advantage in winning office or influencing society. This advantage is particularly important in a polarized environment where few minds are changing and the decisive question is which side has the more active constituency. For this reason, the psychological dynamics of sacred rhetoric have important partisan consequences as well as meaning for American democracy.

Democratic Consequences: The Conflicting Demands of Participation and Deliberation

> "Of the challenges that American democracy faces today, none is more formidable than the problem of moral disagreement. Neither the theory nor the practice of democratic politics has so far found an adequate way to cope with conflict about fundamental values." —Amy Gutmann and Dennis Thompson[2]

It has become a common belief that citizen engagement in America has declined, leaving us with a lamentably underdeveloped civil society. The ideal of civil society depends on both cohesion and compromise—on citizens holding beliefs that inspire them to engage with other members of society, and on these same citizens nonetheless maintaining their ability to tolerate others' beliefs that conflict with their own. Strong belief systems are often what inspire citizens to participate in politics. However, strong beliefs that do not allow for compromise may also degrade civil society and lessen the prospects for democratic deliberation. In this sense a healthy democracy requires a balance between too little political intensity and too much. The dilemma that sacred rhetoric provides is that it increases intensity and engagement at the same time that it degrades deliberation. So which do we value more, a participatory democracy or a deliberative one? As Isaiah Berlin points out in his incisive commentary on value conflict, "Some among the Great Goods cannot live together."[3] Different versions of democratic theory may well have this same character. Because of their contradictions, we cannot have all of the positive aspects of democracy, but must choose among them. Democratic deliberation can discourage participation because of its messy and discordant nature. Likewise, participation can discourage deliberation when it is strident or unyielding. The influence of sacred rhetoric presents us with the second case, when we cannot necessarily have our participation and our deliberation too.

When we judge between the conflicting demands of participation and deliberation there is no simple choice. We can compare their goals and advantages, but the normative quandary only deepens rather than lifts. Like many facets of democratic politics, it is a trade-off. Perhaps one of the ironies of the study of sacred rhetoric is that the same absolutist claims that reject value trade-offs create one that is irresolvable.

Sacred Rhetoric and Political Power

The effects of sacred rhetoric are important for both the psychology of persuasion and the nature of democracy, but they also have implications for partisan politics. The same effects that decrease deliberation and increase participation improve the prospects of the social movements and politicians who employ sacred appeals. Political leaders who can raise the intensity and engagement of their followers or recruits while lessening their degree of negotiability gain a distinct advantage. The valorization effect of increasing the perceived virtue of absolutist speakers also provides politicians with a vital edge. By merely speaking in sacred terms (and especially avoiding antisacred gaffes) they become more principled, more determined, more virtuous than their consequentialist-speaking rivals. If sacred appeals were employed equally by different parties and movements, there would be no advantage to be had. But a benefit accrues to one group over another if their use is unequal. Some of the clear beneficiaries of sacred rhetoric have been social movements on the left as well as the right. Successful movement activists understand the close connection between absolutist language and political motivation. Which movements will attempt to gain the absolutist advantage in the future is a question to be answered, but what is clear in American politics is that not all groups will be represented equally. One of the flaws in James Madison's vision of many competing factions within our society balancing each other's influence is that some potential interests are never mobilized. But those who do organize are often driven by powerful beliefs that transcend mere economic interest, focusing on absolute or sacred claims.

In contemporary partisan politics it is clearly Republicans who have seized the absolutist advantage. An analysis of the competing party rhetoric suggests that while Democrats employ sacred language on some occasions,

Republicans by far employ the greater degree of sacred appeals. This allows them to gain the advantages in activation and valorization that sacredness creates. The dominance of Republicans is one of the abiding features of presidential politics in the post-Vietnam era. The conservative advantage may be grounded in their rhetorical distinction: the emphasis on sacred claims that for many citizens are meaningful and motivational. The consequentialist rhetoric favored by Democrats has neither the same power to influence the process of reasoning nor the same persuasive ability to inspire political engagement. Contemporary Democrats focus on several political domains in which they could employ sacred rhetoric as well, but so far have failed to do so. Political leaders on the left may be wedded to the perspective that things are complex, that there are no absolutes, and that outcomes of policy trump expressions of protected values.

Whether the balance of sacredness among current parties and movements will alter remains to be seen, but the influence of sacred rhetoric will likely continue to play a strong role in American politics. What all of this suggests is that contemporary citizens have not lost touch with the sacred, and perhaps what is more important, that the sacred has not lost its influence over them. Sacred rhetoric has abiding consequences for the prospects of competing parties and movements, as well as for the nature of American democracy.

Methodological Appendix

Subjects, an Experimental Approach

"If we are to talk about the human mind, let us start with human beings." With these words, Robert Lane starts his classic text on American thought, *Political Ideology: Why the Common Man Believes What He Does*. Like Lane, our purpose is to understand a facet of political thinking—in this case how citizens respond to sacred rhetoric. Do human minds react to sacredness in the same way they respond to other political appeals, or does sacredness have a distinct form of influence? It should be clear immediately that this is a fundamentally empirical question. To pursue it, we cannot assume away the nature of human psychology, either in motivation or mechanics. Most of the empirical evidence from Hume to Tversky and Kahneman suggests that humans cannot be described as purely rational creatures. Moreover, the workings of the mind are more a question than a given; human psychology is illuminated by empirical study rather than logical analysis. But an empirical approach nonetheless leaves a broad range of specific methods that could be employed.

Our explicit interest in this study is causation—what are the effects of hearing sacred rather than negotiable appeals? This leads us toward experimental methods, which are most suited to this task. However, this is only the case when we can manipulate the causal variable. If, for example, we thought that income explained the variation in our object of study, we could not assign different citizens to different levels of wealth in order to observe its effects. Hence we could not be sure that it is wealth rather than another factor associated with it that is really the causal agent. In these cases we turn from experiments to more inferential methods, such as the statistical analysis of survey data, attempting to control for confounding variables. In our case, however, we can simply manipulate citizens' exposure to different forms of rhetoric, establishing a clear causal test.

The primary advantage of experiments is this ability to isolate causal mechanisms. This is accomplished through the establishment of a control group to compare to the treatment group, and the random assignment of subjects to one group or the other, removing selection bias and randomizing out other possible causal factors.[4] These procedures establish the internal validity that is the hallmark of experimental approaches. We can be sure that any observed differences between the control and treatment groups are due to the experimental manipulation, because the two groups are otherwise identical; the only difference between them is the one that we introduced. The associated disadvantage is the lack of external validity or generalizability to circumstances outside the lab. Although experimenters strive to recreate or mimic real-world conditions, only so much can be achieved. In our case the corollary to real-world political persuasion is strong; the rhetorical statements employed are similar to actual political appeals that citizens hear in the course of their daily lives.

Which brings us back to the citizens under study: our experimental subjects. The first study employs 237 students at the University of Pittsburgh, drawn from the Psychology Department subject pool, and the second sample comprises 136 students at Colgate University, drawn from the student research pool. Although the citizens in both studies are students, they represent a broader spectrum of Americans. Their representativeness relies not on the essential similarity between these students and other Americans, but on the essential similarity in how they react to political stimuli—in how their minds operate. One of the modern criticisms of laboratory experiments is the "sophomores in the lab" effect.[5] The argument is that the narrow subject pool of college undergraduates may bias the results of contemporary psychology because of the unusual characteristics of that demographic, especially a susceptibility to peer pressure, less solidified attitudes, and political liberalism. Whenever any of these biases are related to the specific research question at hand, we must be especially careful about our conclusions.

Of those three traits, the first is irrelevant for our manipulation, the second should not bias our specific question, and the third, if anything, biases results against our hypotheses, making the test more rigorous. Whereas some social psychology experiments regarding group dynamics and other public interactions may be biased by undergraduates' greater susceptibility to peer pressure, our experiments are done individually, without regard to group opinion. That students have less solidified attitudes than older Americans may seem at first to bias our results, but our test is not whether sacred rhetoric will persuade, but whether it does so more or less than negotiable rhetoric. If students are biased toward being persuaded, they should be more persuaded by both equally. Differences in the effects of the two forms of rhetoric should not be a result of undergraduate biases. If anything, students should hold fewer sacred values than older citizens, and be *less* persuaded by appeals to sacredness. The third trait—greater political liberalism—should if anything bias students against sacred appeals and absolutist reasoning. If our third hypothesis, that Democrats employ less sacred rhetoric than Republicans, is correct, we could assume that if there is a bias, it is toward liberals being less fond of sacredness and if anything less persuaded by it. The specific character of the sophomores (and juniors, seniors, and fifth-year students) in our lab will not determine our results, so an experimental approach is viable.

The Sacred Rhetoric Statements

Gay Marriage Sacred (Anti): The institution of marriage is under attack, and we must save it before the one man–one woman definition of marriage is completely and radically redefined. We cannot allow the imposition of gay marriage and the degradation of one of our most sacred institutions. This is true regardless of the unsubstantiated claims by some groups that not changing the definition of marriage limits the rights of homosexuals. That claim ignores the greater good of our community and the right to protect our most foundational principles. Marriage as it is currently defined is ordained by the Bible and also by our longest traditions. We should be angry that it is being threatened and not stand for it any longer.

Protected status	Yes	Relativism	No
Boundary	Yes	Denial of boundaries	No
Authority	Yes	Denial of authority	No
Moral Outrage	Yes	Denial of moral outrage	No
Noninstrumentalism	No	Instrumentalism	No
Nonnegotiability	Yes	Negotiability	No
Nonconsequentialism	No	Consequentialism	No

Reasoning Scale = 5

Gay Marriage Nonsacred (Anti): Changing the law to allow for gay marriage is not a step that we should take lightly without considering its consequences. After gay marriage, what will become of marriage itself? One of the possible effects of gay marriage is to take us down a slippery slope to legalized polygamy and group marriage. Marriage could be transformed into a variety of relationship contracts, linking two, three, or more individuals (however weakly and temporarily) in every conceivable combination of male and female. In a democratic society, we can protect the institutions that are in the best interests of the majority.

Protected status	No	Relativism	No
Boundary	No	Denial of boundaries	No
Authority	No	Denial of authority	No
Moral Outrage	No	Denial of moral outrage	No
Noninstrumentalism	No	*Instrumentalism*	Yes
Nonnegotiability	No	Negotiability	No
Nonconsequentialism	No	*Consequentialism*	Yes

Reasoning Scale = –2

Death Penalty Sacred (Pro): The death penalty makes a clear moral statement about what we will and will not allow in our society. Heinous crimes cannot be tolerated. We must be clear about what sort of justice they require. Both the victims and especially their families are due the form of justice that both our religious and secular traditions call for. The Bible is clear about the demands of an eye for an eye, and the Constitution itself specifically mentions capital punishment as part of our legal system. The issue is not deterrence; it is the strongest possible statement of what outrages the community—of what is allowable and what is not.

Protected status	Yes	Relativism	No
Boundary	Yes	Denial of boundaries	No
Authority	Yes	Denial of authority	No
Moral Outrage	Yes	Denial of moral outrage	No
Noninstrumentalism	No	Instrumentalism	No
Nonnegotiability	No	Negotiability	No
Nonconsequentialism	Yes	Consequentialism	No

Reasoning Scale = 5

Death Penalty Nonsacred (Pro): The death penalty is our last line of defense against the most violent and dangerous criminals in our society. Some argue that capital punishment is not a deterrent to crime, but common sense tells you that at least some potential murderers will be stopped by the knowledge that they may be put to death. We must also protect society by removing the most vicious criminals from our midst, which cannot be done with certainty by imposing long prison sentences that later parole boards can lessen. Opponents argue that if one innocent man is executed then the system must be stopped. But how different is this from one innocent man who is held in prison for the rest of his life? We cannot stop from determining justice only because a mistake might rarely be made. Even if an innocent man is executed in the rare case of a mistake, this is more than balanced by the number of lives saved by making sure that the most vicious criminals cannot kill again.

Protected status	No	*Relativism*	Yes
Boundary	No	Denial of boundaries	No
Authority	No	Denial of authority	No
Moral Outrage	No	Denial of moral outrage	No
Noninstrumentalism	No	*Instrumentalism*	Yes
Nonnegotiability	No	Negotiability	No
Nonconsequentialism	No	*Consequentialism*	Yes

Reasoning Scale = –3

Environment Sacred (Pro): The environment is a sacred trust that we must not allow to be destroyed. Natural wonders like our wilderness areas, national parks, and the wildlife themselves must be left for future generations to enjoy. Species that are lost are gone forever, as are natural settings that have been despoiled. The Bible entrusts the earth to us to husband. In that sense it is not ours to destroy, any more than we can deny its beauty to our grandchildren who will inhabit it in the future. In addition to religious authority, our secular traditions teach the same lesson—some of our greatest presidents, such as Teddy Roosevelt, were also our greatest environmentalists. Greed is not an adequate excuse for destroying nature. We can achieve both preservation and profits without sacrificing what is irreplaceable. We should be angry at the destruction of our natural environment and tolerate it no longer.

Protected status	Yes	Relativism	No
Boundary	Yes	Denial of boundaries	No
Authority	Yes	Denial of authority	No
Moral Outrage	Yes	Denial of moral outrage	No
Noninstrumentalism	Yes	Instrumentalism	No
Nonnegotiability	No	Negotiability	No
Nonconsequentialism	Yes	Consequentialism	No

Reasoning Scale = 6

Environment Nonsacred (Pro): Protecting the environment is not a matter of beauty or nature or the fate of owls or any other motive that could be thought of as soft-hearted. It is purely self-interested, as our own health and welfare depend on a clean environment in which to live. Industrial pollutants in air and water are one of the major sources of cancer-causing agents. Our lives are shortened now by the build-up of toxins in our bodies, and in many cases this has led directly to early deaths for thousands of people. This is likely to only increase in the future, as pollutants continue to build up. Protecting the environment is not a small concern for the welfare of a few animals. It is a major concern for the health of all humans.

Protected status	No	Relativism	No
Boundary	No	Denial of boundaries	No
Authority	No	Denial of authority	No
Moral Outrage	No	Denial of moral outrage	No
Noninstrumentalism	No	*Instrumentalism*	Yes
Nonnegotiability	No	Negotiability	No
Nonconsequentialism	No	*Consequentialism*	Yes

Reasoning Scale = –2

Guns Sacred (Pro): The ability to keep and bear arms is a protected right of free citizens. The Constitution gave us that right because our forefathers knew that it must be preserved against future encroachments. It is this principle that counts. The Second Amendment is no better or no worse than the other parts of the Bill of Rights. We must preserve it just as we must preserve First Amendment rights to free speech, and Fifth Amendment rights against self-incrimination. We should be angry at the efforts by false leaders to take away our long-standing freedoms, and refuse to allow ourselves to go down the slippery slope of one concession after another. We cannot negotiate away our sacred rights.

Protected status	Yes	Relativism	No
Boundary	Yes	Denial of boundaries	No
Authority	Yes	Denial of authority	No
Moral Outrage	Yes	Denial of moral outrage	No
Noninstrumentalism	Yes	Instrumentalism	No
Nonnegotiability	Yes	Negotiability	No
Nonconsequentialism	No	Consequentialism	No

Reasoning Scale = 6

Guns Nonsacred (Pro): Citizens must be allowed to keep firearms in order to protect themselves. Allowing citizens to own guns is simply a matter of weighing the consequences of law-abiding citizens having them versus what would happen if solid citizens did not have guns. Having firearms may lead to some accidental deaths by some who do not store their guns properly or teach their children how to respect them. But the consequence of not upholding gun rights is the inability of citizens to protect themselves against criminals, as well as the increased boldness of criminals because they know that home owners are not armed. This would result in a larger number of deaths and a more violent society. It is simply not true that we can rely on the police to protect us. They do not, and we must be able to protect ourselves.

Protected status	No	*Relativism*	Yes
Boundary	No	Denial of boundaries	No
Authority	No	Denial of authority	No
Moral Outrage	No	Denial of moral outrage	No
Noninstrumentalism	No	*Instrumentalism*	Yes
Nonnegotiability	No	*Negotiability*	Yes
Nonconsequentialism	No	*Consequentialism*	Yes

Reasoning Scale = −4

NOTES

Introduction

1 George Lakoff, *The Political Mind* (New York: Viking, 2008), 231. Lakoff is a prominent linguist at Berkeley who refers to himself as a "cognitive activist," or a scholar who applies cognitive science to advancing progressive causes (*Don't Think of an Elephant* [White River Junction, Vt.: Chelsea Green, 2004], 73). His major works on the nature of metaphor and political reasoning include *Metaphors We Live By* (with Mark Johnson; Chicago: University of Chicago Press, 1980); *Women, Fire, and Dangerous Things* (Chicago: University of Chicago Press, 1987); and *Moral Politics* (Chicago: University of Chicago Press, 1996). His more recent works applying these concepts to contemporary politics include *Thinking Points* (New York: Farrar, Straus & Giroux, 2006), and *Whose Freedom?* (New York: Farrar, Straus & Giroux, 2006). For a discussion of his influence among Democratic strategists, see Evan R. Goldstein, "Who Framed George Lakoff?," *Chronicle of Higher Education*, August 15, 2008, B6-B9.
2 Lakoff, *Thinking Points*, 111; *Political Mind*, 53.
3 Lakoff, *Political Mind*, 232.

Chapter 1

1 Mircea Eliade, *The Sacred and the Profane* (New York: Harcourt, 1957), 15.
2 "Let every nation know, whether it wishes us well or ill, that we shall pay any price, bear any burden, meet any hardship, support any friend, oppose any foe, in order to assure the survival and the success of liberty" (inaugural address, January 20, 1961). These lines are paraphrased frequently. The

second sentence of the Democratic response (by Richard Gephardt) to the president's State of the Union address in 2002 was, "Like generations that came before us, we will pay any price and bear any burden to make sure that this proud nation wins the first war of the twenty-first century."

3 "We shall go on to the end, we shall fight in France, we shall fight on the seas and oceans, we shall fight with growing confidence and growing strength in the air, we shall defend our island, whatever the cost may be, we shall fight on the beaches, we shall fight on the landing grounds, we shall fight in the fields and in the streets, we shall fight in the hills; we shall never surrender" (address to the House of Commons, June 4, 1940).

4 See Charlton Heston's 2000 NRA presidential address in Charlotte, N.C. (transcript on the NRA website at http://www.nrahq.org/transcripts/hestonam.asp), which not only concludes with this statement but also refers to the concept of sacredness elsewhere: "We know that there is sacred stuff in that wooden stock and blued steel" (a reference to the wooden cross and iron nails of the crucifixion). Religious symbolism, both clear and subtle, is an important part of NRA rhetoric, as discussed in chap. 5.

5 Michael Alvarez and John Brehm, *Hard Choices, Easy Answers* (Cambridge, Mass.: Harvard University Press, 2003); Stanley Feldman and John Zaller, "The Political Culture of Ambivalence: Ideological Responses to the Welfare State," *American Journal of Political Science* 36 (1992): 268–307; Jennifer Hochschild, *What's Fair? American Beliefs about Distributive Justice* (Cambridge, Mass.: Harvard University Press, 1981).

6 Philip Tetlock, "Thinking the Unthinkable: Sacred Values and Taboo Cognitions," *Trends in Cognitive Sciences* 7, no. 7 (2003): 320, emphasis original.

7 "Sacred values are often ultimately religious in character, but they need not have divine sanction. Sacred values can range from fundamentalists' faith in God to the liberal-social democratic dogma of racial equality to the radical libertarian commitment to the autonomy of the individual" (Philip Tetlock, Orie Kristel, Beth Elson, Melanie Green, and Jennifer Lerner, "The Psychology of the Unthinkable: Taboo Trade-Offs, Forbidden Base Rates, and Heretical Counterfactuals," *Journal of Personality and Social Psychology* 78, no. 5 [2000]: 853). Many seemingly secular values may have older religious foundations from which they have evolved to become ostensibly secular. The natural rights foundations of the Constitution are a prominent example (Locke held that the unalienable rights to life, liberty, and property were granted by God; in contemporary politics many Americans insist on these rights while rejecting the original view of their source).

8 John Green, James Guth, Lyman Kellstedt, and Corwin Schmidt, *Religion and the Culture Wars* (Lanham, Md.: Rowman & Littlefield, 1996); James

Davison Hunter, *Culture Wars: The Struggle to Define America* (New York: Basic Books, 1991); Hunter, *Before the Shooting Begins: Searching for Democracy in America's Culture War* (New York: Free Press, 1994); Geoffrey Layman, "Culture Wars in the American Party System," *American Politics Quarterly* 27, no. 1 (1999): 89-121; John Kenneth White, *The Values Divide* (Washington, D.C.: CQ Press, 2003); but see Morris Fiorina, *Culture War? The Myth of a Polarized America* (New York: Pearson, Longman, 2005).

9 Even economic policy disputes are increasingly expressed in moral terms. One way to characterize the Tea Party movement is as an explicit attempt to recast issues of taxation and public debt as moral boundaries.

10 "Sometime after 1968, analysts and participants began to speak of 'new social movements' that worked outside of the formal institutional channels and emphasized lifestyle, ethical, or identity concerns rather than narrowly economic goals"; these movements are "concerned largely with values, norms, language, identities and collective understandings" (Craig Calhoun, "'New Social Movements' of the Nineteenth Century," in *Repertoires and Cycles of Collective Action*, ed. Mark Traugott [Durham, N.C.: Duke University Press, 1995], 173, 176). See also Alberto Melucci, "The Symbolic Challenge of Contemporary Movements," *Social Research* 52, no. 4 (1985): 789-816.

11 Claus Offe, "New Social Movements: Challenging the Boundaries of Institutional Politics," *Social Research* 52, no. 4 (1985): 831.

12 David Barker, *Rushed to Judgment: Talk Radio, Persuasion, and American Political Behavior* (New York: Columbia University Press, 2002); Robert Davis and Diana Owen, *New Media and American Politics* (New York: Oxford University Press, 1998); Robert Davis, *Politics Online: Blogs, Chatrooms, and Discussion Groups in American Democracy* (New York: Routledge, 2005).

13 William Butler Yeats, "The Second Coming" (ca. 1920).

14 These three scholars are central figures in the sociology of religion, but each also discusses the concept of sacredness outside the explicitly religious realm. I take three of their works to be classic statements, beginning with Emile Durkheim, *The Elementary Forms of Religious Life* (New York: Free Press, 1995 [1912]); followed by Eliade, *The Sacred and the Profane*; and Peter Berger, *The Sacred Canopy: Elements of a Sociological Theory of Religion* (New York: Anchor Books, 1967), which built on his and Thomas Luckmann's *The Social Construction of Reality* (New York: Anchor Books, 1966).

15 Durkheim, *Elementary Forms of Religious Life*, 44; Berger, *Sacred Canopy*, 25-26; Eliade, *The Sacred and the Profane*, 11.

16 Durkheim, *Elementary Forms of Religious Life*, 36-37.

17 Eliade, *The Sacred and the Profane*, 14. There is some question about the best term for the nonsacred, or the residual outside the sacred realm. One

possibility is *material*, though its technical opposite is *ideational* rather than sacred, and material objects often have a sacred quality. Another possibility is *secular*, but this is a misleading term because its opposite is *religious*, and it bears repeating that the sacred is *not* coterminous with the religious, allowing for a significant realm of the secular sacred. Durkheim, Eliade, and Berger prefer the term *profane*, but I find this to be inaccurate or at least limiting, as the profane connotes those things that explicitly contravene the sacred, violating sacred boundaries. I suggest that the best term is the *mundane*, or the inoffensive world of the everyday, as opposed to the sacred or its explicit violation. Hence I would argue that it is more meaningful to discuss three identifiable concepts: the sacred, the mundane, and the profane. But the greater distinction is between the realm imbued with sacred concerns (both sacred and its opposite, the truly profane) and the mundane realm of the everyday.

18 Eliade describes it as "an absolute reality, *the sacred*, which transcends this world but manifests itself in this world, thereby sanctifying it and making it real" (202). Establishing the sacred provides a point of reference to potentially disconnected humans, giving them "an absolute fixed point, a center" (21). "The sacred reveals absolute reality and at the same time makes orientation possible; hence it *founds the world* in the sense that it fixes the limits and establishes the order of the world" (30; emphasis in original).

19 Readers may recognize this dispute in the nominalist/realist debate in Greek and Christian philosophy. Note that in the Platonic and medieval scholastic traditions, *realism* refers to the position that abstractions or ideals, not empirical observations, are most real.

20 Berger, *Sacred Canopy*, 89.

21 Durkheim, *Elementary Forms of Religious Life*, 35. See also Berger, *Sacred Canopy*: "This quality may be attributed to natural or artificial objects, to animals, or to men, or to the objectivations of human culture. There are sacred rocks, sacred tools, sacred cows. The chieftain may be sacred, as may be a particular custom or institution. Space and time may be assigned the same quality, as in sacred localities and sacred seasons . . . The historical manifestations of the sacred vary widely" (25).

22 In this sense sacredness can be compared to the concept of perfectionism, which also originated in religious thought but infused broader American thinking to such a degree that it has tremendous secular implications. Perfectionism can be understood as the human desire for completeness, manifested in the belief that individual humans or human institutions can be improved successively and brought to a state of excellence. This idea in both its distinctly religious and its secular forms has been a foundation of progressive politics throughout American history, highlighted by the abolitionist

movement, the reform movements of the Progressive Era, and the peace, environmental, and civil rights movements, as well as the development of the welfare state up through the recent health care reforms. For an important discussion of the role of perfectionism and especially its rhetorical implications, see Michael Hyde, *Perfection: Coming to Terms with Being Human* (Waco, Tex.: Baylor University Press, 2010).

23   Durkheim, *Elementary Forms of Religious Life*, 35, xlvi.
24   Berger, *Sacred Canopy*, 24, 17.
25   See Berger and Luckmann, *Social Construction of Reality*, part III. Because "man is capable of forgetting his own authorship of the human world . . . it is experienced by man as a strange facticity, an *opus alienum* over which he has no control"; he "does not internalize the world as one of many possible worlds. He internalizes it as *the* world, the only existent and only conceivable world, the world *tout court*" (89, 134).
26   Berger and Luckmann, *Social Construction of Reality*, 9.
27   Durkheim, *Elementary Forms of Religious Life*, 6.
28   Eliade, *The Sacred and the Profane*, 50, 23. "Profane man cannot help preserving some vestiges of the behavior of religious man, though they are emptied of religious meaning. Do what he will, he is an inheritor" (204). Therefore "even the most avowedly nonreligious man, in his deeper being, shares in a religiously oriented behavior" (211).
29   Peter Berger, *The Desecularization of the World: Resurgent Religion and World Politics* (Washington, D.C.: Ethics and Public Policy Center, 1999), 2–3.
30   It may be the very profanity, not mundanity, of the modern world that instigates a counter-secularization. This implies that the contemporary resurgence of religion is a direct reaction against the profanity spawned by a more permissive secular culture.
31   "Sacred values are those values that a moral community treats as possessing transcendental significance that precludes comparison, trade-offs, or indeed any mingling with secular values" (Tetlock, "Thinking the Unthinkable," 320). On value pluralism, see Tetlock, "A Value Pluralism Model of Ideological Reasoning," *Journal of Personality and Social Psychology* 50 (1986): 819–27; on sacred values, see Philip Tetlock, Randall Peterson, and Jennifer Lerner, "Revising the Value Pluralism Model: Incorporating Social Content and Context Postulates," in *The Psychology of Values: The Ontario Symposium, Volume 8*, ed. Clive Seligman, James Olson, and Mark Zanna, 25–52 (Mahwah, N.J.: Lawrence Erlbaum, 1996); and Tetlock et al., "Psychology of the Unthinkable."
32   See Timur Kuran, *Private Truths, Public Lies: The Social Consequences of Preference Falsification* (Cambridge, Mass.: Harvard University Press, 1995).

33 Sidney Tarrow, *Power in Movement: Social Movements and Contentious Politics* (Cambridge: Cambridge University Press, 1998), 113.
34 Alan Fiske and Philip Tetlock, "Taboo Trade-Offs: Reactions to Transactions That Transgress Spheres of Justice," *Political Psychology* 18, no. 2 (1997): 255–97; see also Fiske, *Structure and Social Life: The Four Elementary Forms of Human Relations* (New York: Free Press, 1991).
35 See Tetlock, "Thinking the Unthinkable." Research conducted by psychologist Jonathan Baron also provides evidence that initial claims of sacred status sometimes do not hold up when citizens are pushed to clarify their views further (Jonathan Baron and Sarah Lesher, "How Serious Are Expressions of Protected Values?," *Journal of Experimental Psychology: Applied* 6 [2000]: 183–94).
36 Eric Hoffer, *The True Believer: Thoughts on the Nature of Mass Movements* (New York: Harper & Brothers, 1951), 15.
37 410 U.S. 113 (1973).
38 "The issue is not revenge or retribution exactly, so much as moral order. The death penalty maintains its hold on the American conscience because of its intensely symbolic nature. Values count enormously in our lives. But it is essential to recognize that our adherence to the death penalty arises not because it provides proven tangible benefits like deterrence but rather from our belief that capital punishment makes an unequivocal moral statement" (Scott Turow, *Ultimate Punishment: A Lawyer's Reflections on Dealing with the Death Penalty* [New York: Farrar, Straus & Giroux, 2003], 64).
39 Constitutionalism can be defined as the primacy of the Constitution as the source of basic law. Donald Lutz defines it as treating the written document "as the summary of our political commitments and as the standard by which we assess, develop, and run our political system. To use a constitution in this way is the essence of constitutionalism" (*The Origins of American Constitutionalism* [Baton Rouge: Louisiana State University Press, 1988], 3). Rousseau argues in *The Social Contract* that all societies need a foundation myth (book II, chap. 7). A constitution as the essence of a Founding and a symbol of that mythology can clearly gain sacred status. As "a bureaucratic form of the claim to moral authority" a constitution offers "new organizational vehicles for assessing national history against some standard of ultimate values. This helps assure political life of a sacred or quasi-sacred aspect so that politics is not merely a matter of force and fraud" (John Markoff and Daniel Regan, "Religion, the State and Political Legitimacy in the World's Constitutions," in *Church-State Relations: Tensions and Transitions*, ed. Thomas Robbins and Roland Robertson [New Brunswick, N.J.: Transaction, 1987], 168, 171). That constitutionalism in this sense is a mainstream article of faith in American society, as well as an aspect of perceptions of American exceptionalism, is

evident in comments such as Peter Jennings' remark in an ABC news broadcast that "in no other society does such a document have the quality of a sacred text" (*World News Tonight*, July 3, 2003).

40   William Lloyd Garrison, *Resolution Adopted by the Antislavery Society*, 1843.
41   Garrison, *Salutatory of the Liberator*, January 1, 1831.
42   Isaiah Berlin, *The Crooked Timber of Humanity: Chapters in the History of Ideas* (New York: Vintage Books, 1992), 11.
43   This is in contrast to the great majority of Americans, who seem to think that some balancing is in order, as illustrated by the high numbers who favor legal abortion with some restrictions, and the high variability in survey responses when introducing different conditions based on the pregnancy's origins or the woman's situation.

Chapter 2

1   Berlin, *Crooked Timber of Humanity*, 10.
2   "Values are backstops of belief systems. When we press people to justify their political preferences, all inquiry ultimately terminates in values that people find it ridiculous to justify any further" (Tetlock et al., "Revising the Value Pluralism Model," 26). This suggests not only a definition but also a method of identifying core values.
3   Clyde Kluckhohn, "Values and Value-Orientations in the Theory of Action," in *Toward a General Theory of Action*, ed. Talcott Parsons and Edward A. Shils (New York: Harper, 1951); Gordon Allport, *Pattern and Growth in Personality* (New York: Harcourt, 1961); Milton Rokeach, *The Nature of Human Values* (New York: Free Press, 1973).
4   Shalom Schwartz, "Value Priorities and Behavior: Applying a Theory of Integrated Value Systems," in *The Psychology of Values: The Ontario Symposium, Volume 8*, ed. Clive Seligman, James Olson, and Mark Zanna (Mahwah, N.J.: Lawrence Erlbaum, 1996); Meg Rohan, "A Rose by Any Name? The Values Construct," *Personality and Social Psychology Review* 4, no. 3 (2000): 255-77.
5   Mark Peffley and Jon Hurwitz, "A Hierarchical Model of Attitude Constraint," *American Journal of Political Science* 29 (1985): 871-90; Jon Hurwitz and Mark Peffley, "How Are Foreign Policy Attitudes Structured: A Hierarchical Model," *American Political Science Review* 81 (1987): 1099-120; William Jacoby, "Issue Framing and Public Opinion on Government Spending," *American Journal of Political Science* 44, no. 4 (2000): 750-67.
6   Isaiah Berlin, *Four Essays on Liberty* (New York: Oxford University Press, 1970), 170.
7   Berlin, *Crooked Timber*, 11. See also Jon Elster, *Sour Grapes: Studies in the Subversion of Rationality* (Cambridge: Cambridge University Press, 1983), on

the "plurality of ultimate values" (38), and Joseph Schumpeter, *Capitalism, Socialism, and Democracy* (New York: Harper & Brothers, 1942): "Ultimate values—or conceptions of what life and society should be—are beyond the range of mere logic. They may be bridged by compromise in some cases but not in others" (251).

8   Berlin, *Crooked Timber*, 12, 13; *Four Essays on Liberty*, 171.
9   Gaetano Mosca, *The Ruling Class* (New York: McGraw-Hill, 1939), 163.
10 Berlin, *Crooked Timber*, 12, 17.
11 See Tetlock, "Value Pluralism Model."
12 Robert Lane, *Political Ideology: Why the Common Man Believes What He Does* (New York: Free Press, 1962), 102.
13 See Max Weber, *Economy and Society: An Outline of Interpretive Sociology* (Berkeley: University of California Press, 1978 [1922]), 25, for a discussion of value rationality as opposed to instrumental rationality. A great deal has been written about the nature of instrumental and noninstrumental thought from the perspective of different disciplines and subdisciplines. Here the word is meant to describe only the distinction between calculated self-interest and uncalculated adherence to principle—only one possible meaning of instrumentality, but I think the best available term for the distinction under consideration.
14 See Samuel Walker, *In Defense of American Liberties: A History of the ACLU* (Carbondale: Southern Illinois University Press, 1990).
15 Weber, *Economy and Society*, 25. See also Jon Elster, *Ulysses and the Sirens* (Cambridge: Cambridge University Press, 1984), in which Elster describes the concept of binding, or precommitments limiting what one can or cannot do regardless of circumstances or consequences. James G. March and Johan P. Olsen describe different forms of decision making conforming to the logic of consequences (instrumentalism) or the logic of appropriateness (cultural norms) (March and Olsen, *Rediscovering Institutions: The Organizational Basis of Politics* [New York: Free Press, 1989]). Each of these distinctions helps illuminate the concept of nonconsequentialism.
16 Hunter, *Culture Wars*, 322.
17 See Morgan Marietta and Mark Perlman, "The Uses of Authority in Economics: Shared Intellectual Legacies as the Foundation of Persuasion," *American Journal of Economics and Sociology* 59, no. 2 (2000): 151-89, on "authority systems, traceable to specific intellectual or cultural precursors, or authorities" (151). These "may be a reference to a person, a definitive published work, or an interpretation of a seminal thought ... Our use of the term 'authority' as interchangeable with an intellectual legacy may be misconstrued because of its dual meaning—connoting both that a certain person or line of thought serves *as* an authority, and they *assert* authority over us ... Once ingrained,

however, the authority may be fully self-imposed, without any need for external support" (153 and n4).

18 Robert Lane, *Political Man* (New York: Free Press, 1972), 182; and Schumpeter, *Capitalism, Socialism, and Democracy*, 251.

19 William Trotter, *Instincts of the Herd in Peace and War* (New York: Macmillan, 1916), quoted in James Harvey Robinson, "The Still Small Voice of the Herd," *Political Science Quarterly* 32, no. 2 (1917): 316.

20 Mohammed Arkoun, "Emergences et problems dans le monde musulman contemporain (1960-1985)," *Islamochristiana* 12 (1986): 151-73, cited in Kuran, *Private Truths, Public Lies*, 176.

21 The "mere contemplation effect"; see Tetlock et al., "Psychology of the Unthinkable."

22 A sacred thing is "the mandatory recipient of elaborated deference" (Durkheim, *Elementary Forms of Religious Life*, xlvi); to not show that deference is profane.

23 Tetlock et al., "Revising the Value Pluralism Model"; Tetlock et al., "Psychology of the Unthinkable." See also the work by psychologist Jonathan Baron, which employs the term *protected values*, or values that "are protected from being traded off for other values . . . The defining property of protected values is absoluteness" (Jonathan Baron and Mark Spranca, "Protected Values," *Organizational Behavior and Decision Processes* 70, no. 1 [1997]: 1-16). Baron and Spranca's definition also includes nonnegotiability ("Protected values are different. They are treated as commitments") and nonconsequentialism (such values "apply to certain behavior 'whatever the consequences'") (5, 3). Baron and others define five other properties of protected values that derive from this status: (1) *quantity insensitivity* (the degree of violation is irrelevant to the reaction); (2) *agent relativity* (violations are judged by the degree of personal participation; hence protected values are asymmetric around commissions and omissions, an example of the omission bias; (3) *moral obligation* (values are seen as universals, not cultural constructs); (4) *denial* (citizens engage in wishful thinking to avoid admitting a need for a trade-off; this is similar to what I described as sacred blindness, which refers to refusing to notice evidence of sacrilege); and (5) *anger* at violations of the value—i.e., moral outrage. See Ilana Ritov and Jonathan Baron, "Protected Values and Omission Bias," *Organizational Behavior and Human Decision Processes* 79, no. 2 (1999): 79-94; Baron and Lesher, "How Serious Are Expressions of Protected Values?"

24 Tetlock et al., "Psychology of the Unthinkable."

25 "They are hard to resolve because, unlike quarrels over money, religious and ethnic quarrels are not easily solved by fractional relief, a redivision of the

pie" (Lane, *Political Man*, 203). "Various political activities having to do with drugs, abortion, the teaching of evolution in public schools, prayer in the classroom, and religious observance as sanctioned by the government are fundamentally symbolic. That is, they are struggles over what activities—and hence what kinds of people—will be publicly defined as righteous, respectable, and worthy, and which will be bracketed in the opposite ways . . . Political participation tells who we are and what we stand for—to the world at large and to ourselves. Thus the stakes are very high, even when they have nothing to do with the kinds of interests allocated by lobbies and other 'economic' action" (James Rule, *Theories of Civil Violence* [Berkeley: University of California Press, 1988], 40).

26 This is the alleged conundrum of Thomas Frank's *What's the Matter with Kansas? How Conservatives Won the Heart of America* (New York: Henry Holt, 2004). But see Hunter, *Culture Wars*, and David Barker, "The Spirit of Capitalism? Religious Doctrine, Values, and Economic Attitude Constructs," *Political Behavior* 22, no. 1 (2000): 1-19, which explains the strong belief system connection between Evangelical Protestantism and respect for wealth accumulation.

Chapter 3

1 For this observation I am indebted to John Markoff, who suggested the example of flag washing.
2 491 U.S. 397 (1989).
3 This illustration was employed in remarks by Sir Zelman Cowen, former governor-general of Australia and provost of Oriel College, Oxford University. He argued that harvesting is a metaphor from farming rather than butchering, thereby invoking growth rather than destruction.
4 Graham Greene, *The End of the Affair* (New York: Viking, 1951), 182.
5 Durkheim, *Elementary Forms of Religious Life*, 322.
6 Durkheim, 328.
7 Durkheim, 322.
8 Durkheim, 328.
9 "The causes of those feelings are entirely foreign to the nature of the object on which they eventually settle . . . By themselves, these emotions are not bound to the idea of any definite object" (Durkheim, 328).
10 David Barker, "Values, Frames, and Persuasion in Presidential Nomination Campaigns," *Political Behavior* 27, no. 4 (2005): 375-94.
11 For a clear summary of attitude change, see Alice Eagly and Shelly Chaiken, *The Psychology of Attitudes* (New York: Harcourt, Brace, Jovanovich, 1993); for framing, see Robert Entman, "Framing: Toward Clarification of a Fractured

Paradigm," *Journal of Communication* 43, no. 4 (1993): 51-58, and *Projections of Power: Framing News, Public Opinion and US Foreign Policy* (Chicago: University of Chicago Press, 2004); for priming, see Shanto Iyengar and Donald Kinder, *News That Matters* (Chicago: University of Chicago Press, 1987); for preference falsification, Kuran, *Private Truths, Public Lies*; and for activation, Steven E. Finkel, "Reexamining the 'Minimal Effects' Model in Recent Presidential Campaigns," *Journal of Politics* 55, no. 1 (1993): 1-21.

12 "Issue frames affect opinion by selectively enhancing the *psychological importance, relevance,* or *weight* accorded to specific beliefs with respect to the issue at hand" (Thomas E. Nelson and Zoe M. Oxley, "Framing Effects on Belief Importance and Opinion," *Journal of Politics* 61, no. 4 [1999]: 1043; emphasis in original). The terminology can be confusing because of the different use of the term *framing* by political psychology, judgment and decision making (JDM), and communication scholars. Framing as described here refers to *issue framing*, or what is sometimes called *emphasis framing*. This is distinct from *equivalence framing*, or when wording that is different but logically equivalent leads listeners to different decisions, as in the famous Kahneman and Tversky experiments (see the distinction made by James Druckman, "Political Preference Formation: Competition, Deliberation, and the (Ir)relevance of Framing Effects," *American Political Science Review* 98, no. 4 [2004]: 671-86). Framing can also be distinguished from *priming*, which is the effect of inducing the hearer to remember or consider a given factor, whereas framing changes the weight given to one factor rather than another among considerations already in play. Priming can be particularly effective when media sources emphasize a single consideration, such as one aspect of presidential performance (Jon Krosnick and Donald Kinder, "Altering the Foundations of Support for the President through Priming," *American Political Science Review* 84, no. 2 [1990]: 497-512).

13 Thomas E. Nelson and Donald R. Kinder, "Issue Frames and Group Centrism in American Public Opinion," *Journal of Politics* 58 (1996): 1055-78; Thomas E. Nelson, Zoe M. Oxley, and Rosalee A. Clawson, "Toward a Psychology of Framing Effects," *Political Behavior* 19, no. 3 (1997): 221-46; James Druckman, "The Implications of Framing Effects for Citizen Competence," *Political Behavior* 23 (2001): 225-56.

14 Thomas E. Nelson, Rosalee A. Clawson, and Zoe M. Oxley, "Media Framing of a Civil Liberties Conflict and Its Effect on Tolerance," *American Political Science Review* 91, no. 3 (1997): 567-84.

15 Paul Brewer, "Value Words and Lizard Brains: Do Citizens Deliberate about Appeals to Their Core Values?," *Political Psychology* 22, no. 1 (2001): 45-64; James Druckman, "On the Limits of Framing Effects: Who Can Frame?," *Journal of Politics* 63 (2001): 1041-67.

16 Druckman, "Political Preference Formation."
17 Classic papers making the cognitive miser argument are Amos Tversky and Daniel Kahneman, "Judgment under Uncertainty: Heuristics and Biases," *Science* 185 (1974): 1124–31, as well as Herbert Simon, "Human Nature in Politics: The Dialogue of Psychology with Political Science," *American Political Science Review* 79 (1985): 293–304. For the role of heuristics, see Paul Sniderman, Richard Brody, and Philip Tetlock, *Reasoning and Choice: Explorations in Political Psychology* (Cambridge: Cambridge University Press, 1991); Samuel Popkin, *The Reasoning Voter* (Chicago: University of Chicago Press, 1991); and Arthur Lupia, "Shortcuts vs. Encyclopedias: Information and Voting Behavior in California Insurance Reform Elections," *American Political Science Review* 88 (1994): 63–76. For political ignorance, see Michael X. Delli Carpini and Scott Keeter, *What Americans Know about Politics and Why It Matters* (New Haven, Conn.: Yale University Press, 1996); Jeffrey Friedman, "Introduction: Public Ignorance and Political Theory," *Critical Review* 12, no. 4 (1998): 397–412; and Samuel DeCanio, "Bringing the State Back In . . . Again," *Critical Review* 14, no. 2 (2000): 139–46.
18 Durkheim, *Elementary Forms of Religious Life*, 328.
19 The usual biblical references are Genesis 9:6: "Whoso sheddeth man's blood, by man shall his blood be shed"; Exodus 21:12: "He that smiteth a man, so that he die, shall be surely put to death"; and Leviticus 24:17: "And he that killeth any man shall surely be put to death" (King James Version). The phrase "shall surely be put to death" or a close variant is repeated more than forty times in the first five books of the Bible.
20 These are grounded in the Noadic covenant to husband the earth (Gen 9:1-2: "And God blessed Noah and his sons, and said unto them, Be fruitful, and multiply, and replenish the earth. And the fear of you and the dread of you shall be upon every beast of the earth, and upon every fowl of the air, upon all that moveth upon the earth, and upon all the fishes of the sea; into your hand are they delivered"). This is often interpreted to mean that we are under obligation to preserve that which God has given us; the resources of the earth are ours to employ but not to destroy, as they ultimately belong to God and have been given to us to husband. While this line of thought was prevalent in the early days of the conservation movement, more contemporary strands of environmentalism seem much more secular.
21 An exception to the lack of sacredness on the antienvironmental side is in regard to property rights, which many citizens as well as intellectuals view as inviolable. However, this provides a sacred argument only in some situations that impinge directly on property rights.
22 $F = 3.44$ ($p = .065$), $F = 9.96$ ($p = .002$), and $F = 7.77$ ($p = .006$). The statistical tests employ an analysis of variance (one-way ANOVA), comparing the

sacred rhetoric group to the nonsacred rhetoric group. This is a straightforward way of comparing the variance in categorization, reasoning, opinion, or other variables between the sacred rhetoric and nonsacred rhetoric groups.

23 The coding of these responses was carried out separately from subjects' other responses in order to maintain blind coding procedures. A random subset of participants' responses (100 out of the 237) were then coded by another researcher to test the reliability of the measures. The average correlation between the two coders across the four domains was 0.86, meeting the usual levels of intercoder reliability.

24 $F = 9.37$ ($p = .002$), $F = 15.93$ ($p = .001$), $F = 16.56$ ($p = .001$), $F = 8.37$ ($p = .004$).

25 $F = 5.35$ ($p = .02$), $F = 6.61$ ($p = .01$).

26 Theda Skocpol and Morris Fiorina, *Civic Engagement in American Democracy* (Washington, D.C.: Brookings, 1999), 12.

27 See Jurgen Habermas, *The Theory of Communicative Action* (Boston: Polity, 1984), developed in more detail in *Between Facts and Norms: Contributions to a Discourse Theory of Law and Democracy* (Cambridge, Mass.: MIT Press, 1996). Other major works in this tradition include John Dryzek, *Discursive Democracy: Politics, Policy, and Political Science* (Cambridge: Cambridge University Press, 1990), and James Fishkin, *Democracy and Deliberation: New Directions for Democratic Reform* (New Haven, Conn.: Yale University Press, 1991).

28 On reciprocity, see especially Amy Gutmann and Dennis Thompson, *Democracy and Disagreement* (Cambridge, Mass.: Harvard University Press, 1996). Gutmann and Thompson argue that fundamental value conflict can be overcome through deliberation, but see Seyla Benhabib, *The Claims of Culture: Equality and Diversity in the Global Era* (Princeton, N.J.: Princeton University Press, 2002), who is not as sanguine on this point.

29 The seminal work in this tradition is Carole Pateman, *Participation and Democratic Theory* (Cambridge: Cambridge University Press, 1970), followed by Benjamin Barber, *Strong Democracy: Participatory Politics for a New Age* (Berkeley: University of California Press, 1984).

30 Diana Mutz, *Hearing the Other Side: Deliberative versus Participatory Democracy* (Cambridge: Cambridge University Press, 2006). See also Nina Eliasoph, *Avoiding Politics: How Americans Produce Apathy in Everyday Life* (Cambridge: Cambridge University Press, 1998), and Melanie Green, Penny Visser, and Phil Tetlock, "Coping with Accountability Cross-Pressures: Low-Effort Evasive Tactics and High-Effort Quests for Complex Compromises," *Personality and Social Psychology Bulletin* 26 (2000): 1380–91.

31 John Hibbing and Elizabeth Theiss-Morse, *Congress as Public Enemy: Public Attitudes toward Political Institutions* (Cambridge: Cambridge University Press, 1995).

Chapter 4

1. Anthony Downs, *An Economic Theory of Democracy* (New York: Harper & Row, 1957).
2. Mancur Olson, *The Logic of Collective Action: Public Goods and the Theory of Groups* (Cambridge, Mass.: Harvard University Press, 1965).
3. Olson, 160–61.
4. Olson, 160–61; emphasis added.
5. Tetlock et al., "Psychology of the Unthinkable," 855.
6. Finkel, "Reexamining the 'Minimal Effects' Model."
7. Framing as it is usually understood presupposes a weighing process (which might pit consequence x against consequence y, or consequence x against value z, or even two values against each other). Sacred appeals imply that the process of weighing is itself illegitimate.
8. N = 38 and 44, respectively.
9. Robert Weissberg, "Democratic Political Competence: Clearing the Underbrush and a Controversial Proposal," *Political Behavior* 23, no. 3 (2001): 276.
10. "The only regulations and ways of acting that can claim legitimacy are those to which all who are possibly affected could assent as participants in rational discourse. In light of this 'discourse principle' citizens test which rights they should mutually accord one another" (Habermas, *Between Facts and Norms*, 458).
11. Seyla Benhabib, "Toward a Deliberative Model of Democratic Legitimacy," in *Democracy and Difference: Contesting the Boundaries of the Political*, ed. Seyla Benhabib (Princeton, N.J.: Princeton University Press, 1996), 67.
12. Benhabib, "Toward a Deliberative Model of Democratic Legitimacy," 68.
13. Habermas, *Between Facts and Norms*, 458. "Law can be preserved as legitimate only if enfranchised citizens switch from the role of private legal subjects and take the perspective of participants who are engaged in the process of reaching an understanding about the rules for their life in common" (461).
14. Dryzek, *Discursive Democracy*, 20.
15. "It is not the use of power or the habit of obedience that depraves men, but the use of power that they consider illegitimate, and obedience to a power they regard as usurped and oppressive" (Alexis de Tocqueville, *Democracy in America*, trans. and ed. Harvey C. Mansfield and Delba Winthrop [Chicago: University of Chicago Press, 2000 (1835)], 8).
16. Habermas, *Between Facts and Norms*, 97.
17. A salient example is the recent pathbreaking U.S. Supreme Court decision that includes homosexuality under the generalized right to privacy; fully one-third of the controlling opinion is a discussion of the history and traditions

(or lack thereof) of specific types of government control, as an explicit basis of their legitimacy or illegitimacy (*Lawrence et al. v. Texas* [2003]).

18   Jacques Barzun, *Is Democratic Theory for Export?* (New York: Carnegie Council on Ethics and International Affairs, 1986), 19.

Chapter 5

1   Robert Wuthnow, *Meaning and Moral Order: Explorations in Cultural Analysis* (Berkeley: University of California Press, 1987), 4.
2   See Mayer Zald, "Culture, Ideology, and Strategic Framing," in *Comparative Perspectives on Social Movements*, ed. Doug McAdam, John McCarthy, and Mayer Zald (Cambridge: Cambridge University Press, 1996). The focus on materialism may be an intellectual legacy of Marxism—a propensity to see change and causation in materialist terms, neglecting ideational approaches, what Francis Fukuyama describes as "our disinclination to believe in the autonomous power of ideas" (Fukuyama, *The End of History* [New York: Free Press, 1992], 21).
3   Michael McGee, "Social Movement: Phenomenon or Meaning?," *Central States Speech Journal* 31 (1980): 238.
4   For other ideational or culture-based approaches to social movements, see William Gamson, *Talking Politics* (Cambridge: Cambridge University Press, 1992); Alberto Melucci, *Nomads of the Present: Social Movements and Individual Needs in Contemporary Society* (Philadelphia: Temple University Press, 1989); and Serge Moscovici, *The Invention of Society* (London: Polity, 1993).
5   Bert Klandermans, "The Social Construction of Protest," in *Frontiers in Social Movement Theory*, ed. Aldon Morris and Carol McClurg Mueller (New Haven, Conn.: Yale University Press, 1992), 89.
6   See Charles Tilly and Sidney Tarrow, *Contentious Politics* (Boulder, Colo.: Paradigm, 2007); Frances Fox Piven and Richard Cloward, *Poor People's Movements: Why They Succeed, How They Fail* (New York: Pantheon Books, 1977); Paul Burstein and April Linton, "The Impact of Political Parties, Interest Groups, and Social Movement Organization on Public Policy," *Social Forces* 81 (2002): 380–408; and Paul Burstein and Sarah Sausner, "The Incidence and Impact of Policy-Oriented Collective Action: Competing Views," *Sociological Forum* 20 (2005): 403–19.
7   Tilly and Tarrow, *Contentious Politics*, 11.
8   David Snow and Robert Benford, "Master Frames and Cycles of Protest," in *Frontiers in Social Movement Theory*, ed. Aldon Morris and Carol McClurg Mueller (New Haven, Conn.: Yale University Press, 1992).
9   Tilly and Tarrow, *Contentious Politics*, 8; Hank Johnston and Bert

Klandermans, *Social Movements and Culture* (Minneapolis: University of Minnesota Press, 1995), 12.

10 See Charles Tilly, *Social Movements, 1768–2004* (Boulder, Colo.: Paradigm, 2004).

11 On accountability, see Green et al., "Coping with Accountability Cross-Pressures"; on the spiral of silence, Elisabeth Noelle-Neumann, *The Spiral of Silence: Public Opinion—Our Social Skin* (Chicago: University of Chicago Press, 1984); and on preference falsification, Kuran, *Private Truths, Public Lies*.

12 Some scholarship suggests that Rosa Parks' refusal may not have been as spontaneous as it was portrayed, but instead was orchestrated ahead of time among civil rights leaders (see Douglas Brinkley, *Rosa Parks* [New York: Viking, 2000]). Regardless, it and many other acts during the civil rights era can be counted as examples of civil courage.

13 See Richard Swedberg, "Civil Courage (*Zivilcourage*): The Case of Knut Wicksell," *Theory and Society* 28 (1999): 501–28. No other reference to the term *civil courage* seems to exist in English, but Swedberg cites several sources in German and Swedish.

14 See the Fourteenth Amendment: "No State shall make or enforce any law which shall abridge the privileges or immunities of citizens of the United States," and *Black's Law Dictionary*, 6th ed.: "A power, privilege, or immunity guaranteed under a constitution, statutes or decisional laws, or claimed as a result of long usage."

15 For a discussion of rights and their origins within American beliefs, see Barry Shain, ed., *The Nature of Rights at the American Founding and Beyond* (Charlottesville: University of Virginia Press, 2007).

16 See Charles Epp, *The Rights Revolution* (Chicago: University of Chicago Press, 1998): "Sustained judicial attention and approval for individual rights grew primarily out of pressure from below, not leadership from above" (2). See also Roy Fleming, "The Public and the Supreme Court," *American Journal of Political Science* 41 (1997): 468–98; Fleming argues that there is a strong connection between prevailing public opinion and Supreme Court decision making.

17 Observers since Tocqueville have commented that the more significant brake on the discussion and dissemination of unpopular ideas in America is public opinion rather than government. In this view it is the high cultural regard for mainstream beliefs, and the suspicion that accrues to those who go against them, that is the more functional limit to free expression (see Tocqueville, *Democracy in America*, vol. 1, part II, chap. 9, 243–45, and vol. 2, part I, chap. 2, 407–10).

18 Alexander Bickel, *The Least Dangerous Branch* (New York: Bobbs-Merrill, 1962), 266.

19 Tilly and Tarrow, *Contentious Politics*, 114-19.
20 Hunter, *Culture Wars*; Mark Brewer and Jeffrey Stonecash, *Split: Class and Cultural Divides in American Politics* (Washington, D.C.: CQ Press, 2006).
21 For this reason there are explicitly Jewish gun rights organizations. A well-known poster with the slogan "All in favor of 'gun control' raise your right hand" displays Hitler doing a Nazi salute, a reference to the Nazi-era restrictions on firearms among Jews, inhibiting their ability to resist persecution (see the Jews for the Preservation of Firearms Ownership website, http://jpfo.org).
22 Sacred rhetoric may be particularly suited to the medium of bumper stickers, as they are provocative by design and require short statements that do not allow complex expression but instead encourage short evocations of bounds and authorities. Noteworthy gun rights bumper stickers include "God, Guts and Guns Keep America Free" (an alternative to God + Guns = Freedom), "Only Crooked Politicians Fear Armed Citizens," "A Man With a Gun Is a Citizen. A Man Without a Gun Is a Subject," and "Democide—What Happens When People Are Disarmed." Humor and ridicule are other powerful aspects of bumper-sticker rhetoric, as in "I Support the Right to Arm Bears." Other highly sacralized issues such as abortion also display the same tendency to find expression on bumper stickers—for example, "Choose Life, Your Mother Did," the opposite of "Keep Your Hands Off My Body."
23 This understanding of the Second Amendment has been endorsed by the recent landmark decisions of the Supreme Court. In *District of Columbia v. Heller* (2008), the Court ruled that the amendment protects an individual right to self-defense, alongside the collective right of bearing arms against potential government tyranny. For the first time in 2010, the Court addressed the question of whether bearing arms was a fundamental right under the Fourteenth Amendment, according it the highest level of constitutional protection. In *McDonald v. Chicago* (2010), the Court recognized this fundamental individual right, placing it on par with freedom of speech and religion. Two notes are worth emphasizing in regard to the meaning of these rulings in relation to social movements and sacred rhetoric. The first is that during the long lull in the Supreme Court's decisions on the Second Amendment (from *U.S. v. Miller* in 1939 to 2008), the gun rights movement had popularized its interpretation of the amendment, which was increasingly validated by scholarly and now judicial authorities. But the movement preceded the Court's agreement. A second crucial point is that assuming the Supreme Court's current rulings are synonymous with the meaning of the Constitution is a common error. The Court has made and does make mistakes. In one sense it is appropriate to grant the Court its due respect,

as we understand the Constitution through its interpretations. In another sense it is not the current view of the Court but the binding meaning of the Constitution that is at issue, and the two may not be the same. Social movement activists are more likely to argue that the *Constitution* is sacred, not the Supreme Court's rulings on it, a point that is taken seriously by antiabortion activists on the right and antigun activists on the left, among others. For a further clarification of the individual and collective rights protected by the Second Amendment, see the influential book by Akhil Amar, *The Bill of Rights* (New Haven, Conn.: Yale University Press, 1998).

24 *The Omega Man* was remade in 2007 with Will Smith as the central character, though more in keeping with the story line of the original novel and with its title, *I Am Legend*. Some argue that the recent resurgence of post-apocalyptic films, including the zombie genre, is driven by post-9/11 worries about challenges to modernity.

25 Compare this to Mao's well-known quote: "Power comes from the barrel of a gun." While these two lines may seem at first to express similar sentiments, on closer examination it is more accurate to say that Heston's line is the antithetical response to Mao's. If government tyranny (Mao's power) comes from the barrel of a gun, this is precisely why freedom requires an armed citizenry, so that that form of power can be resisted.

26 A transcript of this speech can be found on the NRA website at http://www.nrahq.org/transcripts/hestonam.asp. Emphasis added.

27 See the transcripts on the NRA website (http://www.nrahq.org/transcripts).

28 This argument was made explicitly by the more militant wings of the civil rights movement, especially the Black Panthers. Another connection of civil rights to gun rights is the argument about the racist origins of gun control, essentially that gun control legislation in the United States began as an attempt to keep firearms away from freedmen following the Civil War. Again, the historical veracity of this argument is not the point; what it illustrates is the rhetorical connection of gun rights to civil rights.

29 Durkheim, *Elementary Forms of Religious Life*, 100, 118.

30 Durkheim, 236.

31 Heston, 2000 NRA convention speech.

32 Durkheim, *Elementary Forms of Religious Life*, 139.

33 Durkheim, 139.

34 Stephen E. Lucas and Martin J. Medhurst, *Words of a Century: The Top 100 American Speeches, 1900–1999* (New York: Oxford University Press, 2009).

35 Kennedy's inaugural address was given on January 20, 1961. Reagan's speech in front of the Brandenburg Gate in Berlin took place on June 12, 1987.

36 The famous mural of John Brown by John Steuart Curry is in the Kansas Statehouse.

Chapter 6

1. Otis M. Walter and Robert L. Scott, *Thinking and Speaking: A Guide to Intelligent Oral Communication* (New York: Macmillan, 1962); emphasis in original.
2. Unlike the participants' responses in the experiments described earlier, the candidates were not coded for both sacred and negotiable rhetoric, but instead only their invocation of sacredness. The question here is not whether they are influenced toward one mode of reasoning or the other, but whether they do or do not employ the elements of sacred rhetoric that could aid their message.
3. $t = 5.16$, which with thirty-three degrees of freedom represents a p level of .001, or a 99.9% chance that Bush and Gore employ different levels of sacred rhetoric. Three of the exchanges were excluded from the analysis because they were in response to fluff questions, producing no meaningful response. These were on whether the candidates could handle unexpected events, whether they had credibility, and whether they would keep their pledges if elected. The answers offered by both candidates were essentially yes, yes, and yes.
4. Mentions of God by Bush: "I'm asking for your vote, and God bless" (end of debate 2); "I, too, want to extend my prayers and blessings, God's blessings, on the families whose lives were overturned" (beginning of debate 3, regarding the death of Missouri governor Mel Carnahan); "Should I be fortunate enough to become your president, when I put my hand on the Bible, I will swear to not only uphold the laws of the land, but I will also swear to uphold the honor and the dignity of the office to which I have been elected, so help me God. Thank you very much" (end of debate 3). By Gore: "Tipper and I have four children. And God bless them, every one of them decided on their own to come here this evening" (debate 3, regarding morality and Hollywood).

    Mentions of faith by Bush: "faith-based programs being a part of after-school programs" (debate 2 on guns); "I think that after-school money ought to be available for faith-based programs and charitable programs" (debate 3 on morality). By Gore: reference to Matthew quoted in the text.

    Mentions of the Bible by Bush: reference to swearing in on the Bible just quoted. By Gore: reference to Matthew quoted earlier.

    References to God, the Bible, or faith were considered an element of sacred rhetoric only if they were a clear citation of authority, so pro forma references such as "God bless America" were not counted. If the meaningful examples are removed from the analysis, Bush's average of absolutist reasoning per response only drops from 2.0 to 1.9.
5. Outside the presidential debates, the 2000 campaign may have been remarkably more religious than many contemporary campaigns, driven by Bush's

religiosity and the unusual degree of religious rhetoric on the Democratic side, especially from Joe Lieberman (see Martin Medhurst, "Religious Rhetoric and the *Ethos* of Democracy: A Case Study of the 2000 Presidential Campaign," in *The Ethos of Rhetoric*, ed. Michael J. Hyde (Columbia: University of South Carolina Press, 2004), 114-35.

6   This is similar to another narrative employed by Gore: "There is a man here tonight named George McKinney from Milwaukee. He's seventy years old, has high blood pressure, his wife has heart trouble. They have an income of $25,000 a year. They can't pay for their prescription drugs. They're some of the ones that go to Canada regularly in order to get their prescription drugs. Under my plan, half of their costs would be paid right away. Under Governor Bush's plan, they would get not one penny for four to five years and then they would be forced to go into an HMO or to an insurance company and ask them for coverage, but there would be no limit on the premiums or the deductibles or any of the terms and conditions."

7   Popkin, *Reasoning Voter*.

8   On the role of certainty in presidential rhetoric, see Roderick Hart, *Verbal Style and the Presidency* (New York: Academic, 1984); Hart analyzes four major variables in presidential speech from Truman to Reagan, including activity, optimism, realism, and certainty, or "statements indicating resoluteness, inflexibility, and completeness" (16).

9   On the influence of character assessments, see Kathryn Doherty and James Gimpel, "Candidate Character vs. the Economy in the 1992 Election," *Political Behavior* 19, no. 3 (1997): 177-96; Carolyn Funk, "Bringing Candidates into Models of Candidate Evaluation," *Journal of Politics* 61 (1999): 700-720; Paul Goren, "Character Weakness, Partisan Bias, and Presidential Evaluation," *American Journal of Political Science* 46, no. 3 (2002): 627-41; Arthur Miller, Martin Wattenberg, and Oksana Malanchuk, "Schematic Assessments of Presidential Candidates," *American Political Science Review* 80, no. 2 (1986): 520-40; Barbara Norrander, "Correlates of Vote Choice in the 1980 Presidential Primaries," *Journal of Politics* 48 (1986): 156-67; and David C. Barker, Adam Lawrence, and Margit Tavits, "Values, Partisanship, and 'Candidate Centered Politics' in U.S. Presidential Nominations," *Electoral Studies* 25 (2006): 599-610.

10 *Wall Street Journal*, December 21, 2004, A1, column 3.

Chapter 7

1   The debates are now an expected norm in presidential politics, under the auspices of the Commission on Presidential Debates, which took over from the League of Women Voters in 1988. While candidates are under no legal

obligation to participate, the norm seems to have become powerful enough that they are unlikely to refuse, though each campaign season includes negotiations over the number of debates, the operating rules, the selection of moderators, and whether third-party candidates will be included.

2. The only direct reference to God in all three debates is by Carter (in his closing statement of the foreign policy debate). Ford refrains from almost any religious reference.

3. For an interesting discussion of Carter's moralism in foreign policy rhetoric, see Mary Stuckey, *Jimmy Carter, Human Rights, and the National Agenda* (College Station: Texas A&M University Press, 2008).

4. President Carter agreed to only one debate in the 1980 campaign. An earlier debate took place between only Ronald Reagan and the independent candidate John Anderson.

5. Jeffrey K. Tulis, *The Rhetorical Presidency* (Princeton, N.J.: Princeton University Press, 1987).

6. Tulis, 189.

7. Tulis, 189–202.

8. The Willie Horton ad (sponsored by the National Security Political Action Committee) played the following script: *Announcer:* "Bush and Dukakis on crime. Bush supports the death penalty for first-degree murderers. Dukakis not only opposes the death penalty, he allowed first-degree murderers to have weekend passes from prison. One was Willie Horton, who murdered a boy in a robbery, stabbing him nineteen times. Despite a life sentence, Horton received ten weekend passes from prison. Horton fled, kidnapped a young couple, stabbing the man and repeatedly raping his girlfriend. Weekend prison passes. Dukakis on crime."

9. The Bush campaign sponsored two ads that addressed the same topic without mentioning Horton directly. The "Revolving Door" ad: *Announcer:* "As Governor, Michael Dukakis vetoed mandatory sentences for drug dealers. He vetoed the death penalty. His revolving-door prison policy gave weekend furloughs to first-degree murderers not eligible for parole. While out, many committed other crimes like kidnapping and rape, and many are still at large. Now Michael Dukakis says he wants to do for America what he's done for Massachusetts. America can't afford that risk." The "Credibility" ad: *Announcer:* "One person has released killers sentenced to life without parole on unsupervised weekend passes, pardoned forty-nine convicted drug dealers and offenders, and commuted the sentences of a record fifty-three murderers. But how did Michael Dukakis defend his record in the debate?" *Dukakis:* "I'm opposed to the death penalty. I think everybody knows that. I'm also very tough on violent crime." *(Audience laughter). Announcer:* "Even Michael Dukakis can't say he's tough on crime with a straight face."

Chapter 8

1. Ron Suskind, "Without a Doubt: Faith, Certainty, and the Presidency of George W. Bush," *New York Times Magazine*, October 17, 2004, 44–51.
2. The five other candidates for the Democratic nomination were Joe Biden (senator from Delaware since 1972, chair of the Foreign Relations Committee), Chris Dodd (senator from Connecticut since 1980, Democratic National Committee chair 1994–1997), Mike Gravel (senator from Alaska 1968–1981, noted for his role in releasing the Pentagon Papers and leading a filibuster to end the Vietnam draft), Dennis Kucinich (congressman from Ohio since 1996, former mayor of Cleveland), and Bill Richardson (governor of New Mexico since 2002, former congressman 1982–1997, ambassador to the UN and secretary of energy under Clinton).
3. The other candidates were Sam Brownback (senator from Kansas since 1996, replacing Bob Dole), James Gilmore (former governor of Virginia and chair of the National Council on Readiness and Preparedness [inheritor of the Gilmore Commission on homeland security]), Mike Huckabee (governor of Arkansas 1996–2007 and Baptist minister), Duncan Hunter (congressman since 1980 and Vietnam veteran), Ron Paul (nine-term congressman, former U.S. Air Force flight surgeon, and 1988 candidate for the Libertarian Party), Tom Tancredo (congressman since 1998), and Tommy Thompson (four-time governor of Wisconsin, secretary of health and human services 2001–2003).
4. It is important to note that the gauges of sacred rhetoric for these debates are not directly comparable to those of the presidential debates examined earlier. In the presidential exchanges, each candidate answered all questions and had approximately ninety seconds plus often additional follow-up time. In the primary debates, questions were often directly to only one or two candidates, and time allotted was much shorter, often thirty seconds or less. Hence direct comparisons of the number of facets of sacred rhetoric per answer are not comparable, and for the primary debates the tables center on the total number of facets for the whole debate.
5. See Denise Bostdorff's detailed examination of Republican war rhetoric in the primary debates (Bostdorff, "Judgment, Experience, and Leadership: Candidate Debates on the Iraq War in the 2008 Presidential Debates," *Rhetoric and Public Affairs* 12, no. 2 [2009]: 223–78). She concludes that unlike Democrats, the Republican candidates, especially John McCain, increasingly discussed the Iraq War as an issue of moral resolve and determination.
6. "Giuliani Tempers Tough Image, Trading Growl for a Smile," *New York Times*, May 20, 2007, A1. Powell argues that Giuliani makes the same biting retorts he employed in his New York City days, but in a kinder fashion now. On his radio talk show as mayor, when challenged about his antiferret

policy, he said, "The excessive concern that you have with ferrets is something you should examine with a therapist, not with me. You are devoting your life to weasels. There is something really, really very sad about you."

7   For a concise summary of this transition, see Kirkpatrick Sale, *The Green Revolution: The American Environmental Movement 1962–1992* (New York: Hill & Wang, 1993).

8   The comparative brevity of the third debate is reflected in the number of words spoken. The word counts for debates 1 and 2 are 15,229 and 20,250, respectively, but the count for debate 3 is only 12,915 words.

9   The only sacred mention outside of the third debate was by Chris Dodd, who invoked moral outrage at the status of health care in America: "There's not a person in this audience or who's watching this program who wouldn't tell you that they've encountered the problems of the health care system in this country. It is shameful. We rank forty-second in infant mortality in the United States worldwide. We rank forty-fifth in life expectancy. It is shameful that in the twenty-first century we have forty-seven million of our fellow citizens without health care coverage; nine million children. And the number's growing every single day."

10 Warren is the founder of Saddleback Church in Lake Forest, California, one of the largest congregations in America at over twenty thousand members. He is the author of *The Purpose Driven Life* (Grand Rapids: Zondervan, 2002), which has sold more than thirty million copies.

11 See, for example, "Obama Says He Was Too Flip on Abortion Issue," *MSNBC.com*, September 7, 2008, http://www.msnbc.msn.com/id/26593948; Mary Lu Carnevale, "Obama Says 'Above My Pay Grade' Comment Was Too Flip," Washington Wire, *Wall Street Journal*, September 7, 2008, http://blogs.wsj.com/washwire/2008/09/07/obama-says-above-my-pay-grade-comment-was-too-flip/tab/article; and Ken Kusmer, "Palin Slams Obama: Abortion Isn't Above My Pay Grade," *HuffPost Politics*, April 16, 2009, http://www.huffingtonpost.com/2009/04/16/palin-slams-obama-abortio_n_188026.html.

12 "Round 1 in Debates Goes to Obama, Poll Says," *CNNPolitics.com*, September 27, 2008, http://www.cnn.com/2008/POLITICS/09/27/debate.poll/index.html.

13 See Shailagh Murray and Charles Babington, "Democrats Struggle to Seize Opportunity," *New York Times*, March 7, 2006, A1.

14 See George Lakoff's important book *Thinking Points*: "In surveying conservative and progressive arguments, we have noticed another important regularity. Conservatives seem to argue on the basis of direct, individual causation, while progressives tend to argue on the basis of systemic, complex causation" (62).

15 Compare this to Obama's response on Iran in the presidential debates: "I will do everything that's required to prevent it."

16 See especially Lakoff, *Political Mind*, ch. 8.
17 Lakoff, *Political Mind*, 153.
18 Jodi Wilgoren, "Kerry on Hunting Photo-Op to Help Image," *New York Times*, October 22, 2004, http://www.nytimes.com/2004/10/22/politics/campaign/22kerry.html. The photo and the mocking tone of the story were even picked up by the foreign press, including the BBC ("Kerry Goes Hunting for Ohio Votes," *BBC News*, October 22, 2004, http://news.bbc.co.uk/2/hi/americas/3762770.stm). In her book *Picture Perfect: Life in the Age of the Photo Op* (Princeton, N.J.: Princeton University Press, 2008), Kiku Adatto describes the event as an example of "failed photo ops," which, "like successful ones, function as metaphors, symbols, or condensed arguments in public debate": "Pictures, like words, are fair game, part of the language of partisan politics in a democracy. For example, when the Democratic nominee John Kerry went goose hunting in Iowa to boost his appeal to hunters and rural voters during the 2004 presidential campaign, the Republicans were quick to strike back" (16).
19 Lakoff, *Moral Politics*, *Don't Think of an Elephant*, *Thinking Points*, *Whose Freedom?*, and *The Political Mind*.
20 Lakoff, *Political Mind*, 82.
21 Lakoff, *Whose Freedom?*, 11, 16.
22 It may be useful to distinguish between Lakoff's use of the term *framing* and how political psychologists have employed the same term. What political psychologists such as Tom Nelson and his colleagues call framing is what Lakoff calls "surface framing" rather than his emphasis on "deep framing." Whereas surface framing entails crafting each message so that it changes the considerations that are consciously in play, deep framing involves crafting all political messages so that they invoke the same central nonconscious metaphor (the nurturant parent). The more the deep frame (government as protector) is established in the public mind, the more effective subsequent surface frames will be. Lakoff's use of the term *frame* may be more akin in political psychology usage to *schema* or *script*.
23 In a review of Lakoff's *Whose Freedom?*, Geoffrey Nunberg, also a linguist at Berkeley, writes, "Why should the 'nation-as-family' metaphor be paramount in dividing the sides, and why should everything follow from that one schema? . . . Lakoff doesn't give any direct evidence for that hypothesis: no surveys, interviews, case studies or ethnographic investigations; no database counts or empirical investigation of language use; no historical or contrastive analyses; no experiments that support the centrality of the family metaphor over others" (Nunberg, "Frame Game," Open University blog, *New Republic*, November 4, 2006, http://www.tnr.com/blog/open-university/frame-game).

24 For empirical support, see David Barker and James Tinnick, "Competing Visions of Parental Roles and Ideological Constraint," *American Political Science Review* 100, no. 2 (2006): 249-63.

Conclusion and Methodological Appendix

1 Aaron Wildavsky, "A Cultural Theory of Preference Formation," *American Political Science Review* 81, no. 1 (1987): 3-22.
2 Gutmann and Thompson, *Democracy and Disagreement*.
3 Berlin, *Crooked Timber*, 13.
4 Donald Kinder and Thomas Palfrey, *Experimental Foundations of Political Science* (Ann Arbor: University of Michigan Press, 1993); David Martin, *Doing Psychology Experiments* (New York: Brooks/Cole, 1996).
5 David Sears, "College Sophomores in the Laboratory: Influences of a Narrow Data Base on Psychology's View of Human Nature," *Journal of Personality and Social Psychology* 51 (1986): 515-30.

References

Adatto, Kiku. *Picture Perfect: Life in the Age of the Photo Op*. Princeton, N.J.: Princeton University Press, 2008.
Allport, Gordon. *Pattern and Growth in Personality*. New York: Harcourt, 1961.
Alvarez, Michael, and John Brehm. *Hard Choices, Easy Answers*. Cambridge, Mass.: Harvard University Press, 2003.
Amar, Akhil. *The Bill of Rights*. New Haven, Conn.: Yale University Press, 1998.
Arkoun, Mohammed. "Émergences et problèmes dans le monde musulman contemporain (1960–1985)." *Islamochristiana* 12 (1986): 151–73.
Barber, Benjamin. *Strong Democracy: Participatory Politics for a New Age*. Berkeley: University of California Press, 1984.
Barker, David. *Rushed to Judgment: Talk Radio, Persuasion, and American Political Behavior*. New York: Columbia University Press, 2002.
———. "The Spirit of Capitalism? Religious Doctrine, Values, and Economic Attitude Constructs." *Political Behavior* 22, no. 1 (2000): 1–19.
———. "Values, Frames, and Persuasion in Presidential Nomination Campaigns." *Political Behavior* 27, no. 4 (2005): 375–94.
Barker, David, and James Tinnick. "Competing Visions of Parental Roles and Ideological Constraint." *American Political Science Review* 100, no. 2 (2006): 249–63.
Barker, David C., Adam Lawrence, and Margit Tavits. "Values, Partisanship, and 'Candidate Centered Politics' in U.S. Presidential Nominations." *Electoral Studies* 25 (2006): 599–610.
Baron, Jonathan, and Sarah Lesher. "How Serious Are Expressions of Protected Values?" *Journal of Experimental Psychology: Applied* 6 (2000): 183–94.

Baron, Jonathan, and Mark Spranca. "Protected Values." *Organizational Behavior and Decision Processes* 70, no. 1 (1997): 1-16.
Barzun, Jacques. *Is Democratic Theory for Export?* New York: Carnegie Council on Ethics and International Affairs, 1986.
Benhabib, Seyla. *The Claims of Culture: Equality and Diversity in the Global Era.* Princeton, N.J.: Princeton University Press, 2002.
———. "Toward a Deliberative Model of Democratic Legitimacy." In *Democracy and Difference: Contesting the Boundaries of the Political,* edited by Seyla Benhabib. Princeton, N.J.: Princeton University Press, 1996.
Berger, Peter. *The Desecularization of the World: Resurgent Religion and World Politics.* Washington, D.C.: Ethics and Public Policy Center, 1999.
———. *The Sacred Canopy: Elements of a Sociological Theory of Religion.* New York: Anchor Books, 1967.
Berger, Peter, and Thomas Luckmann. *The Social Construction of Reality.* New York: Anchor Books, 1966.
Berlin, Isaiah. *The Crooked Timber of Humanity: Chapters in the History of Ideas.* New York: Vintage Books, 1992.
———. *Four Essays on Liberty.* New York: Oxford University Press, 1970.
Bickel, Alexander. *The Least Dangerous Branch.* New York: Bobbs-Merrill, 1962.
Bostdorff, Denise. "Judgment, Experience, and Leadership: Candidate Debates on the Iraq War in the 2008 Presidential Debates." *Rhetoric and Public Affairs* 12, no. 2 (2009): 223-78.
Brewer, Mark, and Jeffrey Stonecash. *Split: Class and Cultural Divides in American Politics.* Washington, D.C.: CQ Press, 2006.
Brewer, Paul. "Value Words and Lizard Brains: Do Citizens Deliberate about Appeals to Their Core Values?" *Political Psychology* 22, no. 1 (2001): 45-64.
Brinkley, Douglas. *Rosa Parks.* New York: Viking, 2000.
Burstein, Paul, and April Linton. "The Impact of Political Parties, Interest Groups, and Social Movement Organization on Public Policy." *Social Forces* 81 (2002): 380-408.
Burstein, Paul, and Sarah Sausner. "The Incidence and Impact of Policy-Oriented Collective Action: Competing Views." *Sociological Forum* 20 (2005): 403-19.
Calhoun, Craig. "'New Social Movements' of the Nineteenth Century." In *Repertoires and Cycles of Collective Action,* edited by Mark Traugott. Durham, N.C.: Duke University Press, 1995.
Davis, Robert. *Politics Online: Blogs, Chatrooms, and Discussion Groups in American Democracy.* New York: Routledge, 2005.

Davis, Robert, and Diana Owen. *New Media and American Politics*. New York: Oxford University Press, 1998.
DeCanio, Samuel. "Bringing the State Back In . . . Again." *Critical Review* 14, no. 2 (2000): 139–46.
Delli Carpini, Michael X., and Scott Keeter. *What Americans Know about Politics and Why It Matters*. New Haven, Conn.: Yale University Press, 1996.
Doherty, Kathryn, and James Gimpel. "Candidate Character vs. the Economy in the 1992 Election." *Political Behavior* 19, no. 3 (1997): 177–96.
Downs, Anthony. *An Economic Theory of Democracy*. New York: Harper & Row, 1957.
Druckman, James. "The Implications of Framing Effects for Citizen Competence." *Political Behavior* 23 (2001): 225–56.
———. "On the Limits of Framing Effects: Who Can Frame?" *Journal of Politics* 63 (2001): 1041–67.
———. "Political Preference Formation: Competition, Deliberation, and the (Ir)relevance of Framing Effects." *American Political Science Review* 98, no. 4 (2004): 671–86.
Dryzek, John. *Discursive Democracy: Politics, Policy, and Political Science*. Cambridge: Cambridge University Press, 1990.
Durkheim, Emile. *The Elementary Forms of Religious Life*. New York: Free Press, 1995. First published 1912.
Eagly, Alice, and Shelly Chaiken. *The Psychology of Attitudes*. New York: Harcourt, Brace, Jovanovich, 1993.
Eliade, Mircea. *The Sacred and the Profane*. New York: Harcourt, 1957.
Eliasoph, Nina. *Avoiding Politics: How Americans Produce Apathy in Everyday Life*. Cambridge: Cambridge University Press, 1998.
Elster, Jon. *Sour Grapes: Studies in the Subversion of Rationality*. Cambridge: Cambridge University Press, 1983.
———. *Ulysses and the Sirens*. Cambridge: Cambridge University Press, 1984.
Entman, Robert. "Framing: Toward Clarification of a Fractured Paradigm." *Journal of Communication* 43, no. 4 (1993): 51–58.
———. *Projections of Power: Framing News, Public Opinion and US Foreign Policy*. Chicago: University of Chicago Press, 2004.
Epp, Charles. *The Rights Revolution*. Chicago: University of Chicago Press, 1998.
Feldman, Stanley, and John Zaller. "The Political Culture of Ambivalence: Ideological Responses to the Welfare State." *American Journal of Political Science* 36 (1992): 268–307.

Finkel, Steven E. "Reexamining the 'Minimal Effects' Model in Recent Presidential Campaigns." *Journal of Politics* 55, no. 1 (1993): 1-21.
Fiorina, Morris. *Culture War? The Myth of a Polarized America.* New York: Pearson, Longman, 2005.
Fishkin, James. *Democracy and Deliberation: New Directions for Democratic Reform.* New Haven, Conn.: Yale University Press, 1991.
Fiske, Alan. *Structure and Social Life: The Four Elementary Forms of Human Relations.* New York: Free Press, 1991.
Fiske, Alan, and Philip Tetlock. "Taboo Trade-Offs: Reactions to Transactions That Transgress Spheres of Justice." *Political Psychology* 18, no. 2 (1997): 255-97.
Fleming, Roy. "The Public and the Supreme Court." *American Journal of Political Science* 41 (1997): 468-98.
Frank, Thomas. *What's the Matter with Kansas? How Conservatives Won the Heart of America.* New York: Henry Holt, 2004.
Friedman, Jeffrey. "Introduction: Public Ignorance and Political Theory." *Critical Review* 12, no. 4 (1998): 397-412.
Fukuyama, Francis. *The End of History.* New York: Free Press, 1992.
Funk, Carolyn. "Bringing Candidates into Models of Candidate Evaluation." *Journal of Politics* 61 (1999): 700-720.
Gamson, William. *Talking Politics.* Cambridge: Cambridge University Press, 1992.
Garrison, William Lloyd. *Resolution Adopted by the Antislavery Society.* 1843.
———. *Salutatory of the Liberator,* January 1, 1831.
Goldstein, Evan R.. "Who Framed George Lakoff?" *Chronicle of Higher Education,* August 15, 2008, B6-B9.
Goren, Paul. "Character Weakness, Partisan Bias, and Presidential Evaluation." *American Journal of Political Science* 46, no. 3 (2002): 627-41.
Green, John, James Guth, Lyman Kellstedt, and Corwin Schmidt. *Religion and the Culture Wars.* Lanham, Md.: Rowman & Littlefield, 1996.
Green, Melanie, Penny Visser, and Phil Tetlock. "Coping with Accountability Cross-Pressures: Low-Effort Evasive Tactics and High-Effort Quests for Complex Compromises." *Personality and Social Psychology Bulletin* 26 (2000): 1380-91.
Greene, Graham. *The End of the Affair.* New York: Viking, 1951.
Gutmann, Amy, and Dennis Thompson. *Democracy and Disagreement.* Cambridge, Mass.: Harvard University Press, 1996.
Habermas, Jurgen. *Between Facts and Norms: Contributions to a Discourse Theory of Law and Democracy.* Cambridge, Mass.: MIT Press, 1996.

———. *The Theory of Communicative Action*. Boston: Polity, 1984.
Hart, Roderick. *Verbal Style and the Presidency*. New York: Academic, 1984.
Hibbing, John, and Elizabeth Theiss-Morse. *Congress as Public Enemy: Public Attitudes toward Political Institutions*. Cambridge: Cambridge University Press, 1995.
Hochschild, Jennifer. *What's Fair? American Beliefs about Distributive Justice*. Cambridge, Mass.: Harvard University Press, 1981.
Hoffer, Eric. *The True Believer: Thoughts on the Nature of Mass Movements*. New York: Harper & Brothers, 1951.
Hunter, James Davison. *Before the Shooting Begins: Searching for Democracy in America's Culture War*. New York: Free Press, 1994.
———. *Culture Wars: The Struggle to Define America*. New York: Basic Books, 1991.
Hurwitz, Jon, and Mark Peffley. "How Are Foreign Policy Attitudes Structured: A Hierarchical Model." *American Political Science Review* 81 (1987): 1099-120.
Hyde, Michael. *Perfection: Coming to Terms with Being Human*. Waco, Tex.: Baylor University Press, 2010.
Iyengar, Shanto, and Donald Kinder. *News That Matters*. Chicago: University of Chicago Press, 1987.
Jacoby, William. "Issue Framing and Public Opinion on Government Spending." *American Journal of Political Science* 44, no. 4 (2000): 750-67.
Johnston, Hank, and Bert Klandermans. *Social Movements and Culture*. Minneapolis: University of Minnesota Press, 1995.
Kennedy, Christopher. *Trouble with the Machine*. New York: Low Fidelity, 2003.
Kinder, Donald, and Thomas Palfrey. *Experimental Foundations of Political Science*. Ann Arbor: University of Michigan Press, 1993.
Klandermans, Bert. "The Social Construction of Protest." In *Frontiers in Social Movement Theory*, edited by Aldon Morris and Carol McClurg Mueller. New Haven, Conn.: Yale University Press, 1992.
Kluckhohn, Clyde. "Values and Value-Orientations in the Theory of Action." In *Toward a General Theory of Action*, edited by Talcott Parsons and Edward A. Shils. New York: Harper, 1951.
Krosnick, Jon, and Donald Kinder. "Altering the Foundations of Support for the President through Priming." *American Political Science Review* 84, no. 2 (1990): 497-512.
Kuran, Timur. *Private Truths, Public Lies: The Social Consequences of Preference Falsification*. Cambridge, Mass.: Harvard University Press, 1995.

Lakoff, George. *Don't Think of an Elephant*. White River Junction, Vt.: Chelsea Green, 2004.
———. *Moral Politics*. Chicago: University of Chicago Press, 1996.
———. *The Political Mind*. New York: Viking, 2008.
———. *Thinking Points*. New York: Farrar, Straus & Giroux, 2006.
———. *Whose Freedom?* New York: Farrar, Straus & Giroux, 2006.
———. *Women, Fire, and Dangerous Things*. Chicago: University of Chicago Press, 1987.
Lakoff, George, and Mark Johnson. *Metaphors We Live By*. Chicago: University of Chicago Press, 1980.
Lane, Robert. *Political Ideology: Why the Common Man Believes What He Does*. New York: Free Press, 1962.
———. *Political Man*. New York: Free Press, 1972.
Layman, Geoffrey. "Culture Wars in the American Party System." *American Politics Quarterly* 27, no. 1 (1999): 89–121.
Lucas, Stephen E., and Martin J. Medhurst. *Words of a Century: The Top 100 American Speeches, 1900–1999*. New York: Oxford University Press, 2009.
Lupia, Arthur. "Shortcuts vs. Encyclopedias: Information and Voting Behavior in California Insurance Reform Elections." *American Political Science Review* 88 (1994): 63–76.
Lutz, Donald. *The Origins of American Constitutionalism*. Baton Rouge: Louisiana State University Press, 1988.
March, James G., and Johan P. Olsen. *Rediscovering Institutions: The Organizational Basis of Politics*. New York: Free Press, 1989.
Marietta, Morgan, and Mark Perlman. "The Uses of Authority in Economics: Shared Intellectual Legacies as the Foundation of Persuasion." *American Journal of Economics and Sociology* 59, no. 2 (2000): 151–89.
Markoff, John, and Daniel Regan. "Religion, the State and Political Legitimacy in the World's Constitutions." In *Church-State Relations: Tensions and Transitions*, edited by Thomas Robbins and Roland Robertson. New Brunswick, N.J.: Transaction, 1987.
Martin, David. *Doing Psychology Experiments*. New York: Brooks/Cole, 1996.
McGee, Michael. "Social Movement: Phenomenon or Meaning?" *Central States Speech Journal* 31 (1980): 233–44.
Medhurst, Martin. "Religious Rhetoric and the *Ethos* of Democracy: A Case Study of the 2000 Presidential Campaign." In *The Ethos of Rhetoric*, edited by Michael J. Hyde. Columbia: University of South Carolina Press, 2004.

Melucci, Alberto. *Nomads of the Present: Social Movements and Individual Needs in Contemporary Society*. Philadelphia: Temple University Press, 1989.
———. "The Symbolic Challenge of Contemporary Movements." *Social Research* 52, no. 4 (1985): 789–816.
Miller, Arthur, Martin Wattenberg, and Oksana Malanchuk. "Schematic Assessments of Presidential Candidates." *American Political Science Review* 80, no. 2 (1986): 520–40.
Mosca, Gaetano. *The Ruling Class*. New York: McGraw-Hill, 1939.
Moscovici, Serge. *The Invention of Society*. London: Polity, 1993.
Mutz, Diana. *Hearing the Other Side: Deliberative versus Participatory Democracy*. Cambridge: Cambridge University Press, 2006.
Nelson, Thomas E., and Donald R. Kinder. "Issue Frames and Group Centrism in American Public Opinion." *Journal of Politics* 58 (1996): 1055–78.
Nelson, Thomas E., and Zoe M. Oxley. "Framing Effects on Belief Importance and Opinion." *Journal of Politics* 61, no. 4 (1999): 1040–67.
Nelson, Thomas E., Rosalee A. Clawson, and Zoe M. Oxley. "Media Framing of a Civil Liberties Conflict and Its Effect on Tolerance." *American Political Science Review* 91, no. 3 (1997): 567–84.
Nelson, Thomas E., Zoe M. Oxley, and Rosalee A. Clawson. "Toward a Psychology of Framing Effects." *Political Behavior* 19, no. 3 (1997): 221–46.
Noelle-Neumann, Elisabeth. *The Spiral of Silence: Public Opinion—Our Social Skin*. Chicago: University of Chicago Press, 1984.
Norrander, Barbara. "Correlates of Vote Choice in the 1980 Presidential Primaries." *Journal of Politics* 48 (1986): 156–67.
Offe, Claus. "New Social Movements: Challenging the Boundaries of Institutional Politics." *Social Research* 52, no. 4 (1985): 817–68.
Olson, Mancur. *The Logic of Collective Action: Public Goods and the Theory of Groups*. Cambridge, Mass.: Harvard University Press, 1965.
Pateman, Carole. *Participation and Democratic Theory*. Cambridge: Cambridge University Press, 1970.
Peffley, Mark, and Jon Hurwitz. "A Hierarchical Model of Attitude Constraint." *American Journal of Political Science* 29 (1985): 871–90.
Piven, Frances Fox, and Richard Cloward. *Poor People's Movements: Why They Succeed, How They Fail*. New York: Pantheon Books, 1977.
Popkin, Samuel. *The Reasoning Voter*. Chicago: University of Chicago Press, 1991.
Ritov, Ilana, and Jonathan Baron. "Protected Values and Omission Bias." *Organizational Behavior and Human Decision Processes* 79, no. 2 (1999): 79–94.

Robinson, James Harvey. "The Still Small Voice of the Herd." *Political Science Quarterly* 32, no. 2 (1917): 312-19.
Rohan, Meg. "A Rose by Any Name? The Values Construct." *Personality and Social Psychology Review* 4, no. 3 (2000): 255-77.
Rokeach, Milton. *The Nature of Human Values.* New York: Free Press, 1973.
Rule, James. *Theories of Civil Violence.* Berkeley: University of California Press, 1988.
Sale, Kirkpatrick. *The Green Revolution: The American Environmental Movement 1962-1992.* New York: Hill & Wang, 1993.
Schumpeter, Joseph. *Capitalism, Socialism, and Democracy.* New York: Harper & Brothers, 1942.
Schwartz, Shalom. "Value Priorities and Behavior: Applying a Theory of Integrated Value Systems." In *The Psychology of Values: The Ontario Symposium, Volume 8*, edited by Clive Seligman, James Olson, and Mark Zanna. Mahwah, N.J.: Lawrence Erlbaum, 1996.
Sears, David. "College Sophomores in the Laboratory: Influences of a Narrow Data Base on Psychology's View of Human Nature." *Journal of Personality and Social Psychology* 51 (1986): 515-30.
Shain, Barry, ed. *The Nature of Rights at the American Founding and Beyond.* Charlottesville: University of Virginia Press, 2007.
Simon, Herbert. "Human Nature in Politics: The Dialogue of Psychology with Political Science." *American Political Science Review* 79 (1985): 293-304.
Skocpol, Theda, and Morris Fiorina. *Civic Engagement in American Democracy.* Washington, D.C.: Brookings, 1999.
Sniderman, Paul, Richard Brody, and Philip Tetlock. *Reasoning and Choice: Explorations in Political Psychology.* Cambridge: Cambridge University Press, 1991.
Snow, David, and Robert Benford. "Master Frames and Cycles of Protest." In *Frontiers in Social Movement Theory*, edited by Aldon Morris and Carol McClurg Mueller. New Haven, Conn.: Yale University Press, 1992.
Stuckey, Mary. *Jimmy Carter, Human Rights, and the National Agenda.* College Station: Texas A&M University Press, 2008.
Swedberg, Richard. "Civil Courage (*Zivilcourage*): The Case of Knut Wicksell." *Theory and Society* 28 (1999): 501-28.
Tarrow, Sidney. *Power in Movement: Social Movements and Contentious Politics.* Cambridge: Cambridge University Press, 1998.
Tetlock, Philip. "Thinking the Unthinkable: Sacred Values and Taboo Cognitions." *Trends in Cognitive Sciences* 7, no. 7 (2003): 320-24.

———. "A Value Pluralism Model of Ideological Reasoning." *Journal of Personality and Social Psychology* 50 (1986): 819-27.
Tetlock, Philip, Orie Kristel, Beth Elson, Melanie Green, and Jennifer Lerner. "The Psychology of the Unthinkable: Taboo Trade-Offs, Forbidden Base Rates, and Heretical Counterfactuals." *Journal of Personality and Social Psychology* 78, no. 5 (2000): 853-70.
Tetlock, Philip, Randall Peterson, and Jennifer Lerner. "Revising the Value Pluralism Model: Incorporating Social Content and Context Postulates." In *The Psychology of Values: The Ontario Symposium, Volume 8*, edited by Clive Seligman, James Olson, and Mark Zanna. Mahwah, N.J.: Lawrence Erlbaum, 1996.
Tilly, Charles. *Social Movements, 1768-2004*. Boulder, Colo.: Paradigm, 2004.
Tilly, Charles, and Sidney Tarrow. *Contentious Politics*. Boulder, Colo.: Paradigm, 2007.
Tocqueville, Alexis de. *Democracy in America*. Translated and edited by Harvey C. Mansfield and Delba Winthrop. Chicago: University of Chicago Press, 2000. First published 1835.
Trotter, William. *Instincts of the Herd in Peace and War*. New York: Macmillan, 1916.
Tulis, Jeffrey K. *The Rhetorical Presidency*. Princeton, N.J.: Princeton University Press, 1987.
Turow, Scott. *Ultimate Punishment: A Lawyer's Reflections on Dealing with the Death Penalty*. New York: Farrar, Straus & Giroux, 2003.
Tversky, Amos, and Daniel Kahneman. "Judgment under Uncertainty: Heuristics and Biases." *Science* 185 (1974): 1124-31.
Walker, Samuel. *In Defense of American Liberties: A History of the ACLU*. Carbondale: Southern Illinois University Press, 1990.
Walter, Otis M., and Robert L. Scott. *Thinking and Speaking: A Guide to Intelligent Oral Communication*. New York: Macmillan, 1962.
Warren, Rick. *The Purpose Driven Life*. Grand Rapids: Zondervan, 2002.
Weber, Max. *Economy and Society: An Outline of Interpretive Sociology*. Berkeley: University of California Press, 1978. First published 1922.
Weissberg, Robert. "Democratic Political Competence: Clearing the Underbrush and a Controversial Proposal." *Political Behavior* 23, no. 3 (2001): 257-84.
White, John Kenneth. *The Values Divide*. Washington, D.C.: CQ Press, 2003.
Wildavsky, Aaron. "A Cultural Theory of Preference Formation." *American Political Science Review* 81, no. 1 (1987): 3-22.

Wuthnow, Robert. *Meaning and Moral Order: Explorations in Cultural Analysis*. Berkeley: University of California Press, 1987.
Zald, Mayer. "Culture, Ideology, and Strategic Framing." In *Comparative Perspectives on Social Movements*, edited by Doug McAdam, John McCarthy, and Mayer Zald. Cambridge: Cambridge University Press, 1996.

INDEX

abortion, 8, 17, 19, 21, 29, 32, 33, 48, 49, 50, 77, 82, 86, 107, 108, 113, 129, 130, 153, 164, 167, 168, 172, 187-88
absolutist reasoning, 23, 33-34, 42, 46, 47, 54-56, 59, 63, 71, 72, 135, 217
activation effect, 22, 23, 43, 44, 63-68, 138
affirmative action, 112, 130, 144
Arab boycott, 142, 143
authenticity, 197, 203

Barzun, Jacques, 71
Benford, Robert, 78
Benhabib, Seyla, 57, 69
Berger, Peter, 10, 11, 12, 14, 162
Berlin, Isaiah, 25, 26, 27, 202, 212
Bible, 31, 36, 53, 55, 102, 105, 116, 130, 131, 180, 201, 217, 218, 219
Bickel, Alexander, 83
Biden, Joe, 164-65, 176, 179, 181, 184, 198, 199,
Blackmun, Harry, 17
Blitzer, Wolf, 198, 199, 201
Book of Mormon, 31
Brady Campaign to Prevent Gun Violence, 86
Brandenburg Gate, 7, 101

Brewer, Mark, 39
Brown, John, 102
Brownback, 169, 170, 172
Burnham, Daniel, 79
Bush, George H. W., 140, 152-59
Bush, George W., 18, 104-38, 151, 161-62

Carter, Jimmy, 139-48, 156, 158, 159, 185, 204, 207
Churchill, Winston, 7
civil courage, 82, 83, 90
Civil War, 19, 81, 84, 116
Clinton, Bill, 139, 140, 151, 152, 155-59, 194
Clinton, Hillary, 163, 164-65, 179-84, 193, 198-201
Coen Brothers, 33
Columbine, 95, 96, 97, 114
consequentialist reasoning, 33-34, 42
Constitution, 18, 19, 30, 31, 36, 37, 41, 49, 54, 71, 83, 86, 89, 92, 101, 102, 110, 113, 131, 137, 142, 143, 146, 173, 175, 178, 179, 180, 181, 184, 218, 220
contagion, 43, 47
content analysis, 106
culture, 12-13, 76, 77, 78, 99-100, 114

259

culture wars, 8-9, 30, 33, 39, 53, 88

Darfur, 128, 165, 178, 181, 187, 198
death penalty, 17, 21, 33, 36, 48-56, 65, 66, 72, 86, 112, 136, 152-54, 218, 219
deliberative democracy, 1, 41, 57-58, 69-72, 212-13
Democratic Party, 2, 39, 116, 127, 131, 137-39, 147, 148, 159, 161-207
Dodd, Chris, 164-65, 179, 181, 184
Dole, Bob, 140, 152, 158
Dorr, Professor G. H., 33
Downs, Anthony, 61
Dryzek, John, 70
Dukakis, Michael, 140, 152-56, 194
Durkheim, Emile, 10, 11, 12, 13, 22, 43, 98, 99

Earth Day, 174
Earth First!, 78
Edwards, John, 163, 164-65, 174, 175, 176, 179, 180, 181, 183, 184, 185, 193, 198, 199, 200
Eliade, Mircea, 7, 10, 13
Enlai, Zhou, 82
environmentalism, 17, 49, 50, 51, 52, 53, 54, 55, 56, 65, 66, 77, 78, 79, 90, 107, 116-17, 119, 125, 127, 174, 183, 204, 206, 207, 219, 220
Episcopal Church, 17
experimental methods, 46, 48, 215-17

fairness, 112, 121, 174, 175, 178, 181, 182, 183, 184, 205
Fiorina, Morris, 57
flag washing, 41
flip-flopping, 125, 133-35
Ford, Gerald, 123, 140, 141-47; and Soviet Union domination of Eastern Europe, 145, 159; and tamale incident, 123

foreign policy, 119, 125, 127, 128, 131, 140, 141, 142-44, 146, 147, 148, 151, 167, 177, 188-92, 194-96
Foucault, Michel, 80
framing, 43-46, 64, 205
fuzzy math, 122-23

Garrison, William Lloyd, 19
gay marriage, 8, 17, 48, 49, 50, 51, 52, 53, 54, 55, 56, 65, 66, 75, 80, 86, 107, 108, 113, 130, 136, 188, 217-18
Gilmore, James, 166-69
Giuliani, Rudy, 163, 166-69, 170, 171, 172, 173
Goldwater, Barry, 141, 178, 180, 182
Gorbachev, Mikhail, 100, 189
Gore, Al, 18, 78, 98, 104-25, 127, 131, 132, 140, 148, 149, 153, 156, 158, 174, 188, 190, 194, 204
Gramsci, Antonio, 80
Grant, Ulysses S., 84
Gravel, Mike, 164-65, 176, 177, 179, 180, 183, 193
Greene, Graham, 43
gun rights, 50, 51, 84-100, 113-15
Gutmann, Amy, 57, 212

Habermas, Jurgen, 57, 69, 70, 71
health care, 107, 109, 112, 122, 130, 132, 155, 156, 164, 174, 175, 178, 179, 181, 183, 184, 191, 192, 193
Hemingway, Ernest, 202
Heston, Charlton, 84-85, 89-98
Hibbing, John, 58
HIV, 165, 182, 184
Hoffer, Eric, 16
Horton, Willie, 153-54
Huckabee, Mike, 166-69, 170, 172, 174
Hunter, Duncan, 166-69
Hunter, James Davison, 30

identity politics, 8, 39

immigration, 130, 164, 168, 172, 201
inequality, 165, 185
inheritance tax, 108, 109, 112
Iran, 126, 129, 147, 166, 168, 171, 181, 189, 191, 192, 193, 199, 200
Iraq War, 2, 125–27, 128, 129, 132–34, 151, 164, 166, 167, 168, 170–71, 174, 176, 177, 178, 179, 181, 182, 183, 186, 188, 189, 191, 200
Israel, 126, 142, 150, 189, 192

Jennings, Peter, 152
Jesus, 93, 94, 116, 174

Kennedy, John F., 7, 100, 101, 130, 131, 141, 178, 181
Kerry, John, 125–35, 140, 148, 153, 156, 158, 175, 176, 188, 190, 194, 202, 203
King, Martin Luther, 7, 90, 92, 93, 94, 96, 101, 163, 181
Kissinger, Henry, 143, 148, 189
Kucinich, Dennis, 165, 175, 176, 177, 178, 179, 180, 181, 184, 193, 200
Kuran, Timur, 44, 81

Lakoff, George, 2, 201, 204–6
Lane, Robert, 22, 215
Lehrer, Jim, 105, 176
Lincoln, Abraham, 94, 180
Lucas, Stephen, 100
Luther, Martin, 1, 170, 180

Marshall, Thurgood, 180, 182
master frames, 75, 78, 102, 175
McCain, John, 116, 163, 166–69, 170, 171, 175, 185–96, 199
McCarthy, Joseph, 94, 156
Medhurst, Martin, 100
Medicare, 109, 122, 123, 132, 149, 191
Mencken, H. L., 197
mere contemplation effect, 31, 63

Mondale, Walter, 140, 148–50
Mosca, Gaetano, 27
Mutz, Diana, 58

NARAL, 86
nation-building, 116–19
National Rifle Association (NRA), 7, 84–100
Nelson, Tom, 44, 45
new media, 8–9, 39, 53
Nixon, Richard, 139, 141, 143, 148, 180, 189

Obama, Barack, 163, 164–65, 179–96, 199, 200, 201, 207
Olson, Mancur, 61, 62
Operation Rescue, 86
organ donation, 41, 63
outcome effects, 43–46

Parks, Rosa, 82
participatory democracy, 1, 58, 61–62, 68–72, 211–13
Patriot Act, 95, 129, 151, 175
Paul, Ron, 166, 168, 172, 173
persuasion, 22, 42–47, 56, 75, 104, 123, 132, 209–13, 216
Planet of the Apes, 89, 90
plans, 121–22, 131–32, 137, 153, 163, 202
political engagement, 23, 62–72, 135
political intensity, 23, 62–72, 137, 211
Popkin, Samuel, 123
preference falsification, 15, 43, 44, 80, 81
presidential election of 1976, 141–47; of 1980, 147–48; of 1984, 148–52; of 1988, 152–55; of 1992, 155–58; of 1996, 158; of 2000, 104–25; of 2004, 125–35; of 2008, 185–97
primary campaign of 2008, 162–85
priming, 43, 44

process effects, 22, 23, 43–46, 211

Quayle, Dan, 153

"Read my lips," 140, 153, 156, 157
Reagan, Ronald, 7, 90, 98, 100, 101, 140, 147–51, 152, 153, 155, 158, 159, 171, 173, 178, 180, 189, 194
"reality-based community," 161, 162
reasoning effect, 21, 22, 44, 53–56, 211
religion, 8, 10–12, 14, 90, 98–100, 115–17, 159, 166, 168, 205
Republican Party, 2–3, 23, 72, 103, 104, 106, 108, 109, 114, 119, 135, 137–38, 149, 161–73
Richardson, Bill, 164, 165, 174, 177, 179, 181, 184, 185
rights, 75, 78–79, 81–84
Roe v. Wade, 17, 130, 131, 166, 172, 187, 192
Romney, Mitt, 163, 166, 168, 169, 172, 199
Roosevelt, Franklin D., 98, 100, 178, 180
Roosevelt, Teddy, 174, 180, 219
Russert, Tim, 199, 200
Russia, 125, 145, 156, 189, 190, 191, 192, 193

sacralization, 16, 79, 82
sacred blindness, 32
sacred rhetoric, 33–38; effects, 20, 23, 72; facets, 35; single-sided vs. double sided, 46, 47
Sacred Value Protection Model (SVPM), 32, 63
sacred values, 14–20, 28; facets, 28–33; single-sided and double-sided, 19
Saddleback Forum, 186
Second Amendment, 17, 37, 86–89, 92, 93, 95, 97, 114, 220
second-term decline, 159

Shaw, Bernard, 153
Skocpol, Theda, 57
Snow, David, 78
social construction, 12–13, 162
social movements, 38–40, 75–79, 100–102, 213
Social Security, 107, 109, 110, 120, 122, 130, 137, 149, 150, 191
Solzhenitsyn, Alexander, 143
Soviet Union, 143, 145, 147, 150
spiral of silence, 15, 80, 81
stem-cell research, 129, 130, 171
Stevens, John Paul, 41
Stonecash, Jeffrey, 39
Strategic Defense Initiative, 149
Supreme Court, 18, 39, 83, 129, 184
Suskind, Ron, 161
Swedberg, Richard, 82

Tancredo, Tom, 166, 169, 172
Tarrow, Sidney, 15, 78, 84
taxes, 29, 108 109, 110, 111, 112, 120, 122, 127, 129, 130, 140, 153, 157, 159, 165, 167, 181, 182
terrorism, 39, 49, 118, 119, 125, 129, 148, 170, 175, 200
Tetlock, Philip, 8, 14, 15, 16, 31, 32, 64, 80
Texas v. Johnson, 41
Thatcher, Margaret, 135
Theiss-Morse, Elizabeth, 58
Thompson, Dennis, 57, 212
Thompson, Tommy, 166
Tilly, Charles, 78, 79, 84
Tocqueville, Alexis de, 70, 80
Totemism, 98–100
Trotter, William, 31
Tulis, Jeffrey, 151
"Two Americas," 183

valorization, 21, 44, 62–63, 135–37, 138, 213, 214

values, 25–26; conflictual and consensus, 18; value conflict, 26–27; value pluralism, 19
veterans, 164, 182
Vietnam, 152, 156

Warren, Rick, 186–87
Watergate, 140, 141, 143, 148

wealth, 39, 68, 111, 142, 165, 182, 183, 184, 185, 190
Weber, Max, 28, 30
Weissberg, Robert, 69
Wildavsky, Aaron, 210, 211

Yeats, W. B., 9

www.ingramcontent.com/pod-product-compliance
Lightning Source LLC
Chambersburg PA
CBHW021822300426
44114CB00009BA/278